LAND POLICIES
for GROWTH
and POVERTY
REDUCTION

A World Bank Policy Research Report

LAND POLICIES
for GROWTH
and POVERTY
REDUCTION

Klaus Deininger

A copublication of the World Bank and
Oxford University Press

Oxford University Press

OXFORD   NEW YORK   ATHENS   AUCKLAND   BANGKOK   BOGOTÁ   BUENOS AIRES
CALCUTTA   CAPE TOWN   CHENNAI   DAR ES SALAAM   DELHI   FLORENCE   HONG KONG
ISTANBUL   KARACHI   KUALA LUMPUR   MADRID   MELBOURNE   MEXICO CITY   MUMBAI
NAIROBI   PARIS   SÃO PAULO   SINGAPORE   TAIPEI   TOKYO   TORONTO   WARSAW

and associated companies in

BERLIN   IBADAN

Library of Congress Cataloguing-in-Progress Data
            p. cm. – (A World Bank policy research report)
   Includes bibliographical references.
   ISBN 0-8213-5071-4
      1. Land tenure—Developing countries. 2. Land use—Government policy—Developing
   countries. 3. Land reform—Developing countries. 4. Farm ownership—Developing
   countries. 5. Right of property—Developing countries. 6. Rural poor—Developing
   countries. 7. Poverty—Developing countries. 8. Developing countries—Economic
   conditions. I. World Bank. II. Series.

   HD1131.L345 2003
   333'.009172'4—dc21

                                                                              2003050076

Credit for front cover photo: World Bank
Credit for back cover photos: IFAD/R. Grossman (top photo); IFAD/A. Hossain (second photo from
top); Klaus Deininger (third and fourth photos from top)

Contents

Foreword   ix

Acknowledgments   xiii

Executive Summary   xvii
   The Importance of Land Policies   xvii
   Property Rights to Land   xxii
   Land Transactions   xxix
   Socially Desirable Land Use   xxxviii
   Challenges Ahead   xliv

1   Introduction   1
   The Relevance of Land Rights   1
   Land Policy in Different Regional Contexts   3
   The Role of This Report   5

2   Property Rights to Land   7
   The Historical Context   8
   Conceptual Framework   22
   Demand for and Impact of Secure Property Rights   36
   Policy Implications   51
   Conclusion   74
   Notes   76

3   Land Transactions   79
   Key Factors Affecting the Functioning of Rural Land Markets   80
   Implications for Land Rental Markets   84
   Implications for Land Sales Markets   93
   Empirical Evidence on Land Markets in Different Regions   98
   Policy Implications   115
   Conclusion   129
   Notes   131

4   Fostering Socially Desirable Land Use   133
Restructuring the Farm Sector in CEE and CIS Countries   134
Enhancing Land Access through Land Reform   143
Reducing the Incidence and Impact of Land-Related Conflict   157
Land Taxation   165
Devolution of Control of State Land   169
Land Use Regulation and Zoning   174
Putting Land Policy in Context   178
Conclusion: Continuity and Change since 1975   185
Notes   190

Appendix: Regional Workshops   193
Regional Workshop on Land Issues in Central and Eastern Europe
    Budapest, Hungary, April 3–6, 2002   193
Regional Workshop on Land Issues in Africa and the Middle East
    Kampala, Uganda, April 29–May 2, 2002   195
Regional Workshop on Land Issues in Latin America and the Caribbean
    Pachuca (Hidalgo), Mexico, May 19–22, 2002   199
Regional Workshop on Land Issues in Asia
    Phnom Penh, Cambodia, June 3–6, 2002   202

Glossary   205

References   207

Boxes
2.1   A decentralized two-step system for registering property rights:
        the case of Lithuania   34
2.2   Land tenure security under state ownership   55
2.3   Innovative gender legislation in Latin America   60
2.4   The scope for gradually upgrading tenure security over time   65
2.5   Key differences between deed and title registration   71
3.1   The scope and flexibility of land rental contracts in West Africa   105
3.2   The impact of eliminating restrictions on land rental   121
3.3   Dangers of land privatization in an environment
        with multiple market imperfections   123
4.1   Changes in land reform policy in Colombia   147
4.2   Brazil: land reform to combat poverty
        in a middle-income country   148
4.3   Challenges of land reform in South Africa   150
4.4   The many facets of land conflict throughout history   158
4.5   Land tax reform in Kenya and Indonesia   169
4.6   The continuing challenge of state ownership   172
4.7   Ghana: an example of a comprehensive land policy   180
4.8   Elaborating and monitoring a land policy framework:
        key issues and indicators   182

Figures

2.1   Initial land distribution and economic growth, selected countries   18

2.2   Informal land occupation in urban areas, by region   37

2.3   Impact of title status on land values, selected countries and years   44

2.4   Impact of title status on investment, selected countries and years   46

2.5   Impact of title status on access to credit, selected countries and years   49

2.6   Impact of titling and wealth on credit access, Paraguay, 1990–95   51

3.1   Actual and desired rental land, China   110

3.2   Land rental before and after agricultural market liberalization, Nicaragua   112

4.1   Productivity of plots with and without conflict, Uganda, 2001   161

Tables

2.1   Intervention to establish and support large farms, selected locations and periods   12–13

2.2   Impact of land ownership distribution in four Latin American countries   21

2.3   Status of customary tenure in new land laws, selected African countries   63

4.1   Nature of land rights, selected CEE and CIS countries   137

4.2   Share of land held privately, selected CEE and CIS countries, 1990 and 2000   139

4.3   Extent and characteristics of land reforms, selected economies and years   144

Foreword

LAND POLICIES ARE OF FUNDAMENTAL IMPORTANCE TO sustainable growth, good governance, and the well-being of and the economic opportunities open to rural and urban dwellers—particularly poor people. Therefore, research on land policy and analysis of specific interventions relating to land have long been of interest to the World Bank's Research Department and other academic and civil society institutions. However, the results of such research have not always been disseminated to policymakers and other key stakeholders as effectively as they might have been. As a result, discussions on land policies are often characterized by preconceived notions and ideological viewpoints rather than by careful analysis of the potential contribution of land policies to broader development, the scope for interventions in the area, and the mechanisms that can be used to achieve broader social and economic goals. Given this lack of analysis, the potential for using land policies as a catalyst for social and economic change is often not fully realized.

This report aims to strengthen the effectiveness of land policy in support of development and poverty reduction by setting out the results of recent research in a way that is accessible to a wide audience of policymakers, nongovernmental organizations, academics in World Bank client countries, donor agency officials, and the broader development community. Its main message rests on three principles.

First, providing secure tenure to land can improve the welfare of the poor, in particular, by enhancing the asset base of those, such as women, whose land rights are often neglected. At the same time it creates the incentives needed for investment, a key element underlying sustainable economic growth. In addition to highlighting these advantages, the report discusses different mechanisms that can be used to promote tenure security, their advantages and disadvantages, and the ways in which they can fit into a broader development strategy.

Second, facilitating the exchange and distribution of land, whether as an asset or for current services, at low cost, through markets as well as through nonmarket channels, is central to expediting land access by productive but land-poor producers and, once the economic environment is right, the development of financial markets that rely on the use of land as collateral. The report demonstrates the importance of rental market transactions and argues that removing impediments to these can help generate considerable equity advantages and at the same time establish the basis for a positive investment climate and the diversification of economic activity, especially in the rural nonfarm sector. It also recognizes that nonmarket mechanisms for transferring land, such as inheritance, award of public and state lands, and expropriation of land by the state for the broader public good, have historically played a major role in either facilitating or obstructing broad land access and effective land use and that policymakers should take careful account of these processes.

Third, governments have a clear role to play in promoting and contributing to socially desirable land allocation and utilization. This is clearly illustrated by farm restructuring in the context of decollectivization and land reform and postconflict land policy in economies with a highly unequal distribution of land ownership where land issues are often a key element of social strife. Appropriate incentives for sustainable land use are also required to avoid negative externalities and irreversible degradation of nonrenewable natural and cultural resources. The report illustrates mechanisms, ranging from taxation to regulation and land use planning, to address these issues.

Given the cross-cutting nature, far-reaching implications, and often long time horizon of interventions in the area of land policies, effective dissemination of knowledge and experience requires that research be informed by the broad range of problems policymakers face and be integrated into a broader dialogue with the Bank's development partners. For this reason I am particularly pleased that this policy research report builds on four regional workshops and an electronic discussion that allowed civil society and donor representatives, policymakers, and academics to discuss the role of land issues in a regional context. These workshops and discussion provide a strong basis for using the report as an input into the development of strategies and activities at the country level.

The Bank issued its last comprehensive overview of land policies in 1975. Since that time the world has changed profoundly. The policy research report illustrates how these changes affect the issues decision-makers have to be concerned about and the implications this will have for specific policy advice. We and our development partners are now more aware of the importance of taking a comprehensive and integrated approach to development that includes attention to issues such as land policy that require a long-term approach. This, together with the consensus already achieved, encourages us to hope that the report will be widely used in the policy debate on land and provide the basis for integrating land into broader strategies and implementing specific land policies that will help increase growth in a way that benefits poor people.

Nicholas H. Stern
Senior Vice President,
    Development Economics,
    and Chief Economist,
The World Bank
May 2003

Acknowledgments

THIS REPORT WAS WRITTEN BY KLAUS DEININGER IN the Development Research Group under the guidance and supervision of Gershon Feder. We would like to thank the external technical advisory committee consisting of Michael Carter, Alain de Janvry, Gustavo Gordillo de Anda, Michael Kirk, Keijiro Otsuka, Jean-Philppe Platteau, Scott Rozelle, Elisabeth Sadoulet, and Jo Swinnen for providing guidance and critical feedback throughout the process. The report also benefited greatly from the comments received in the context of a three-week electronic discussion.[1] We thank all the contributors to this discussion for their valuable inputs, as well as Michael Carter, Jonathan Conning, Alain de Janvry, Robin Palmer, and Elisabeth Sadoulet, who moderated it. We are grateful for discussions with and continuing support from the Bank's Land Policy and Administration Thematic Group, in particular Hans Binswanger, John Bruce, Frank Byamugisha, Ed Cook, Li Guo, Lynn Holstein, Hoonae Kim, Isabel Lavadenz, Shem Migot-Adholla, Jessica Mott, Jorge Munoz, Jeeva Perumalpillai-Essex, Idah Pswarayi-Riddihough, Iain Shuker, Rogier van den Brink, Dina Umali-Deininger, and Wael Zakout. Many other Bank staff, too numerous to acknowledge by name, provided thoughtful comments at various stages of report preparation, and we are grateful for their input. The management of ESSD, in particular, the Agriculture and Rural Development Department, led by Kevin Cleaver and Sushma Ganguly, has been very supportive and has provided valuable inputs throughout the process.

---

1. The archive of this discussion can be accessed at http://www.worldbank.org/devforum/forum_prr-landpolicy.html.

The report builds on the insights gained from background papers presented and feedback received at four regional workshops in Hungary (April 3–6, 2002), Uganda (April 29–May 2, 2002), Mexico (May 19–22, 2002), and Cambodia (June 3–6, 2002), as well as a follow-up meeting with representatives from civil society, client governments, and donors in Washington (March 13–14, 2003). To thank the presenters, discussants, and chairs during these workshops, and at the same time illustrate the wealth of experience that these workshops brought together, the appendix presents an abbreviated program of these events. For providing the leadership that made these workshops feasible in the host countries, we thank Im Chhun Lim, Minister of Land Management, Urban Planning, and Construction, Cambodia; Tamas Eder, State Secretary, Ministry of Agriculture, Hungary; Maria Teresa Herrera Tello, Secretary of Agrarian Reform, Mexico; Miguel Angel Nuñez Soto, Governor of the State of Hidalgo, Mexico; and Ruhakana Rugunda, Minister of Land, Water, and the Environment, Uganda.

We particularly thank the French Ministry of Foreign Affairs, the German Agency for Technical Cooperation, the U.K. Department for International Development, and the U.S. Agency for International Development, which were the main sponsors for the regional workshops. In these institutions, Christian Graefen, Lena Heron, Philippe Ospital, Julian Quan, Jolyne Sanjak, Bruno Vindel, and Willi Zimmermann provided substantive and logistical input for which we are most grateful. We would also like to acknowledge the sponsorship of participants from civil society organizations to attend these workshops by the International Land Coalition and Oxfam, as well as the substantive support received from the European Union, the Food and Agriculture Organization of the United Nations, and regional development banks. We are also indebted to the World Bank's regional managers, country directors, and field office staff who provided invaluable support to the conduct of the workshops. Thanks for coordinating logistics locally are due to Susana Becerril,, Michael Becker, Tamara de Mel, Vivien Gyuris, Viktoria Kovacs, Gabriele Kruk, Judy Longbottom, Eugenio Montiel, and Placid Ssekamatte.

For their untiring assistance in organizing the workshops and dealing with the many other logistical challenges that had to be overcome in preparing this report, we would like to thanks Catalina Ramos-Cunanan, Aban Daruwala, Maria Fernandez, Pauline Kokila, Liliana

Longo, Anna Maranon, Karen McHugh, Renata Mohriak, Jason Paiement, Alfredo Revilak, Anna Regina Rillo Bonfield, Patricia Sader, and Radhika Yeddanapudi, as well as Raffaella Castagnini, Sara Savastano, and Oliver Taft, who, in addition, provided expert assistance with editing. We also would like to thank Lynn Brown, Ronald Kim, Polly Means, Rosemary O'Neill, and Melissa Williams for technical assistance; Alice Faintich for the final editing; Melissa Edeburn, Santiago Pombo, and Stuart Tucker from the Office of the Publisher for coordinating the editorial process; and Lawrence MacDonald for assisting with dissemination.

Executive Summary

The Importance of Land Policies

LAND IS A KEY ASSET FOR THE RURAL AND URBAN POOR. IT provides a foundation for economic activity and the functioning of market (for example, credit) and nonmarket institutions (for instance, local governments and social networks) in many developing countries. Given this importance, institutions dealing with land have evolved over long periods, and land policies will invariably be affected by the presence of multiple market imperfections. Policy advice that is oblivious of either the complexity of these issues or the historical and political repercussions of policy interventions in this area can lead to unintended negative consequences. Research has long pointed to the need for a careful and differentiated approach as a precondition for making clear policy recommendations in relation to land that can help improve both efficiency and equity. Frequently, however, this message does not seem to have been clearly communicated to policy analysts and decisionmakers, with negative consequences. This report aims to summarize key insights from research and practical experience, not only to highlight the importance of careful and nuanced policy advice, but also to illustrate some general principles for formulating such policy advice in specific country settings.

Origins and Evolution of Property Rights

Understanding the origins of property rights and their evolution over time is important to appreciate how property rights to land affect households' behavior and can, in turn, be influenced by government policy. Historically, one reason property rights evolved was to respond to increased payoffs from investment in more intensive use of land resulting from population growth or opportunities arising from greater market integration and technical advances. In the course of development virtually everywhere, the need to sustain larger populations or to make use of economic opportunities associated with trade will require investments in land that cultivators will be more likely to make if land rights are secure. Appropriate institutional innovations to provide such rights can lead to a virtuous cycle of increasing population and successively greater investment in land, economic growth, and increased welfare. At the same time, failure of the institutions administering land rights to respond to these demands can lead to land grabbing, conflict, and resource dissipation that, in extreme circumstances, can undermine societies' productive and economic potential.

In addition to this evolutionary perspective, the imposition of property rights to land by outside forces or local overlords has affected the nature of such rights in many countries of the developing world. The goal of such intervention was to obtain surpluses from local smallholder populations or to force independent smallholders into wage labor by preventing them from acquiring independent land rights. To do so, a variety of mechanisms, often supported by distortions in other markets, was used. Not surprisingly, such imposition of rights often disrupted the evolution of land rights as a response to population growth or has, by co-opting local institutions or changing how they functioned, implied vast changes in the way land was allocated and managed at the local level.

Given that the historical evolution of property rights is not only a response to purely economic forces, it is not surprising that the arrangements found in many countries are often not optimal from either an economic or a social perspective. For example, in Africa, the vast majority of the land area is operated under customary tenure arrangements that, until very recently, were not even recognized by the state and therefore remained outside the realm of the law. In Eastern Europe, collective production structures have failed to contribute to rural growth. In Latin America and parts of Asia, highly unequal land ownership and access to assets have made it difficult to establish inclusive patterns of growth. As a consequence, there is concern that in many of these countries economic growth may widen pre-existing inequalities and tensions rather than reduce them. Despite such shortcomings, socially suboptimal and economically inefficient property rights arrangements have often remained in place for long periods of time. In fact, far-reaching changes of land relations have generally been confined to major historic transitions.

Importance of Property Rights for Economic Growth

Property rights affect economic growth in a number of ways. First, secure property rights will increase the incentives of households and individuals to invest, and often will also provide them with better credit access, something that will not only help them make such investments, but will also provide an insurance substitute in the event of shocks. Second, it has long been known that in unmechanized agriculture, the operational distribution of land affects output, implying that a highly unequal land distribution will reduce productivity. Even though the ability to make productive use of land will depend on policies in areas beyond land policy that may warrant separate attention, secure and well-defined land rights are key for households' asset ownership, productive development, and factor market functioning.

If property rights are poorly defined or cannot be enforced at low cost, individuals and entrepreneurs will be compelled to spend valuable resources on defending their land, thereby diverting effort from other purposes such as investment. Secure land tenure also facilitates the transfer of land at low cost through rentals and sales, improving the allocation of land while at the same time supporting the development of financial markets. Without secure rights, landowners are less willing to rent out their land, which may impede their ability and willingness to engage in nonagricultural employment or rural-urban migration.

Poorly designed land market interventions and the regulation of such markets by large and often corrupt bureaucracies continue to hamper small enterprise startups and nonfarm economic development in many parts of the world. Such interventions not only limit access to land by the landless and poor in rural and urban areas of the developing world, but by discouraging renting out by landlords who are thus unable to make the most productive use of their land, they also reduce productivity and investment. High transaction costs in land markets either make it more difficult to provide credit or require costly development of collateral substitutes, both of which constrain development of the private sector. A recent study estimates that in India, such land market distortions reduce the annual rate of gross domestic product growth by about 1.3 percent.

Role of Secure Property Rights in Poverty Reduction

For most of the poor in developing countries, land is the primary means for generating a livelihood and a main vehicle for investing, accumulating wealth, and transferring it between generations. Land is also a key element of household wealth. For example, in Uganda land constitutes between 50 and 60 percent of the asset endowment of the poorest households. Because land comprises a large share of the asset portfolio of the poor in many developing countries, giving secure property rights to land they already possess can greatly increase the net wealth of poor people. By allowing them to make productive use of their labor, land ownership makes them less reliant on wage labor, thereby reducing their vulnerability to shocks.

Given the key role of land as a determinant of access to economic opportunities, the way in which land rights are defined, households and entrepreneurs can obtain ownership or possession of it, and conflicts pertaining to it are resolved through formal or informal means will have far-reaching social and economic effects. The implications not only influence the structure of governance at the local level, but also affect (a) households' ability to produce for their subsistence and to generate a marketable surplus, (b) their social and economic status and often their collective identity, (c) their incentive to invest and to use land in a sustainable manner, and (d) their ability to self-insure and/or to access financial markets. For this reason, researchers and development practitioners have long recognized that providing poor people with access to land and improving their ability to make effective use of the land they occupy is central to reducing poverty and empowering poor people and communities.

Control of land is particularly important for women, whose asset ownership has been shown to affect spending, for instance, on girls' education. Yet traditionally, women have been disadvantaged in terms of land access. Ensuring that they are able to have secure rights to one of the household's main assets will be critical in many respects. This includes meeting the challenges arising in the context of the HIV/AIDS epidemic, where the absence of clear land rights can lead to costly conflict and hardship regarding possible loss of land by widows.

Impact of Secure Property Rights on Governance and Sustainable Development

The ability of local leaders and authorities to control land has traditionally been a major source of political and economic power. Over and above the economic benefits that may be derived from giving households greater tenure security, measures to increase households' and individuals' ability to control land will have a clear impact on empowering them, giving them greater voice, and creating the basis for more democratic and participatory local development. For example, fiscal decentralization is often hampered by the lack of own revenue and accountability on the part of local governments. Both of these could be increased by taxation of land. In countries where land continues to be a key productive asset, governments could use land taxation more effectively to motivate fiscal discipline and to strengthen the voice of the local population by enhancing the accountability of local officials.

Conflicting interventions in land rights systems by outsiders in the course of history, or a failure to establish legitimate institutions in the face of increasing population pressure and appreciation of land values, have tended to exclude the poor from land access and ownership and resulted in the creation of parallel or overlapping institutions. Therefore ensuring minimum standards for rapid conflict resolution and dispensation of justice, accountability, and transparency in land management and access is critical. Where longstanding, systematic distortions in the area of land overlap with race and ethnicity issues, a buildup of land-related conflict and violence can even result in collapse of the state, with devastating consequences. In Africa, for example, formal tenure covers only between 2 and 10 percent of the land. To avoid leaving the occupants of these lands effectively outside the rule of law, many African countries have recently given legal recognition to customary tenure as well as to the institutions administering it; however, implementing these laws remains a major challenge.

In many countries the state continues to own a large portion of valuable land despite evidence that this is conducive to mismanagement, underutilization of resources, and corruption. Broad and egalitarian asset ownership strengthens the voice of the poor, who are otherwise often excluded from political processes, allowing them greater participation that can not only increase the transparency of institutions, but can also shift the balance of public goods provision, especially at the local level. As appropriation of rents from land appreciation through discretionary bureaucratic interventions and controls remains a major source of corruption and a barrier to the startup of small enterprises in many developing countries, this can help to significantly improve governance.

Property Rights to Land

L AND RIGHTS ARE SOCIAL CONVENTIONS THAT REGULATE THE distribution of the benefits that accrue from specific uses of a certain piece of land. A number of arguments support public provision of such rights. First, the high fixed cost of the institutional infrastructure needed to establish and maintain land rights favors public provision, or at least regulation. Second, the benefits of being able to exchange land rights will be realized only in cases where such rights are standardized and can be easily and independently verified. Finally, without central provision, households and entrepreneurs will be forced to spend resources to defend their claims to property, for example, through guards, fences, and so on, which is not only socially wasteful, but also disproportionately disadvantages the poor, who will be the least able to afford such expenditures.

Desirable Characteristics of Property Rights to Land

Property rights to land need to have a horizon long enough to provide investment incentives and be defined in a way that makes them easy to observe, enforce, and exchange. They need to administered and enforced by institutions that have both legal backing and social legitimacy and are accessible by and accountable to the holders of property rights. Even if property rights to land are assigned to a group, the rights and duties of individuals within this group, and the way in which they can be modified and will be enforced, have to be clear. Finally, as the precision with which property rights will be defined will generally increase in line with rising resource values, the institutions administering property rights need to be flexible enough to evolve over time in response to changing requirements.

Duration

As one of the main effects of property rights is to increase incentives for investment, the duration for which such rights are awarded needs at least to match the time frame during which returns from possible investments may accrue. Clearly this depends on the potential for investment, which is higher in urban than in rural areas. While indefinite property rights are the best option, giving long-term rights that can be renewed automatically is an alternative. Given the long time spans involved, attention to the way in which such rights can be inherited is particularly warranted, and has often proven to be critical to enhance women's ability to control land on their own.

Modalities of Demarcation and Transfer

Property rights to land should be defined in a way that makes them easy to identify and exchange at a cost that is low compared with the value of the underlying land. With limited land values, low-cost mechanisms of identifying boundaries, such as physical marks (hedges, rivers, and trees) that are recognized by the community, will generally suffice, while higher-value resources will require more precise and costly means of demarcation. Similarly, where land is relatively plentiful and transactions are infrequent, low-cost mechanisms to record transactions, such as witnessing by community elders, will be appropriate. More formal mechanisms will normally be adopted once transactions become more frequent and start to extend beyond traditional community and kinship boundaries.

Enforcement Institutions

The key advantage of formal, as compared with informal, property rights is that those holding formal rights can call on the power of the state to enforce their rights. For this to be feasible, the institutions involved need to enjoy legal backing as well as social legitimacy, including accountability to and accessibility by the local population. Yet in many countries, especially in Africa, the gap between legality and legitimacy has been a major source of friction, something that is illustrated by the fact that often more than 90 percent of land remains outside the existing legal system. Failure to give legal backing to land administration institutions that enjoy social legitimacy can undermine their ability to draw on anything more than informal mechanisms for enforcement. By contrast, institutions that are legal but do not enjoy social recognition may make little difference to the lives of ordinary people, and have therefore often proven to be highly ineffective. Bringing legality and legitimacy together is a major challenge for policy that cannot be solved in the abstract.

Subject of Rights

Whether it is more appropriate to give property rights to individuals or to a group will depend largely on the nature of the resource and on existing social arrangements. Group rights will be more appropriate in situations characterized by economies of scale in resource management or if externalities exist that can be managed at the level of the group but not the individual. Group ownership is also often adopted in situations where risk is high and markets for insurance are imperfect or where the resource in question is abundant and the payoff from any land-related investment that individuals could undertake on their own is low. Even if these conditions apply, group rights will be the option of choice only if the group to which such rights are assigned has a clear definition of its membership; if the responsibilities of individuals within the group are well identified; if mechanisms for internal management and enforcement, for example, the imposition of sanctions, are available; and if there is a clear understanding of the ways in which decisions to modify rules can be made.

Evolution over Time

Unless there are clear externalities that can be dealt with most effectively by groups, the relative advantage of group, as compared with individual, land rights will generally decrease in the course of development because of a number of factors. Technical progress reduces the risk of crop failure while at the same time increasing the potential payoff from investments; development of the nonfarm economy provides access to more predictable income streams; and greater access to physical infrastructure reduces not only the risk, but also the cost, of publicly providing property rights. Thus one would expect to see a move toward more individualized forms of property rights with economic development. At the same time, historical evidence suggests that transformation of property toward increased individualization is not automatic. To the contrary, it will be affected by political and economic factors, and thus will often coincide with major conflicts, upheavals, or power struggles.

Exogenous demographic changes, especially in the absence of economic development, will increase the scarcity and value of land. This can challenge traditional authorities and institutions that previously had unquestioned authority over land allocation and dispute resolution. If they coincide with land claims by outsiders and are overlaid with race and ethnicity issues, such situations can lead to serious crises of governance, including civil war. Even neglecting broader noneconomic impacts and possible indirect effects, the direct costs of land conflicts that may arise in this context are high and are borne mostly by the poor, who are generally least able to afford them. Land conflicts often generate large, negative, external effects. In the extreme, they can undermine the state's authority and effectiveness by leading to the creation of a multiplicity of parallel institutions, as illustrated by the fact that unresolved land conflicts have in some cases escalated to become a significant contributor to state failure.

To avoid such consequences, the institutions managing land rights will need to be able to re-interpret traditions and social norms authoritatively and in a way that protects the poor and vulnerable from abuse of their rights by those with political power and economic resources. This requires attention to legal provisions that can instantly eliminate traditional rights or the rights of specific groups, such as women or herders. Even where an appropriate legal and regulatory basis is in place, operational mechanisms for putting laws into practice in a way that protects vulnerable members of society and precludes the elimination of secondary rights will be important. Seemingly simple alterations of the property rights regime can have far-reaching impacts on the poor.

Empirical Evidence on the Impact of Tenure Security

In many countries of the developing world, insecure land tenure prevents large parts of the population from realizing the economic and noneconomic benefits, such as greater investment incentives, transferability of land, improved credit market access, more sustainable management of resources, and independence from discretionary interference by bureaucrats, that are normally associated with secure property rights to land. For example, more than 50 percent of the peri-urban population in Africa and more than 40 percent in Asia live under informal tenure and therefore have highly insecure land rights. While no such figures are available for rural areas, many rural land users are reported to make considerable investments in land as a way to establish ownership and increase their perceived level of tenure security. This illustrates not only that tenure security is highly valued, but also that in many contexts existing land administration systems fail to provide secure tenure. We discuss first the economic and then the noneconomic benefits of more secure tenure.

A first benefit from increased tenure security that can easily be measured is the increase in land users' investment incentives. Some studies have reported a doubling of investment, and values for land with more secure tenure are reported to be between 30 and 80 percent higher than those for land where there is a higher probability of losing it. Transferability of land will greatly increase this effect, something that will be especially important in situations where the scope for transacting land between less and more productive producers has increased, for example, because of development of the nonagricultural economy and rural-urban migration. Higher levels of tenure security, not necessarily formal title, will also reduce the time and resources individuals have to spend trying to secure their land rights, thereby allowing them to invest these resources elsewhere. For example, in Peru the formalization of land rights increased the supply of labor to the market by more than 50 percent.

Where effective demand for credit exists, giving formal title to land can help producers gain access to credit and improve the functioning of financial markets. It has long been noted that the impact of such credit access may be differentiated by the size of landholdings, and therefore that attention to the anticipated equity effects will be required. In situations where the credit effect associated with title is unlikely to materialize in the near future, a more gradual and lower-cost approach to securing land rights and improving tenure security, with the possibility of upgrading once the need arises, will allow for provision of most, if not all, the benefits from increased tenure security at lower cost.

While targeting efforts aimed at increasing tenure security for the poor will therefore automatically lead to greater equity, two additional issues are of interest. First, the ability to make decisions about the allocation of land is a key element of political power wielded by traditional authorities or modern bureaucrats. Devolving some of this authority to democratic decisionmaking within the group or to individuals can greatly improve governance as illustrated by the example of Mexico, where beneficiaries mentioned improved governance as a key benefit of property rights reforms introduced after 1992.

Second, ensuring secure land tenure will be of particular relevance for groups that were traditionally discriminated against. In addition to being warranted based on basic considerations of equity, attention to women's land rights will have far-reaching economic consequences where women are the main cultivators, where out-migration is high, where control of productive activities is differentiated by gender, or where high levels of adult mortality and unclear inheritance regulations could undermine women's livelihood in case of their husbands' death. The importance of doing so is reinforced by strong evidence suggesting that the way in which assets are distributed within the household will affect spending patterns. Greater control of assets by women often translates into higher levels of spending on children's education, health, and food. Similarly, even though the significance of land for indigenous peoples and herders goes beyond economics, even its economic impact has often been underestimated. Transferring property rights to indigenous communities, especially if combined with technical assistance, can allow them to manage these better or to derive greater benefits from the resources associated with their land. For herders, different countries have developed promising approaches to resource tenure and management that recognize the central role of mobility and risk management on an ecological scale that may transcend traditional boundaries.

Ways to Increase Tenure Security

The findings described in the previous section imply that governments have a role to play in providing secure tenure to owners and users of land. Even though formal title will increase tenure security in many situations, experience indicates that it is not always necessary, and often is not a sufficient condition for optimum use of the land resource. The goal of providing tenure security for the long term, administered in a cost-effective way through institutions that combine legality with social legitimacy, can be achieved in a variety of ways depending on the situation.

Customary Land

In customary systems, legal recognition of existing rights and institutions, subject to minimum conditions, is generally more effective than premature attempts at establishing formalized structures. Legally recognizing customary land rights subject to a determination of membership and the codification or establishment of internal rules and mechanisms for conflict resolution can greatly enhance occupants' security. Demarcation of the boundaries of community land can remove the threat of encroachment by outsiders while drawing on well-defined procedures within the community to assign and manage rights within the group. Conflicts historically often erupt first in conjunction with land transfers, especially to outsiders. Where such transfers occur and are socially accepted, the terms should be recorded in writing to avoid ambiguity that could subsequently lead to land-related conflict.

State Land

Occupants on state land have often made considerable efforts to increase their level of security, in some cases through significant investments, but often remain vulnerable to eviction threats. Because of their limited land rights they generally cannot make full use of the land they occupy. Giving them legal rights and regularizing their possession is therefore important, along with ensuring that appropriate means are in place for resolving any conflicts that may arise in the process. In many situations, political or other considerations may preclude the award of full private property rights. If existing institutions can credibly commit to lease contracts, giving users secure, transferable, long-term lease rights will permit the realization of most, if not all, the investment benefits associated with higher levels of tenure security. In these cases, the recognition of long-term, peaceful occupation in good faith (adverse possession) and the award of long-term land leases with provisions for automatic renewal will be the most desirable option. If the leases awarded by state institutions are not credible, measures to increase tenure security or, alternatively, full privatization, will be required to give users sufficient security of tenure and the associated benefits. An indicator of limited credibility of leases is that even where there is strong, effective demand for credit, financial institutions will not accept long-term leases as collateral.

Individual Title

Where, after considering the arguments advanced earlier, formal and individual ownership title will be the option of choice, inefficiencies in the land administration institutions responsible for demarcation of boundaries, registration and record keeping, adjudication of rights, and resolution of conflict can still preclude realization of many of the benefits of secure tenure. If these institutions are not working well or are poorly coordinated, inefficient, or corrupt, transaction costs will be high, thereby reducing the level of transactions below what would be socially optimal, and in many cases excluding the poor completely. In the extreme, lack of clarity about who is responsible for specific areas or infighting between institutions has evolved into a major source of insecurity that has undermined the value and authority of titles or certificates of land ownership distributed during systematic interventions. In such situations, institutional reform, including improved coordination within the government and with the private sector, will be a precondition for the state's ability to deliver property rights effectively.

If no previous records exist, or where these are seriously out of date, a strong case for systematic, first-time registration can be made on the grounds that a systematic approach, combined with wide publicity and legal assistance to ensure that everybody is informed, provides the best way to ensure social control and prevent land grabbing by powerful individuals, which would be not only inequitable, but also inefficient. In addition, interventions should be designed so that they are fiscally sustainable and so that the costs involved do not prevent individuals from subsequent registration of land transactions. Although it is often not necessary to have uniform standards for land administration throughout the whole country, coverage should aim to be comprehensive.

Even though most countries mandate equality of men and women before the law in principle, the procedures used by land administration institutions often discriminate against women, either explicitly or implicitly. To overcome this tendency, a more pro-active stance in favor of awarding land rights to women by governments, together with more rigorous evaluation of innovative approaches aiming to accomplish greater gender equality in control of conjugal land on the ground, would be warranted.

Land Transactions

LAND TRANSACTIONS CAN PLAY AN IMPORTANT ROLE BY allowing those who are productive, but are either landless or own little land, to access land. Land markets also facilitate the exchange of land as the off-farm economy develops and, where the conditions for doing so exist, provide a basis for the use of land as collateral in credit markets. Capital market imperfections and policy distortions have, however, prevented land sales markets from contributing to increased levels of productivity or reduced poverty in many instances. This has led some observers to take a negative stance on any type of land market activity and to support government intervention, despite the considerable scope of rental markets and the evidence on limited effectiveness of government intervention in such markets.

Conceptual Foundations

To understand why in some cases land transactions may fail to contribute to improving productivity and equity, it is necessary to review the conceptual foundations that underlie the operation of land markets and how some of the market imperfections frequently encountered in rural areas of the developing world will have a differential impact on land rental and sales.

Basic Elements

A large literature has demonstrated that unmechanized agriculture generally does not exhibit economies of scale in production, even though economies of scale from marketing may in some cases be transferred back to the production stage. At the same time, the need to closely supervise hired laborers implies that owner-operated farms are more efficient than those that rely predominantly on large numbers of permanent wage workers. However, credit rationing and the scope to use collateral as one means to overcome imperfections that are inherent to credit markets will favor farmers who own larger amounts of land. In environments where access to credit is important, this can lead to the appearance of a positive relationship between farm size and productivity, possibly counteracting the supervision cost advantage of small owner-operated farms. These factors will have different implications for land rental as compared with sales markets.

Rental Markets

Rental markets are characterized by low transaction costs, and in most cases where rent is paid on an annual basis require only a limited initial capital outlay. This, together with participants' ability to adjust contract terms so as to overcome market failures in capital and other markets, implies that rental is a more flexible and versatile means of transferring land from less to more productive producers than sales. Renting is thus more likely to improve overall productivity and, in addition, can provide a stepping stone for tenants to accumulate experience and possibly make the transition to land ownership at a later stage.

The importance of tenure security for rental markets is illustrated by the fact that where land tenure is perceived to be insecure, long-term contracts are unlikely to be entered into. Indeed, relatively insecure tenure has been claimed to be one of the key reasons for the virtual absence of long-term rental contracts in most countries of Latin America.

The literature has long pointed out that rental arrangements based on fixed rather than share rents are more likely to maximize productivity. Poor producers may, however, not be offered fixed rent contracts because of the risk of default. In these circumstances, sharecropping has emerged as a second-best solution. Hypothetically, sharecropping contracts could be associated with sizeable inefficiencies, implying that government action could improve efficiency. In practice, the efficiency losses associated with sharecropping contracts were found to be relatively small, and improving on them through government intervention has proven to be difficult, if not impossible. Given that the contracting parties have considerable flexibility to adjust contract parameters so as to avoid inefficiencies, for example, by entering into long-term relationships or through close supervision, the general view is that prohibiting sharecropping or other forms of rental contracts is unlikely to improve productivity. The welfare impact of rental contracts depends on the terms of the contract, which in turn are affected by the outside options open particularly to the weaker party. Efforts to expand the range of options available to tenants, for instance, via access to infrastructure and nonagricultural labor markets, are likely to have a more beneficial impact on land rental market outcomes and rural productivity than prohibiting certain options.

Sales Markets

Transfer of land use rights through rental markets can go a long way toward improving productivity and welfare in rural economies. At the same time, the ability to transfer ownership of land will be required to use land as collateral in credit markets, and thus to provide the basis for low-cost operation of financial markets. This advantage comes at the cost that sales markets will be more affected than rental markets by imperfections in credit markets as well as by other distortions, such as subsidies to agriculture.

Activity in land sales markets will depend on participants' expectations regarding future price movements, creating a potential for asset price bubbles that are not justified by the underlying productive value, as well as a tendency toward speculative land acquisition by the wealthy in anticipation of major capital gains. Ample historical evidence also shows that in risky environments where small landowners do not have access to credit markets, distress sales of land by the poor can occur, with consequent negative equity and efficiency impacts. The impact of such distress sales is magnified by the fact that where, as in most rural areas, land sales markets are thin, land prices can fluctuate considerably over time. High transaction costs associated with land sales, which are often further increased by government intervention, can result in the segmentation of such markets whereby certain strata deal only with each other or sales remain entirely informal. All these factors imply that land acquisition by the poor through the land sales market will be difficult, and that as a consequence, the potential for productivity-enhancing land redistribution through sales markets is likely to be very limited.

Empirical Evidence

The general conclusions discussed in the foregoing section, and the importance of government policies in shaping the outcomes from land sales markets that can be observed in practice, are supported by empirical evidence from different regions of the world.

Industrial Countries and Eastern Europe

In many industrial nations high levels of activity in rental markets, which cover more than 70 percent of cultivated land in some countries, illustrate that land rental is far from archaic. Indeed, because of lower capital requirements, many producers prefer to rent rather than to buy land. The fact that well-functioning, though often strongly regulated, rental markets in most industrial countries allow households to enter into long-term contracts that do not appear to be associated with a visible reduction of investment incentives, demonstrates the flexibility and possible advantages of land rental. It also highlights that long-term security of tenure is critical to achieve such outcomes.

In countries of Eastern Europe and the Commonwealth of Independent States (CIS), land rental was particularly important in the initial phases of the transition to a market economy, and continues to be relevant for facilitating access to land by younger producers and for consolidating operational holdings in situations where the ownership structure is highly fragmented. The potential for rental markets is particularly high where land plots were restituted to original owners who had little intention of becoming involved in farming, but where macroeconomic uncertainty and shallow financial markets slowed the development of land sales markets. Land rentals are also important to achieve market-based consolidation in countries that distributed extremely small plots of land.

Long-term leases are not common in Eastern Europe and the CIS because of tenure insecurity. Short-term leases of public land are widely applied to privatize enterprise land owned by local governments in Eastern Europe, but doing so may be highly inefficient. The reason is that the need to renew these periodically encourages rent-seeking and causes insecurity about contract terms that is likely to undermine the scope for long-term investment on such lands. In this case, sales or other means of transferring ownership would be preferable to rental. Developing true lease markets is also difficult where land was privatized only in share form, and where a combination of high risk, scant market development, and limited knowledge about their property rights prevents owners from making the most effective use of their endowments or establishing operations different from the former collectives.

The fragmentation of ownership and operational holdings caused by restitution implies that there may be considerable scope for land sales markets to bring about an ownership distribution that more closely matches the operational distribution of land. Furthermore, the high number of landowners in some of these situations increases the transaction costs of rental markets, and in some cases has reportedly led to preferences for sale rather than rental. However, in the absence of long-term credit, and with an uncertain overall economic outlook, the level of activity in land sales markets remains limited, implying that most of the adjustments of operational holding sizes are arrived at through rental.

Africa

The current differences in land market activity across African countries can often be directly traced to past policy interventions. Rental markets, including long-term transactions that are in many respects equivalent to sales, are extremely active in West Africa, even though they mostly remain informal. Land transfers are more limited in East and southern Africa, where colonial policy had outlawed them for a long time. Recent studies suggest that activity in rental markets can nevertheless increase relatively quickly once the opportunities to engage in such activity exist. In most empirical settings rental markets improved efficiency as well as equity, and evidence from Ethiopia indicates that restrictions on the operation of rental markets also tend to undermine the emergence of nonfarm enterprises. This would imply that eliminating remaining restrictions on the operation of rental markets could make a critical contribution not only to better land utilization, but also to accelerated development of the broader rural economy.

While the cross-country variation in activity in land sales markets is even wider than in the case of rental markets, evidence points toward the rising importance of informal land sales in peri-urban locations and in areas with potential for high-value crops. Although long-term land transactions are often recognized by communities, failure to formalize them creates opportunities to raise doubts about their legality at a later time, something that has often given rise to serious conflict. Greater efforts to formalize transactions at the local level could therefore have a beneficial impact, especially where the buyers are from different ethnic groups or are migrants.

Asia

Most South Asian countries have legislation restricting land rentals to avoid exploitation of tenants by landlords. Although such laws may have provided advantages to sitting tenants, they are likely to have a negative impact on the ability of the landless to obtain land through the market, as well as on landowners' incentives to undertake land-related investment. The case for gradual abolition of such restrictions is strengthened by the example of China and Vietnam, where rental markets transfer land to more productive and land-poor producers in a way that is more effective than what was achieved by administrative reallocation. Evidence from Southeast Asian countries also illustrates that active markets in use rights can develop quickly as the availability of nonagricultural labor increases. Indeed, broader economic development provides considerable potential for the development of land rental markets that in many instances has not yet been fully tapped or developed.

In most of Asia, markets for long-term use rights have developed only recently. The scant empirical evidence available suggests that such markets will generally help to improve both equity and efficiency, except in situations where credit markets do not work well and shocks may therefore force households into distress sales of land. The threat of government expropriation without compensation is reported to lead to a large number of informal land sales by individuals who hope to use such sales as an opportunity to recoup at least a small part of the real value of the land. Land sales markets in Asia, especially at the rural-urban fringe, are subject to a variety of restrictions. For example, in many peri-urban areas restrictions on conversion from agricultural to urban land limit the availability of such land for settlement and lead to high prices, which may put such land out of the reach of large portions of the population.

Latin America

In Latin America, a perception of weak property rights and a history of land rental market restrictions imply that rental markets are less effective than one might expect in transforming a highly unequal distribution of land ownership into a more egalitarian operational distribution. Even though evidence suggests that land rental is more effective in bringing land into productive use than government programs, weak and insecure property rights, together with high transaction costs, continue to limit the scope for exchange, in particular, long-term contracts, in many countries. As a consequence, markets remain segmented and thin, and transactions are often limited to close relatives, where private enforcement without recourse to formal authorities is possible.

While in much of Latin America macroeconomic liberalization led to a significant drop in land prices during the 1990s, the expected results in terms of greater land market activity have only partly materialized. Even where sales markets are active, they are often highly segmented in the sense that large and small landowners trade with each other, but trades rarely occur across different size classes of producers. The rather muted impact of land market liberalization would be expected in a situation where confidence in property rights is still low, capital markets are imperfect, and transaction costs are high. It supports the hypothesis that land markets alone will not be able to equalize the land ownership distribution in a sustainable manner, thereby helping to overcome the structural difficulties plaguing rural areas in the region.

Policy Implications

To realize the full benefits that can accrue from rental markets, governments need to ensure that tenure security is high enough to facilitate long-term contracts and eliminate unjustified restrictions on the operation of such markets. Limitations on the operation of land sales markets may, in some cases, be justified on theoretical grounds. In practice, efforts to implement such restrictions have almost invariably weakened property rights, with the result that the unintended negative consequences of sales market restrictions have often far outweighed the positive impacts they were intended to achieve. With few exceptions in the case of rapid structural change, there is little to recommend such restrictions as an effective tool for policy.

Rental Markets

Short-term rental contracts will provide only limited incentives for users to undertake land-related investment. For longer-term contracts to be feasible, long duration of land rights and high levels of tenure security are critical, and finding ways to ensure such tenure security is a key policy issue. Another constraint on land rental markets has been the imposition of rent ceilings or the award of implicit ownership rights to tenants. While effectively implemented tenancy regulation can benefit sitting tenants, implementing such regulation is costly, and may therefore not be an efficient way of transferring resources to the poor, even in the short term. In the longer term, tenancy restrictions will reduce the supply of land available to the rental market and undermine investment, directly hurting the poor. Evidence from countries that have eliminated such restrictions suggests that doing so can not only improve access to land via rental markets, but can also increase households' participation in the nonfarm labor market and, by reducing the discretionary power of bureaucrats, improve governance. A key policy issue is therefore how to sequence the elimination of such restrictions in a way that does not undermine equity.

Sales Markets

Credit market imperfections will affect the functioning of sales markets and may lead to situations where government intervention could, in a hypothetical world of perfect implementation, lead to outcomes that would improve efficiency and equity. Implementing such interventions has, however, proved to be exceedingly difficult in practice. In the vast majority of cases, restrictions on land sales markets have undermined tenure security and ended up making things worse than they were at the outset.

Restrictions on the transferability of land imposed by a central authority have generally limited credit access and often only pushed such transactions into informality. Except in situations of rapid economic transition, they are unlikely to be justified. Local communities are more likely to be able to appreciate the costs of limiting the transferability of land to outsiders or the benefits of eliminating such restrictions than central government institutions. As long as such decisions are reached in a transparent way and can be enforced, allowing communities to decide on whether to maintain or drop the restrictions on land transactions with outsiders that generally characterize customary land tenure systems may be more effective than imposing central restrictions that are difficult or impossible to enforce.

Land ownership ceilings have generally been ineffective as a means to facilitate the breakup of large farms, and instead have led to red tape, spurious subdivisions, and corruption. Where they were low, they have apparently had a negative impact on investment and landowners' ability to access credit, as in the Philippines. The only situation where they can be justified is where high enough land ceilings may help to limit the speculative acquisition of land, something that may be relevant in some CIS countries.

High levels of fragmentation, caused either by successive subdivision in the course of inheritance or by the desire to award at least one plot of a specific quality or use type to each producer in the process of land distribution, are often thought to lead to inefficiencies in agricultural production. The magnitude and importance of such inefficiencies increase as agricultural production becomes more mechanized. Dealing with fragmentation based on individual initiative will incur high transaction costs. This provided the justification for governments to adopt programs to complement market mechanisms in an effort to facilitate more rapid consolidation of holdings at lower costs. Although significant monetary and nonmonetary benefits are reported from Western Europe, such programs have often been costly and slow. Evidence from China highlights that in environments where administrative capacity is limited, programs aiming at consolidation can run into great difficulties and fail to yield the expected benefits. Rigorous evaluation of the costs and benefits of different approaches to consolidation in Eastern Europe would be desirable, and will be required before wider adoption of such measures can be recommended.

Socially Desirable Land Use

DECENTRALIZED TRANSACTIONS BASED ON SECURE LAND rights are likely to be more conducive to efficiency and equity while offering less scope for corruption and other undesirable side effects than administrative intervention, especially as the number of exchanges increases and the contractual arrangements become more complex. At the same time, governments have a clear role to play in a number of respects. Governments need to help establish the legal and institutional frameworks within which land markets can function and create a policy environment that rewards transactions that will increase productivity and welfare rather than the opposite.

Even though the need to do so is particularly obvious in the case of farm restructuring in Central and Eastern European (CEE) and CIS countries, devolution of authority over state land has also emerged as a critical issue in many other contexts. Where the land distribution is highly unequal and large amounts of productive land are unutilized or underutilized, governments may find it necessary to deal with fundamental issues related to the distribution of asset endowments that markets will not be able to address. In view of the large number of failed attempts at doing so in a way that increased efficiency and equity, drawing lessons from experience would be particularly relevant.

Finally, governments have a number of fiscal and regulatory instruments at their disposal to provide incentives for land use that maximize social welfare, for example, by helping to internalize effects that are external to individual land users. Their shortage of administrative capacity notwithstanding, many developing countries rely disproportionately on a regulatory rather than a fiscal approach, often with the result of encouraging discretionary bureaucratic behavior. Awareness of the rationale, mechanisms, and most appropriate level for intervention can help promote an approach that could produce more satisfactory outcomes, both in terms of compliance and in terms of reducing the red tape with which private entrepreneurs have to deal.

Farm Restructuring

The performance of production collectives, as opposed to service cooperatives for marketing, has been dismal worldwide, and many of the production units in CIS and CEE countries were economically unviable long before the political changes of the 1990s. The process of reform was affected by a number of factors. First, many of the production units performed important social functions, and viable local governments to take over these functions have emerged only slowly. Second, establishing the infrastructure and supporting institutions needed to facilitate the smooth operation of other markets is a process that requires time. Finally, the magnitude of the transition and the large number of interests affected implies that progress toward a stable post-transition equilibrium is unlikely to be smooth and linear.

Indeed, rather than being based on economic considerations, the specific modalities of farm restructuring were determined by a political process. Most CEE countries adopted restitution of land, while the majority of CIS countries and Albania opted for equal distribution of land to farm members. The distribution of physically demarcated plots, as adopted in Albania, the Kyrgyz Republic, and Moldova, was slower and caused considerable fragmentation, whereas the distribution of land shares that could be taken out of the collective under specified procedures allowed quick privatization, but led to hardly any change in the production structure.

The experience of farm restructuring illustrates that it is impossible to divorce land tenure from broader policy and institutional issues and access to local as well as global markets. Most of the economic benefits of titling have initially been concentrated in urban areas, where credit markets were much faster to emerge than in rural ones. The malfunctioning of rural output and factor markets in a risky environment has in many cases prevented households from leaving former collectives. Improvements in the legal and institutional environment will therefore be critical. To ensure a gradual improvement in the functioning of rural markets, including those for land, establishing a correspondence between land shares and physical property and eliminating implicit and explicit restrictions on land rental will be important.

Land Reform

The fact that in many countries the current land ownership distribution has its origins in discriminatory policies rather than in market forces has long provided a justification for adopting policies aimed at land reform. The record of such policies is mixed. Land reforms have been very successful in Asia (Japan, Republic of Korea, Taiwan [China]), and positive impacts have been reported from some African countries such as Kenya and Zimbabwe in the early phases of their postindependence land reforms. At the same time, land reforms in Latin America, other Asian countries, and more recently South Africa, failed to live up to their objectives and remain incomplete in many respects. A key reason for such limited impact was that reforms were often guided by short-term political objectives, or that implementation responded more to planners' conceptions than to the needs of beneficiaries, often limiting the reforms' sustainability and their impact on poverty.

Where extreme inequality in land distribution and underutilization of vast tracts of productive land co-exist with deep rural poverty, a case for redistributive measures to increase access to land by the poor can be made, both politically and from an economic perspective. Even in such cases, a number of different instruments (ranging from expropriation with compensation to activation of rental markets) to effect the transfer of land will normally be available. To ensure success of the reform and productive use of the land, land reform needs to be combined with other programs at the government's disposal. Access to nonland assets and working capital and a conducive policy environment are essential. Those benefiting from land reform need to be able to access output markets as well as credit, the selection of beneficiaries needs to be transparent and participatory, and attention needs to be paid to the fiscal viability of land reform efforts.

Governments are more likely to meet these challenges if they use the mechanisms at their disposal in concert and with the objective of maximizing synergies between them. This also implies a need to integrate land reform into the broader context of economic and social policies aimed at development and poverty reduction, and to implement programs in a decentralized way with maximum participation by potential beneficiaries and at least some grant element. Given the continuing relevance of the issue, the often heated political debate surrounding it, and the lack of quantitative evidence on some more recent approaches, rigorous, open, and participatory evaluation of ongoing experiences is particularly important.

Land Conflict

Increasing scarcity of land in the presence of high rates of population growth, possibly along with a historical legacy of discrimination and highly unequal land access, implies that many historical and contemporary conflicts have their roots in struggles over land. This suggests a special role for land policy in many postconflict settings. An ability to deal with land claims by women and refugees, to use land as part of a strategy to provide economic opportunities to demobilized soldiers, and to resolve conflicts and overlapping claims to land in a legitimate manner will greatly increase the scope for postconflict reconciliation and speedy recovery of the productive sector, a key for subsequent economic growth. Failure to put in place the necessary mechanisms can keep conflicts simmering, either openly or under the surface, with high social and economic costs. In such situations, subsequent transactions can lead to rapid multiplication of the conflict potential, which in some rural areas can result in generalized insecurity of land tenure that jeopardizes the broader rule of law.

Although empirical evidence is limited, even comparatively "minor" conflict over land can significantly reduce productivity and, as it is likely to affect the poor disproportionately, equity. Such conflicts are more likely in situations of rapid demographic or economic transition. Where this is an issue, existing institutions must have the authority and legitimacy to re-interpret rules and thereby prevent relatively minor conflicts from evolving into large-scale confrontation. Instead of opening up parallel channels for conflict resolution, something that has often contributed to increasing rather than reducing the incidence of land-related conflict, building on informal institutions that have social legitimacy and can deal with conflicts at low cost may be preferable.

Land Taxation

Local governments' lack of adequate sources of own revenue may not only affect their financial viability, but also limit their responsiveness and accountability to the local population. Land taxes have long been identified as a source of own revenue for local governments that is associated with minimal distortions, the use of which can at the same time encourage more intensive land use. Even though the extent to which land taxes are used varies widely across countries, actual revenues are generally well below their potential. Reasons for this include deficient incentive structures and neglect of capacity building with respect to assessment and administration, in addition to the political difficulty of having significant land taxes.

The high visibility of land taxes implies that establishing them may be difficult politically, especially in settings where landlords still wield considerable political power. In addition to democratic election of local governments and administrative support to the different aspects of tax collection, schemes to encourage fiscal responsibility and tax collection at the local level, for example, by matching local taxes collected with central funds, can help to design and subsequently collect land taxes appropriately. This can have a significant impact on incentives for effective land use, local government revenues, types and levels of public services provided, and governance.

State Land Ownership

Governments should have the right of compulsory land acquisition, with compensation, for the broader public benefit. At the same time, the way in which many developing country governments exercise this right, especially for urban expansion, undermines tenure security and, because often little or no compensation is paid, also has negative impacts on equity and transparency. In a number of cases, anticipation of expropriation without compensation has led landowners to sell their land in informal markets at low prices, thereby not only forcing them to part with a key asset at a fraction of its real value, but also encouraging unplanned development and urban sprawl that will make subsequent provision of services by the government harder and more costly. Limiting the scope for such uncontrolled exercise of bureaucratic power is a precondition for transparent decentralization and improved tenure security in many peri-urban areas.

The state, especially in developing countries, often lacks the capacity needed to manage land and bring it to its best use. Nevertheless, surprisingly large tracts of land continue to be under state ownership and management. In peri-urban areas, this can imply that unoccupied land of high potential lies idle while investment is held up by bureaucratic red tape and nontransparent processes of decisionmaking that can attract corruption. Experience demonstrates that transferring effective control of such land to the private sector could benefit local governments, increase investment, and improve equity. Where public land has been occupied by poor people in good faith for a long time and significant improvements have been made, such rights should be recognized and formalized at a nominal cost to avoid negative equity outcomes. In cases where valuable urban land owned and managed by the state lies unoccupied, auctioning it off to the highest bidder will be the option of choice, especially if the proceeds can be used to compensate original landowners or to provide land and services to the poor at the urban fringes at much lower cost.

Land Use Regulation

Even though direct management of land through government agencies has rarely been effective, there is a clear role for government to ensure that resources that embody broader social and cultural values and benefits, such as landscapes, biodiversity, historic sites, and cultural values, will not be irreversibly destroyed by myopic individual actions. Furthermore, public action is warranted to reduce undesirable externalities and nuisances, provide incentives for the maintenance of positive external effects such as hydrological balances, and facilitate cost-effective provision of government services. Ensuring that these goals can be met requires paying attention to the nature of property rights and to the ability to adopt specific regulations.

External environmental effects can often be internalized if property rights are designed in a way that encourages prudent management of natural resources, for example, by awarding property rights to groups that jointly benefit from optimum resource use, by strengthening the capacity of these groups for collective action, or by making award of property rights either to individuals or to groups subject to certain restrictions or rewards for desirable behavior. With the exception of interventions to obtain environmental benefits, regulatory action to avoid negative externalities from land use is more likely to be justified in urban and peri-urban than in rural areas. The two questions that need to be answered in this context are whether such measures should be imposed by central or local authorities and how specific interventions should be designed.

Zoning and other land use regulations should be established based on a clear assessment of the capacity needed to implement them, the costs of doing so, and the way in which both costs and benefits will be distributed. Failure to do so has often implied that centrally imposed regulations could either not be implemented with existing capacity, that doing so was associated with high costs that were predominantly borne by the poor, or that they degenerated into a source of rent-seeking. Too little thought has often been given to providing mechanisms that would allow local communities to deal with such externalities in a more decentralized, and therefore a less costly, way. To facilitate this, it is essential that local governments have sufficient capacity and be aware of the advantages and disadvantages of different approaches. A gradual devolution of responsibility for land use regulation to local governments, if coupled with capacity building, could make a significant contribution to efforts toward more effective decentralization.

Land in the Broader Policy Context

Land policy addresses structural issues that, in the longer term, will affect the ability of the poor to take advantage of the economic opportunities opened up by broad macroeconomic changes. Measures to increase land tenure security, reduce the transaction costs of transferring land rights, and establish a regulatory framework to prevent undesirable externalities do, however, cut across traditional boundaries. As a consequence, institutional responsibilities are often dispersed among ministries such as those responsible for the environment, land reform, and urban planning, many of which do not have strong capacity. To overcome the compartmentalization that may result from such arrangements, it will be essential to have a long-term vision and to include land issues in the framework of a development strategy that has broad backing, as well as being supported and coordinated by a high political level. The extent to which goals are achieved should be monitored independently, and the results compared with those achieved by other government programs aimed at poverty reduction and economic development.

Land policy issues are complex, country-specific, of a long-term nature, and often controversial politically. Even though specific interventions in the land policy area can make society better off, such measures may be challenged by vested interests that derive benefits from the status quo. To prevent stalemate or inaction, proper sequencing of reforms and attention to their political economy will be critical. To make reforms feasible, strong local capacity, an open and broadly based policy dialogue, carefully chosen and evaluated pilots, and sharing of experience across countries will be essential, and can also help build capacity for policy formulation.

Challenges Ahead

THE LAST PUBLIC PRONOUNCEMENT BY THE WORLD BANK ON land issues was in the 1975 *Land Reform Policy Paper,* which analyzed land largely in terms of agricultural use and productivity, devoting little attention to the importance of land rights for empowering the poor and improving local governance, the development of the private sector outside agriculture, the gender and equity aspects associated with land, and the problems arising on marginal areas and at the interface between rural and urban areas. Review of the extent to which the substantive messages have changed since 1975 and the implications of this for operational approaches can illustrate the challenges ahead as well as the scope for successfully addressing them.

It is now widely realized that the almost exclusive focus on formal title in the 1975 paper was inappropriate, and that much greater attention to the legality and legitimacy of existing institutional arrangements will be required. Indeed, issues of governance, conflict resolution, and corruption, which were hardly recognized in the 1975 paper, are among the key reasons why land is coming to the forefront of the discussion in many countries. While there are more opportunities for win-win solutions than may often be recognized, dealing with efficiency will not automatically also resolve all equity issues. Stronger rights for women, as well as improving access to land by herders, indigenous populations, and other groups that were historically disadvantaged, can be justified on the basis of basic human rights considerations, even if they do not imply an immediate increase in economic efficiency.

Another area where the policy recommendations of the earlier paper needs to be corrected is the uncritical emphasis on land sales, without being aware of the high transaction costs and the many obstacles that might impede the functioning of sales markets, especially for the poor. Transferability of land is more important today than it was earlier, as evidenced by the high incidence of rental markets and the role these markets play in facilitating the development of an off-farm sector. At the same time rental markets, whose outcomes in terms of equity, productivity, and long-term investment are more beneficial than had been assumed, can address nearly all productivity concerns. Eliminating remaining restrictions on the functioning of these markets is of high priority.

Even though the earlier paper acknowledged the scope for land redistribution to improve equity and efficiency, little follow-up action took place and no criteria to make this recommendation operational were proposed. This report goes beyond this position in two respects. First, it acknowledges that land reform can be a viable investment in a country's future, but that to ensure that the potential is fully utilized, there is a need to carefully assess the requirements and scope of this intervention as compared with others to determine both target groups and necessary complementary measures. The targeting and impact on poverty reduction, empowerment, and productivity, as well as the cost of such a program, need to be evaluated carefully and in a transparent and participatory way, explicitly allowing for modifications of program design in response to results. Second, there are many land-related interventions with a clear poverty-reducing impact that are less controversial politically and less demanding in terms of institutional capacity and fiscal resources. Initiating a program of land reform without at the same time exhausting these other options will not be prudent. Moreover, even where redistributive land reform is either not needed or is not politically feasible, much can and may need to be done to improve land rights and access by the poor.

Not surprisingly, in view of the controversial nature of the subject, in 1975 the Bank was very cautious about offering policy advice and did not confront the political dimension of land directly. Few links between land and broader economic development were drawn that could have helped to integrate land issues with a long-term strategy that had broad support at the country level, and little detail was offered on how the insights gained could be made operational. As a consequence, the impact in terms of implementation was limited. This report illustrates not only that substantive policy advice has evolved considerably since then, but also that the general principles and recommendations derived here need to be translated into the local realities prevailing in any specific setting. Doing so will require not only an active policy dialogue, but also the collaboration of all major stakeholders, drawing on their respective comparative advantage. It is hoped that building on the process embarked upon in its preparation, this report will make a contribution toward reaching this goal.

CHAPTER ONE

Introduction

A CCESS TO LAND AND THE ABILITY TO MAKE productive use of such land is critical to poor people worldwide. In addition to its direct effect on households' welfare and their strategies for risk coping, together with other factors, the system of land tenure will also affect the scope for the emergence of markets and the structure of governance at the local level. Over the last decade decollectivization in Eastern Europe; legal and other action to overcome the legacy of colonial administration in Africa; and a mix of structural and macroeconomic reforms, de-collectivization, and postconflict situations in Latin America and Asia have all contributed to increasing the importance of land tenure, land markets, and effective and sustainable governance of the land resource. This importance is reflected in a growing and increasingly sophisticated body of research that goes to great lengths to adopt a methodological approach that does justice to the topic, and can therefore lead to policy recommendations that take the complexity and the politically controversial nature of the issues at stake into account. As insufficient communication of the results from such research to decisionmakers and other interested parties has often given rise to misunderstandings, this report aims to summarize available insights in a form that is relatively easily accessible; to present general recommendations; and to illustrate how these could be translated into specific, real-world situations.

The Relevance of Land Rights

A CCESS TO LAND AND THE ABILITY TO EXCHANGE IT WITH others and to use it effectively are of great importance for poverty reduction, economic growth, and private sector investment as

1

well as for empowering the poor and ensuring good governance. Even though the nature of the issues at stake varies considerably across regions and countries, the last decade has seen a tremendous increase in the demand for policy advice on land. Two reasons underlie this phenomenon. First, stakeholders are now more aware of the need to complement macroeconomic policies with attention to structural issues if the desired response to greater economic opportunities is to be forthcoming. Structural characteristics will affect the way in which the benefits of other policy interventions are distributed among the population and different groups' incentives for long-term investment in physical and human capital. Addressing these issues is critical to ensure that such opportunities will indeed benefit the large majority of the population. Second, policymakers now better understand the shortcomings of past approaches to land policy.

Even though land markets are no longer considered to be exploitative of the poor, poorly designed land market interventions and regulations continue to hamper the development of land markets in many parts of the world. This directly limits access to land by the landless and poor in rural and peri-urban areas and, to the extent that it discourages renting out by landlords who are therefore unable to make the most productive use of their land, reduces productivity and investment. High transaction costs in land markets can also either increase the cost of providing credit or require the costly development of collateral substitutes, in both cases constraining private sector development The far-reaching impact of distortions is, for example, illustrated by a recent study that estimates that taking both direct and indirect effects together, land market distortions reduce the annual rate of gross domestic product growth in India by 1.3 percent.

Empowerment of the Poor and Governance

Historically, the imposition of systematic barriers preventing the poor from accessing land has been a key strategy for limiting the scope for their economic advancement. The ensuing legacy of exclusion and extra-legality is large: in many African countries, the large majority of land (more than 90 percent on average) remains under customary tenure, which often lacks legal recognition. Informality is similarly widespread in urban areas. This is of particular concern, because in many of these countries growing populations and expanding nonagricultural demand lead to an appreciation of land values and increase the potential for land-related conflict. Recent examples from both East and

West Africa illustrate that failure to attend to such conflicts early on can, especially if land issues overlap with ethnicity and race issues, easily lead to broader social strife, including possible state failure, with devastating consequences for household welfare and economic growth.

In situations where access to opportunities and resources is insecure or is distributed in a highly unequal fashion, generating the sense of participation and belonging that researchers now generally believe is a precondition for good and democratic governance at the local level will be difficult. Where households have reason to believe that raising their voice will undermine their access to land and other resources, they are much less likely to do so. This will make ensuring consistent minimum standards of accountability and transparency extremely difficult. Similarly, many of the recent attempts at decentralization have had limited success, partly because of a lack of fiscal discipline, and partly because of limited success in giving voice to the local population and allowing them to effectively articulate their demands. In countries where land continues to be a key element of households' wealth, land taxation could be used more effectively as an incentive to motivate fiscal discipline by local governments, and by enhancing the accountability of local officials can also strengthen the voice of the local population.

Land Policy in Different Regional Contexts

A BRIEF REVIEW OF EVIDENCE ACROSS THE WORLD'S MAIN regions illustrates not only that close links exist between land policy and economic growth, poverty reduction, and empowerment, but also that during the last decade, the relevance of such policy has increased considerably for a variety of often region-specific reasons. Therefore, despite the complexity and long-term nature of land policy issues and the fact that they cut across different institutions, there is now increasing recognition that, in view of their far-reaching implications, ignoring them can jeopardize social peace and efforts at long-term, sustainable development.

Political and Social Changes in Eastern Europe

The political changes Eastern Europe has experienced during the last decade have moved property rights and privatization issues to the center of many policy discussions. Contrary to earlier expectations, the transition from a centrally planned to a market economy has been more difficult than anticipated, highlighting that establishing the infrastructure for markets to function takes considerable time. Even in the most advanced countries much remains to be done and progress differs considerably, especially between Central and Eastern European and Commonwealth of Independent States countries. Often the failure to quickly define clear rules for land access and ownership appears to has negatively affected investment. Other countries have made considerable advances in privatizing land and, through the provision of an enabling institutional environment, in allowing landowners to make better use of land and thereby bring about much needed economic restructuring. In the future, in addition to balancing the goals of equity and productive efficiency in the process of transition, policy advice is needed on how to allow landowners to exchange their rights and thereby improve the efficiency of land use as well as the functioning of other factor markets.

Structural Reforms in Latin America

With many countries in Latin America having undergone significant economic liberalization, second-generation reforms will be required to tackle more deeply rooted structural problems, including the unequal distribution of land, if persistent poverty and destitution are to be overcome. Implementing such reforms will require formalizing the often highly informal property rights held by the poor; improving the security of tenure, and thus the functioning of land rental and possibly also of sales markets; addressing the legacy of reforms that were only partially successful; and making further efforts to redistribute land and nonland assets to the poor. Providing secure land rights and establishing clear rules to guarantee broad access and facilitate the exchange of land have proven critical in postconflict situations where land was often a key contributor to the conflict. Where local institutions that enjoy little legitimacy control access to land, this is clearly linked to broader governance issues.

Colonial Legacies in Africa

Until recently, customary tenure systems have not enjoyed legal recognition in many African countries because of colonial policies that discriminated against customary tenure, reinforced by policy advice that regarded such forms of tenure as anachronistic. As lands under customary tenure continue to account for the vast majority of rural, and often also urban and peri-urban, land, a large part of the population has remained outside the purview of the law, with far-reaching consequences for investment, the scope for formal land transactions and credit access, and the ability to control land conflicts. In many cases the negative consequences of this lack of legal recognition were exacerbated by misguided policies to nationalize land. In recent decades some countries have realized that radical change will be needed to adapt the legal framework to current conditions. Implementation of new laws is, however, seriously lagging. Where adequate laws exist, combining their implementation with interventions to enhance the productivity of rural producers or the transferability of land in peri-urban areas is likely to have a major impact on poverty reduction, investment, and economic growth.

Combination of Situations in South and East Asia

Although South and East Asia are characterized by huge differences in economic development and in policy frameworks, the importance of land policy issues has increased in virtually all of them. Evidence of the positive fiscal and economic impact of long-term programs to modernize land administration, as demonstrated most clearly by the case of Thailand, has led to increased attention to land administration by a number of countries in the region. In South Asia, interventions to increase the security of tenants have a long tradition. The de-collectivization of agricultural production has allowed China to realize tremendous productivity gains, and policy experiments in rural and urban areas have provided the basis for a gradual strengthening of tenure security and an extension of the duration of lease rights given to households, all of which culminated in the 2002 passage of the new Land Contracting Law. Attention to land issues has also proven to be critical for equity in countries that have only recently emerged from conflict and civil war.

The Role of This Report

RESEARCHERS ACROSS A VARIETY OF DISCIPLINES ARE WELL aware of the importance of land issues, and a large body of research has been accumulated that aims to improve understanding of land issues and the scope for and impact of specific interventions. From simple beginnings and often naïve recommendations that showed little awareness of the potential complexities of land markets, there has been a considerable evolution and increased sophistication. As a consequence, researchers now widely recognize that in the presence of multiple market and institutional imperfections, "first-best" policy advice that was based on an ideal world of perfect markets without transaction costs and structural rigidities is unlikely to be appropriate. The need for a more cautious approach is reinforced by the fact that the patterns of land ownership, access, and use observed in most countries are not the product of the interplay of supply and demand in an impersonal market, but rather the result of political power struggles and noneconomic restrictions. All this has led researchers to frame their results carefully and to make policy recommendations that are much more nuanced and differentiated than in the past, and that attempt to take market imperfections and the presence of self-interested actors with limited information into account in any analysis and in the policy conclusions derived from it.

At the same time, the conclusions from such research have not always been sufficiently well disseminated or transmitted to policy analysts and decisionmakers. In some cases this has given rise to policy advice that, because it failed to adequately reflect the need to account for local conditions, may not have been the most appropriate for the goals of pro-poor development. The failure to communicate the results of recent research clearly or to critically evaluate innovative approaches has also created misunderstandings between different groups interested in land policy.

This report aims to summarize recent research and operational experience in the area of land tenure and to illustrate the policy implications arising from it in a way that is accessible to a broader audience. Doing so is expected to have two tangible benefits. First, by showing that disagreement on key principles is less than is often presumed, the report should make it easier to address key policy issues in this area, thereby helping to close the gap between research and practice, improve the integration of land into long-term country strategies, and focus discussion on areas where no unambiguous evidence exists. Second, by highlighting the need for policy discussion and careful evaluation to adapt general principles to local conditions, the report aims to encourage the formulation of policy advice that, by taking the specifics of any given situation into account, will harness the full potential of land policy for poverty reduction, economic growth, empowerment, and improved governance in the Bank's client countries.

CHAPTER TWO

Property Rights to Land

A SOCIETY'S ABILITY TO DEFINE AND, WITHIN A broad system of the rule of law, establish institutions that can enforce property rights to land as well as to other assets is a critical precondition for social and economic development. Better access to markets as well as increased population density tend to increase the value of land and can lead to either the emergence of institutions that facilitate a more precise definition of property rights to this asset or the emergence of costly conflict over land rights. Together with the exogenous imposition of property rights by overlords, these factors determine the evolution of property rights systems throughout history. A review of history illustrates that the way in which land rights are assigned does affect economic and human development in the long term. Moreover, property rights arrangements that may not be conducive from either an economic or a social point of view may stay in place for a long time.

Three reasons account for public involvement in the establishment and guarantee of property rights to land: (a) the elimination of the need for individuals to dissipate resources in trying to establish property rights, (b) the cost and equity advantages normally associated with a systematic approach, and (c) the network effects resulting from consistent availability of information across administrative units. This chapter identifies and discusses key elements such as duration of land rights, identification of boundaries, types of rights, enforcement mechanisms, and scope for gradual evolution of property rights arrangements in response to changing economic and social conditions.

The magnitude of the benefits that result from establishing property rights, and the type of intervention most appropriate in any given setting, will depend on the scope for investment (by locals and outsiders) and transfer of property rights, the possible threats of dispossession or conflict, and the potential for increasing output and efficiency by means of land transfers. Empirical evidence from across the world reveals the demand for greater security of tenure and illustrates that appropriate interventions to increase tenure security can have significant benefits in terms of equity, investment, credit supply, and reduced expenditure of resources on defensive activities.

To increase the security of property rights, legal and institutional issues need to be tackled in tandem or evolve jointly, with reference to the broader social and economic environment within which land rights are embedded. On the legal side, the definition of property rights to land and the way in which people can acquire them must be clear and equitable, in line with practice on the ground; rights must be sufficiently long term; and risks of losing them to discretionary bureaucratic behavior must be eliminated. On the institutional side, procedures need to be formulated, institutions need to be accessible, and services should be provided effectively and at low cost. All this implies that beyond the formulation of general principles, practical implementation of any measures to increase the security of tenure has to start with in-depth analysis of the current situation. If the administrative infrastructure is thin and resources are scarce, this will imply a significant role for local communities.

The Historical Context

Land rights can be understood properly only if viewed against the context of their evolution

A HISTORICAL REVIEW OF LAND TENURE ARRANGEMENTS IS important not only because dealing with current land policy issues is impossible without an awareness of the underlying historical dimensions, but also because many of the systems that have historically been encountered in the evolution of property rights, from the nomadic existence of hunter-gatherers to haciendas and highly mechanized farms, still exist side by side in different regions of the world. Placing these within the broader historical evolution of land rights will help in understanding not only their origins, but also the possible paths of development. Doing so does not aim to substitute for the literature on the subject but rather to build on the available work to identify driving forces that underlie the evolution of land tenure arrangements over time and to use these as a backdrop for the challenges policymakers face and their options for addressing them.

Property rights generally emerge as a result of the interaction of economic and political forces. Economists have long used the concept of induced innovation (Hayami and Ruttan 1985) to explain how, with increased population density, a more precise definition of property rights can reduce open access to and provide individuals with investment incentives. According to this theory, social groups adopt property rights because the benefits from doing so exceed the costs, implying that society will always gain. However, there are many cases where the virtuous cycle of increased scarcity of land leading to more precise definition of property rights has not materialized, but instead conflict has arisen. A second strand of the literature emphasizes that those in power may establish certain types of property rights to exclude others or affect their behavior. In this case, the imposition of property rights will not necessarily be associated with economic benefits and may be extremely sub-optimal from a social perspective. Therefore, institutions that lead to socially undesirable outcomes can originate in the inability to respond to the pressure resulting from increased population or outside intervention. In either case, and irrespective of the original causes, inefficient institutions can prevail for a long period and changing them may be politically difficult. Nonetheless, the impact on economic outcomes may be considerable.

Evolution of Customary Tenure with Population Growth

A key justification for secure property rights is that they provide incentives for investment in land and sustainable resource management. In areas that are naturally suitable for arable cultivation, with low population densities, cultivators have no incentive to invest in soil fertility, and instead will practice shifting cultivation. Under this system the cultivator clears a plot of land and grows food crops for a few years until the soil fertility has been exhausted. At this point the cultivator moves to a new plot and leaves the previous plot fallow to restore its soil fertility (Boserup 1965).[1] Because land is plentiful and no labor input is needed to restore fertility, ownership security is not required. Instead, the general right to cultivate a piece of land is an inseparable, and in principle inalienable, element of tribal membership. Cultivation rights are assigned to individuals on a temporary basis, normally for as long as the cleared plot is cultivated. Once cultivation has ended because soil fertility has been exhausted, the plot falls back to the lineage and the family either selects a new plot or has a plot allocated by the chief of the tribe. There is little

Societies adopt property rights when high population density requires land-related investment or if other factors increase the value of land

incentive to claim individual property rights in land, and the general right to use land, though not specific plots, is available to all members of a lineage. The need to expand the level of agricultural production in line with higher population density implies that fallow cycles will become increasingly short until shifting cultivation is no longer adequate as a method of restoring soil fertility. Other means, such as applying manure, planting trees, terracing, or irrigating, will be needed to do so. Unless property rights to land are defined in a way that will allow those making the investment to reap at least part of the benefit, none of these investment activities will be undertaken voluntarily. Historically, this has been one of the driving forces underlying the adoption of more secure property rights as well as the development of social structures to facilitate collective action to engage in land-related investment.

The diffusion of exogenous technical change and/or expansion of trade generally can have an investment-increasing effect similar to the one caused by increased population density. By increasing the stream of incomes that can be derived from a unit of land, technical change and trade expansion increase incentives for better definition of property rights in land. Indeed, establishment of tree crops, and the associated investment in clearing and leveling of land, was generally undertaken only where institutional innovations had enhanced tenure security adequately so that individuals could be sure to reap the benefits from such investments. Similarly, the transportation revolution caused by the steamship in the late nineteenth century led not only to the involvement of hitherto unexplored countries and states in global trade but also to increased demand for individualized ownership of land. For example, the opening of Thailand to international rice trade through the Bowering treaty of 1826 induced a quantum increase in the demand for rice land in the Thailand plains and brought about the introduction of a formal land registration system (Feeney 1988).

Failure to develop property right institutions will lead to conflict and resource dissipation

The above describes a virtuous cycle where greater resource values lead to an increasingly precise definition of property rights that induces higher levels of investment. However, there are many examples throughout history where failure to establish the necessary property rights institutions has led to conflict and resource dissipation rather than investments that would enhance resource values and productivity. Both conceptual models and empirical evidence suggest that the broader economic impact of the way in which property rights are secured will be significant (Eggertsson 1996; Grossman 2001, 2002; Grossman and Kim 1995).

Outside Interventions

On a global scale, the gradual increase of tenure security described in the previous section was followed only in a few marginal areas where no minerals were available. Most other regions at some time experienced colonial intervention or the imposition of overlords. The nature of such intervention was affected by the level of population density prevailing at the time of colonial conquest, and its impacts can be seen most clearly in the case of low population densities. At low levels of mechanization, and with the exception of a few plantation crops, agricultural production does not entail economies of scale. Smallholder agriculture will therefore maximize both output and social welfare. As long as land can be accessed freely, the establishment of large-scale plantations, for example, coffee plantations, as well as the recruitment of labor for agriculture at wages that are below the marginal return to labor in independent agricultural production, will not be feasible unless governments adopt interventions to systematically reduce the benefits that smallholders can obtain on their own holdings. Such interventions to reduce overall welfare so as to benefit a particular group have been common throughout history (Binswanger, Deininger, and Feder 1995).

Low population density or the drastic decimation of the domestic population in the context of colonial conquest in many of the colonies in the Americas and Africa required the imposition of coercion to obtain labor either for agricultural production on large farms and plantations or for a supply of labor to work in the mines. As shown and formalized in detail elsewhere (Conning 2002), in such landlord economies, getting households that would otherwise engage in higher-productivity family farming to supply labor to mines or large farms requires that the supply of land be artificially restricted. To do so, the colonial powers applied three main strategies, namely:

- *Reducing the land available for peasant cultivation* by allocating rights to "unoccupied" lands so that they went to members of the ruling class only, thereby confining free peasant cultivation to infertile or remote areas with poor infrastructure and market access (table 2.1 lists a variety of cases in which access to high-quality land was restricted). Farm profits or welfare on free peasant lands were thus reduced by the higher labor requirements needed to produce a unit of output on poor land, by increased transport and marketing costs, and by increased prices for consumer goods imported to the region.

Colonial rulers often introduced discriminatory systems of property rights

These systems often reduced efficiency, undermined equity, and had to be maintained by force

Table 2.1 Intervention to establish and support large farms, selected locations and periods

Continent and country	Land market interventions	Taxes and interventions in labor and output markets
Africa		
Algeria	Titling, circa 1840 Land grants under settlement programs, 1871 Settlers' law, 1873	Tax exemption for European farmers' workers, 1849 Credit provision for European settlers
Angola	Land concessions to Europeans, 1838, 1865	Slavery until 1880 Vagrancy laws, 1875
Egypt (Ottomans)	Land grants, 1840	*Corvée* labor from 16th century *Corvée* exemption for farm workers, 1840s Land tax exemption for large landlords, 1856 Credit and marketing subsidies, 1920s and 1930s
Kenya	Land concessions to Europeans, circa 1900 No African land purchases outside reserves, 1926	Hut and poll taxes from 1905 Labor passes, 1908 Squatter laws 1918, 1926, and 1939 Restrictions on Africans' market access from 1930: • Dual price system formalized • Quarantine and forced destocking for livestock • Monopoly marketing associations • Prohibition of African export crop cultivation Subsidies to mechanization, 1940s
Malawi	Land allotments to Europeans, 1894	Tax reductions for farm workers, circa 1910
Mozambique	Comprehensive rights to leases under *prazo,* 19th century	Labor tribute, 1880 Vagrancy law, 1899 Abolition of African trade, 1892 Forced cultivation, 1930
Sokotho Caliphate (Nigeria)	Land grants to settlers, 1804	Slavery, 19th century
South Africa	Native reserves, 19th century Pseudo-communal tenure in reserves, 1894 Native Lands Act, 1912 • Demarcation of reserves • Elimination of tenancy • Prohibition of African land purchases outside reserves	Slavery and indentured labor, 19th century Restrictions on Africans' mobility, 1911, 1951 Monopoly marketing, from 1930 Prison labor, circa 1950 Direct and indirect subsidies, 20th century
Tanganyika (Tanzania)	Land grants to settlers, 1890	Hut tax and *corvée* requirements, 1896 Compulsory cotton production, 1902 Vagrancy laws (work cards), 20th century Exclusion of Africans from credit, 1931 Marketing cooperatives to depress African prices, 1940
Zimbabwe	Reserves, 1896 and 1931	Poll and hut taxes, 1896 Discrimination against tenancy, 1909 Monopoly marketing boards, from 1924 • Dual price system in maize • Forced destocking of livestock, 1939

(table continues on following page)

Table 2.1 *(continued)*

Continent and country	Land market interventions	Taxes and interventions in labor and output markets
Asia		
India (north)	Land grants from 1st century	Hacienda system, 4th century B.C.
		Corvée labor, from 2nd century
China (south)		Limitations on peasant mobility, circa 500
		Tax exemption for slaves, circa 500
		Gentry exemption from taxes and labor services, 1400
Japan	Exclusive land rights to developed wasteland, 723	Tribute exemption for cleared and temple land, 700
Java and Sumatra	Land grants to companies, 1870	Indentured labor, 19th century
		Cultivation system, 19th century
Philippines	Land grants to monastic orders, 16th century	*Encomienda*
		Repartimiento
		Tax exemption for hacienda workers, 16th century
Ceylon (Sri Lanka)	Land appropriation, 1840	Plantations tax exempt, 1818
		Indentured labor, 19th century
Europe		
Prussia	Land grants, from 13th century	Monopolies on milling and alcohol
		Restrictions on labor mobility, 1530
		Land reform legislations, 1750–1850
Russia	Land grants, from 14th century	Restrictions on peasant mobility:
	Service tenure, 1565	• Exit fees, 1400–50
		• Forbidden years, 1588
		• Enserfment, 1597
		• Tradability of serfs, 1661
		Home farm exempt from taxation, 1580
		Debt peonage, 1597
		Monopoly on commerce, until 1830
South America		
Chile	Land grants, 16th century	*Encomienda,* 16th century
		Labor services, 17th century
		Import duties on beef, 1890
		Subsidies to mechanization, 1950–60
El Salvador	Grants of public land, 1857	Vagrancy laws, 1825
	Titling of communal land, 1882	Exemption from public and military services for large landowners and their workers, 1847
Guatemala	Resettlement of Indians, 16th century	Cash tribute, 1540
		Manamiento, circa 1600
		Debt peonage, 1877
Mexico	Resettlement of Indians, 1540	*Encomienda,* 1490
	Expropriation of communal lands, 1850	Tribute exemption for hacienda workers, 17th century
		Debt peonage, 1790
		Return of debtors to haciendas, 1843
		Vagrancy laws, 1877
Peru	Land grants, 1540	*Encomienda,* 1530
	Resettlement of Indians, 1570	Labor service exemption for hacienda workers, 1550
	Titling and expropriation of Indian land, 17th century	Slavery of Africans, 1580

Source: Binswanger, Deininger, and Feder (1995).

- *Imposing differential taxation* by requiring free peasants to pay tribute, hut, head, or poll taxes (in cash, kind, or labor services), while often exempting workers or tenants of manorial estates or taxing them at much lower rates. Such systems were used widely in Western Europe during the feudal period; in ancient Japan; in China, India, and the Ottoman Empire; and by all colonial powers (table 2.1). Tribute systems survived into the second half of the 19th century in Eastern Europe and Japan. As long as free peasants could pay tribute or taxes in kind or in cash and have equal access to output markets, taxation alone may have been insufficient to generate a supply of workers or tenants, and it was therefore often complemented by output market interventions.

- *Restricting market access* or confining public goods (roads, extension, credit) to rulers' farms was often done by setting up cooperative or monopoly marketing schemes to buy only from the farms of the rulers. The *prazo* system in Mozambique combined rights to labor and tribute from peasants with monopolies on inputs and outputs. In Kenya the colonial government prohibited the production of coffee by Africans outright until the 1950s. European monopolies on sales of tobacco in what is now Malawi and Zimbabwe were directly transferred to large farms after the countries gained independence. In some cases this was combined with direct subsidization of these farms to make them competitive with peasant farms that would otherwise have shown superior economic performance.

A fourth strategy was the importation of indentured labor or slaves.[2] The workers had to be indentured to prevent them from establishing plots of their own or going into mining at least for the period of indenture. Once members of the ruling group began to establish viable agricultural production, getting enough workers for their estates required interventions in more than one market. The most common pattern was to combine restrictions on land use with differential taxation. This pattern led to the establishment of haciendas, the defining characteristic of which is that a large landowner manages most of the land and workers have access only to small house plots to ensure their subsistence, emerged as the predominant form in Algeria, Egypt, Kenya, South Africa, and Zimbabwe; in Bolivia, Chile, Honduras, Mexico, Nicaragua, Peru, and other countries in Latin America; in the Philippines; and in Prussia and other parts of Eastern Europe.

A major purpose of the concentration of land by individual landlords was to restrict the indigenous population's possibility of engaging in independent cultivation, something that is illustrated by the fact that the landlord's home farm often vastly exceeded the area actually cultivated and much of the land remained under forest or fallow or was devoted to extensive livestock grazing. At the height of the feudal period in Western Europe, between one-quarter and one-half of the total area on manorial estates was cultivated by the owner of the home farm. On Latin American and African haciendas, that share was initially much lower, in some cases only about one-tenth (Palmer 1977).[3]

By contrast to the case of low population density, in situations where population density was already high at the time of colonization, colonial powers could simply replace pre-existing structures, something that the British did in India, the Dutch did in Indonesia, the Dutch and the Portuguese did in Sri Lanka, and to some extent the French did in West Africa.[4] They either established overlords who would collect tribute in return for cultivation rights or conferred land ownership on the crown or an overlord. The latter in practice converted small farmers into tenants or sharecroppers. Landlord estates were prevalent in China, Egypt, Ethiopia, eastern India, Iran, Japan, the Republic of Korea (henceforth referred to as Korea), and Pakistan. In many of these colonial environments, landlords could easily restrict peasants' alternatives and maintain control over land and labor, and sometimes over output markets.

Reforms of Land Relations

To overcome the long-term effects of outside intervention and noneconomic distortions, land reform measures were often needed. The way in which land relations were transformed from feudal landlord estates or haciendas continues to affect systems in place at present and shape the challenges current land policy efforts face. As land reform involves the transfer of rents from a ruling class to tenant workers, it is not surprising that most large-scale land reforms were associated with revolts (Bolivia), revolutions (Chile, China, Cuba, El Salvador, Mexico, Nicaragua, Russia), conquests (Japan and Taiwan [China]), the demise of colonial rule (eastern India, Kenya, Mozambique, Vietnam, Zimbabwe), or the end of major wars (Hungary and much of Eastern Europe). Attempts at land reform without massive political upheaval

Land reform was often needed to correct the bias introduced by nonmarket intervention

15

have rarely succeeded in transferring much of a country's land or have done so extremely slowly because of a lack of political commitment to provide the funding to compensate owners. This report distinguishes among transformation of landlord estates to smallholder farms, transition to junker estates, and collectivization and de-collectivization. Even in Europe, the reform of land relations has been a lengthy, conflictive, and highly political process (Swinnen 2002), and often the introduction of universal franchise has been essential to constrain the power of landlords (Acemoglu and Robinson 1999). This illustrates not only that greater democratization is often inextricably intertwined with the reform of property rights, but also that, in many instances, far-reaching reforms to the property rights system have been undertaken only in conjunction with major historic events, something that is confirmed by the recent changes of property rights in Eastern European countries.

Land reform was relatively simple in tenancy systems, but much more difficult where haciendas prevailed

Rapid transition from landlord estates to family farms in a market economy has led to stable systems of production relations. The organization of production remains the same family farm system; the only change is that ownership is transferred from large landlords to tenants who already farm the land and have the skills and implements necessary to cultivate their fields. Government involvement in the transition has often been substantial, ranging from a ceiling on the size of landholdings and on the amounts to be paid for the land, to the establishment of beneficiaries' financial obligations. Many reforms that followed this pattern provided stronger incentives for tenant-owners to work and invest in their farms and led to increases in output and productivity. The resulting systems have had great stability. Since the end of World War II landlord estates in Bolivia, large areas of China, eastern India, Ethiopia, Iran, Japan, Korea, and Taiwan (China) have been transferred to tenants in the course of successful land reforms. Theoretically, the productivity gains associated with such reforms come about because of improved work and investment incentives associated with increased security of tenure. These gains may be modest if tenants had to compensate landowners at near market prices, if security of tenure had already been high, if cash rent contracts had prevailed, or if the disincentive effects associated with share tenancy had been low (Otsuka and Hayami 1988). Empirical evidence shows that the reform of landlord estates led to considerable investment, adoption of new technology, and increases in productivity (Callison 1983; Dorner and Thiesenhusen 1990; King 1977; Koo 1973; Warriner 1969) and that costs to the government for complementary investments supporting the transition in ownership structure, such as infrastructure, housing, and training in management skills, were low because the structure of the smallholder production system was already in place.

By contrast with the relatively smooth transition from landlord estates to family farms, the reform of hacienda systems has been slow and difficult. The outcome has frequently been the emergence of large owner-operated junker estates, with greatly increased home farm cultivation, that produce a variety of crops and livestock products using a hierarchy of supervisors. By substituting often subsidized capital for labor, junker estates were transformed into large-scale, mechanized, commercial farms that no longer depended on large amounts of labor. Collective farming was also introduced in a number of countries based on an erroneous belief in the productive superiority of large farms. For example, landlord estates in China, the former Soviet Union, and Vietnam were initially converted into family farms. The redistributed farmlands were later consolidated into collectives, in which land is owned and operated jointly under a single management. In Algeria, Chile, the former Democratic Republic of Germany, Mozambique, Nicaragua, and Peru, junker estates or large commercial farms were converted directly into state farms. In most cases workers continued as employees under a single management, with no change in internal production relations, to maintain the perceived economies of scale and superior management associated with these arrangements.

Importance of Land Rights for Long-Term Development

In view of the far-reaching impact of land tenure arrangements on the economic opportunities open to households, it should come as no surprise that, in the long run, the initial land ownership distribution has decisively affected the scope for broader economic development well beyond the agriculture sector. Land and real estate are major assets in modern societies (Ibbotson, Siegel, and Love 1985), with land being even more important in developing countries, where it often constitutes not only the main element in households' asset portfolios, accounting, for example, for about 60 percent in Uganda, but is also a key determinant of household welfare.[5] The way in which land rights are defined will therefore affect not only the returns from specific investments and the direction and magnitude of technical change, but also the way in which the gains from exogenous increases in land values will be distributed, for example, through infrastructure investment, better opportunities for trade, and economic growth in general (Berry 2001). The desire to have the poor benefit from such

The initial distribution of land affects the nature and rate of long-term economic growth

Figure 2.1 Initial land distribution and economic growth, selected countries

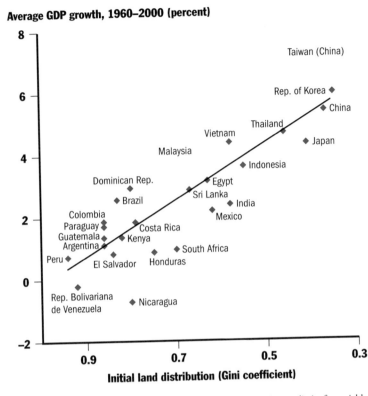

Note: The Gini coefficient measures the degree of concentration (inequality) of a variable in a distribution of its elements. It compares the Lorenz curve of a ranked empirical distribution with the line of perfect equality. This line assumes that each element has the same contribution to the total summation of the values of a variable. The Gini coefficient ranges between 0, where there is no concentration (perfect equality) and 1, where there is total concentration (perfect inequality).

Source: Authors' calculations based on Deininger and Squire (1997); World Bank data (for 2002 from the Statistical Information Management and Analysis database).

investment was the basis for arguments to put redistribution before growth (Adelman, Morris, and Robinson 1976). Indeed, in societies with highly unequal access to assets and opportunities, ensuring that development efforts do not end up benefiting a narrow elite of the rich and powerful, thereby deepening pre-existing inequalities instead of helping the poor, is often extremely difficult (Birdsall and Londono 1997).

Cross-country regressions illustrate not only that the security of property rights does have a significant impact on overall growth (Keefer and Knack 2002), but also that initial access to assets affects subsequent outcomes (Birdsall and Londono 1997; Deininger and Squire 1998; Rodrik 1998).[6] Figure 2.1 illustrates this graphically, highlighting that during 1960–2000, countries that had a more egalitarian distribution of land tended to be characterized by higher levels of economic growth. This general pattern is confirmed if more sophisticated panel techniques are used and other control variables, including the inequality of education, are included (Deininger and Olinto 2000).

The historical importance of land access in the industrial world is illustrated by the divergent reaction of the western and eastern parts of Europe to the plague-induced population declines of the 14th century. As a large body of literature discusses, the associated drop in tribute contributed to the erosion of serfdom in Western Europe, but led to the reimposition of serfdom in Eastern Europe (Brenner 1997; Hilton 1978). Factors held responsible for this difference include a combination of higher wages and urban opportunities, better definition and more equal allocation of property rights, and higher levels of collective action and social capital in the West compared with the East (Allen 1998). In the latter, somewhat similar to what is still encountered in remote, backward areas of some developing countries, a monopoly on the control of land allowed lords to extract tribute and strengthened their political power to claim the land, monopolize output markets, and control the movement of peasants who, without secure and independent land access, and without an entrepreneurial middle class as possible allies, were powerless to resist the imposition of such constraints.

A more recent, but similar, assessment of the long-term importance of land tenure institutions emerges from a comparison of Indonesia, the Philippines, and Thailand. In Indonesia development was based mainly on the exploitation of tropical rain forest under Dutch colonialism, resulting in bifurcation of the rural sector between rice-farming peasant proprietors and large plantations for tropical export crops that were based on hired labor. In the Philippines the exploitation of a similar resource base under Spanish rule resulted in pervasive landlessness among the rural population and successive, though not always successful, attempts at land reform. By contrast, a relatively homogeneous class of land-owning peasants continued to dominate in Thailand, where the delta plains were suitable only for rice production and formed the resource base for development. These different agrarian structures associated with different social value systems have accounted for differential development performance across the three economies in the last 30 years (Hayami 2001).

While cross-country regressions are unable to provide a causal interpretation for such a relationship, two possible explanations stand out. One explanation is that where land is highly concentrated, landlords have an effective monopoly over the labor (as well as the output) market, which makes the accumulation of human capital, or indeed of any other form of investment, much less rewarding.

Land concentration reduces efficiency of resource use

A comparison between Colombia and Costa Rica on the one hand and El Salvador and Guatemala on the other can illustrate this. Even though they share a common colonial history, language, religion, climate, topography, factor endowments, and technology, these countries reacted in quite different ways to the coffee boom of the 19th century. In El Salvador and Guatemala, large landowners who depended on a repressive labor regime to remain economically viable prevailed, and the boom led to land expropriation, especially from Indian and indigenous communities, and concentration of land on a massive scale. Landlords held a monopsony on power in the labor market, which allowed them to pay their workers the bare subsistence minimum, thereby eliminating any incentives for human capital accumulation. By contrast, in Colombia and Costa Rica, two countries characterized by small-scale landholdings where elites depended on trade rather than on large-scale agriculture, the boom led to the emergence of a smallholder coffee economy. As a consequence, literacy rates differed sharply between the two groups of countries from the late 19th century and continue to do so (table 2.2). Table 2.2 also reveals significant gaps with respect to other human development indicators and the establishment of democracy, which occurred about 40 years later in the countries characterized by dominance by large landlords than in those countries that relied on a smallholder production structure.[7]

It can also affect the political economy and provision of local public goods

A second, complementary, interpretation of the link between inequality in initial endowments and subsequent growth is that high concentration of land either reduces the incentives for provision of public goods such as infrastructure and irrigation or biases the provision of such goods in a direction that is more useful to landlords. The literature has long noted that communities' ability to provide public goods may itself be a function of the underlying land ownership distribution (Platteau and Baland 2001). In most cases the total surplus to be derived from land and associated public goods tends to increase with greater equality in the asset distribution (Bardhan and Ghatak 1999), something that is supported empirically by the finding that in Mexico, as well as in India, communities with more egalitarian land access are characterized by higher levels of collective action (Banerjee 1999; Dayton-Johnson 2000). Empirical evidence from India highlights that patterns of land ownership and landlessness will affect the types of public goods provided, as well as how efficiently they are provided (Foster and Rosenzweig 2001). Experimen-

Table 2.2 Impact of land ownership distribution in four Latin American countries

Country	Colombia	Costa Rica	Guatemala	El Salvador
Structural characteristics				
Land privatization	1870–80	1820–40	1870s	1870s
Share of coffee farms smaller than 10 hectares	61.0	42.2	13.1	13.5
Share of coffee farms larger than 50 hectares	14.0	37.5	79.5	57.1
Share of coffee in exports (percent)				
1900	49	76	56	83
1929	55	58	77	93
Adult literacy (percent)				
1900	34	36	12	26
1910	40	50	13	26
1930	52	67	18	27
1980	85	91	54	64
Social and economic development				
GDP per capitia (PPP US $, 1995)	6,130	5,850	3,340	2,610
Rank on Human Development Index (1994)	51	33	117	112
Democracy since	1958	1948	1996	1992

GDP = Gross domestic product.
PPP = Purchasing power parity.
Source: Nugent and Robinson (2002).

tal evidence points in a similar direction, suggesting that in communities where initial asset endowments are highly unequal, the ability to engage in socially optimal collective action is seriously impaired and, as a consequence, welfare losses are incurred (Cardenas forthcoming).

The exogenous imposition of two different kinds of land revenue settlement by the British in colonial India provides a "historical experiment" that allows investigators to make inferences about the long-term impact of land tenure arrangements in an environment where other factors, for instance, endowments and colonial power policy, differ little. Under the *zamindari* or landlord system, revenue collectors (*zamindars*) received full rights to land subject to delivering a fixed amount of revenue to the colonial power. The cultivator-owner (*mahalwari*) system, by contrast, vested land rights in village bodies, essentially establishing individual land ownership by producers. Thus the differences in the concentration of land ownership that were first documented in the late 19th century and persist to this day are not surprising, despite the successful abolition of intermediary interests following independence and more than half a century of land reforms. More interesting, a combination of reduced incentives for investment, constrained credit market access, low effort supply, and little potential for collective action (which is more difficult for extremely heterogeneous groups) associated with the historical assignment of property rights has had far-reaching impacts on long-term development. In particular, differences emerged in the ability to get the state to deliver public goods, the associated human development outcomes, and the adoption of agricultural technology (Banerjee, Gertler, and Ghatak 2002). In non-landlord districts the availability of village schools is 20 to 60 percent above what is found in landlord districts, infant mortality is 40 percent lower, and levels of literacy are 5 percent higher. Adjusting for other characteristics, non-landlord areas were characterized by a higher availability of such public goods as irrigation, which was 25 percent higher than in non-landlord areas, leading to faster adoption of high-yielding varieties, use of inputs such as fertilizer (45 percent higher), and significantly higher yields, even though the differences in land tenure institutions had long been eliminated.

Conceptual Framework

Land rights are social conventions about the distribution of benefits from land use

PROPERTY RIGHTS ARE SOCIAL CONVENTIONS BACKED UP BY the power of the state or the community (at various levels) that allow individuals or groups to lay "a claim to a benefit or income stream that the state will agree to protect through the assignment of duty to others who may covet, or somehow interfere with, the benefit stream" (Sjaastad and Bromley 2000, p. 367). Governments play an important role by determining how property rights are defined, how they can be enforced, and how they evolve in line with changing economic conditions. This, in turn provides a basis for the level of tenure security enjoyed by individual landowners and their ability and willingness to exchange such rights with others. All this suggests that property rights are a social construct. Property is not merely the assets themselves, but consensus between people about how these assets should be held, used, and exchanged (de Soto 2000). Moreover, property rights to land are not static, but evolve in response to changes in the economic and social environment.

By defining who is entitled to reap the benefit streams that flow from a given resource and thereby establishing correspondence between the effort expended in trying to increase the value of this resource and the reward to be had from such activity, land rights are not only a key element of the social fabric of most societies, but also a critical determinant of investment, and thus of economic growth. The nature and characteristics of rights and enforcement institutions together define the perceived security of property rights to land, and it is this security that will affect decisions about land use, land-related investments, and the willingness to engage in land transfers. In many cultures, official land records were among the first documents to appear once a written language had been developed.[8] Indeed, the benefits of well-defined and secure property rights and the advantages of public provision of such rights have, over history, led virtually all economically and politically advanced societies to establish state-managed systems for regulating land ownership and land transfers (Powelson 1988).

Property Rights as a Public Good

Establishing and enforcing a system of property rights to land has benefits that extend beyond the individual landowner. The benefits are to a large extent nonrival; that is, one person's enjoyment will not reduce others' ability to benefit from the system. However, it is possible to exclude some individuals or groups from access to these benefits. The broad distribution of the benefits associated with providing information about the assignment of property rights to land, as well as the enforcement of such rights, provides a strong rationale for government involvement. The infrastructure needed to physically demarcate and delineate plots, to establish and maintain accurate records of land ownership, and to enforce these rights and resolve whatever disputes might arise is associated with high setup costs. The tools used to record land rights, such as maps and inventories of land use, also provide essential inputs for planning and providing other public services. All this implies that significant cost advantages are associated with public provision of information in the form of land records and a judiciary and enforcement system to guarantee property rights to land.

Property rights have public good characteristics

The existence of clear and well-defined property rights to land will prevent the dissipation of valuable economic resources in attempts to secure and define such rights by individuals. This will allow landowners to invest resources in productive activities instead of spending them on defending their land claims. Where property rights are incomplete or

Public establishment of property rights will prevent resource dissipation, providing particular benefits to the poor

23

ill-defined, entrepreneurs and households will need to spend resources to maintain their existing property rights or to establish new ones. Investments such as guards, fences, and other demarcation devices to demonstrate the legitimacy of property claims and to defend such rights against possible intruders often have little direct social or productive value, lead to the dissipation of potential rents, and divert resources from more productive uses of land (Allen and Lueck 1992). Studies show that the privately optimal amount of spending on protection will often be excessive from a social point of view (De Meza and Gould 1992; Feder and Feeny 1991; Hotte 2001; Malik and Schwab 1991). Thus well-defined property rights reduce the need to expend economically valuable resources in defending claims and allow these to be used for productive investment instead (Grossman and Mendoza 2001).

The benefits individual land owners derive from public provision of property rights will be proportional to the amount of land they own. At the same time, in situations where government institutions do not function well, the ability to invoke the powers of the state and to resort to self-enforcement will be highly correlated with individuals' wealth. For this reason, establishing institutions to systematically protect and enforce property rights will generally provide high benefits to the poor and vulnerable. As they have better access to local information than central bodies, communities can in many instances enforce and administer property rights at the local level at very low cost. As it is the poor who are less able to defend their rights in this way, government measures to improve the definition of property rights can have significant potential to improve equity.

Universally recognized rights facilitate transactions with outsiders and offer cost advantages in infrastructure provision

Even though informal rights normally provide security within a well-defined and socially cohesive group, their enforcement is not costless and is generally limited to this group. Similar to common legal standards and the ability to enforce them in different constituencies and administrative entities, broadly recognized property rights facilitate abstract representation and impersonal exchange of rights, thereby increasing the scope for exchange with outsiders. This provides a necessary, though by no means sufficient, condition for participation in a modern economy through mechanisms such as mortgaging and the associated development of financial markets. Legal authority and patterns of conflict resolution allow the state to establish standards of acceptable behavior, and social norms to govern individuals' behavior, that transcend the community and provide the basis for the rule of law.

The establishment of secure property rights, that is, rights that are defined with sufficient precision and can be enforced at low cost so as to instill confidence in economic agents, requires considerable investment in both technical infrastructure, such as boundary demarcation and generation and maintenance of maps and land records, and social infrastructure, such as courts and conflict resolution mechanisms. In view of the fixed costs related mainly to the establishment of a spatial data infrastructure, there are advantages to public delineation and enforcement of property rights to land. Clear cost advantages are associated with public provision of the geographic data infrastructure as well as with the enforcement of rights, because the state can solve the problem of standards and reliability and guarantee enforcement through a legal system and its monopoly on power, and because the spatial data infrastructure required to identify land rights has many applications in related fields.

Key Elements in the Definition of Secure Property Rights to Land

To assess the elements needed for a property rights system conducive to growth and poverty reduction, this section identifies key components of the definition of property rights and briefly describes, at the conceptual level, how such rights are likely to affect economic behavior. In doing so, it focuses on the duration of rights; the identification of boundaries; the need for enforcement institutions, that is, institutions that can interpret land rights in an authoritative manner so as to avoid the emergence of land-related conflict in an environment characterized by demographic and economic transition; and the evolution of rights as relative scarcities change.

Duration of Rights

The "bundle" of property rights defines the nature of legitimate uses that can be made of land and the benefits to be derived from doing so. Such rights may comprise access for gathering, usufruct for a specified period of time, or more complete rights (often referred to as full ownership), with or without the ability to transfer the rights to the resource temporarily or permanently. Not only are there many combinations of rights, but also of the specifications of such rights, which may affect the specific resources covered, the acceptable amount of extraction, and the

The duration of rights needs to match the horizon of expected investment

25

period over which such extraction may occur. Of all of the attributes of land rights, the duration for which use may be enjoyed is one of the most important. Full ownership normally extends in perpetuity and includes the ability to bequeath land across generations. By contrast, use rights may be permanent or of a more limited duration, and many lesser rights, such as seasonal rights to graze animals, may be applicable only for certain periods. The length for which rights to land are awarded, and the mechanisms available for extending them, that is, whether they are automatically renewed or whether extension depends on a discretionary process, will affect the incentive to invest in and manage land in a sustainable fashion. Awarding permanent rights is most appropriate if the intent is to maximize welfare over an infinite horizon, although the extent of investment will also depend on the opportunities available. In practice, most customary systems award permanent land rights to the lineage precisely because of the importance of providing investment incentives.

Land rights in urban and peri-urban areas are generally of longer duration, because of the higher value and longer time horizon of the investments involved. In China use rights to urban lands are given with longer time limits than for rural lands (70 years for residential use and 50 years for industrial and cultural use); are renewable; and can be transferred, bequeathed, and mortgaged within the specified lease period. As a result, an active market in land use rights has emerged in the advanced coastal provinces (Wang and Murie 2000). Similarly, Botswana defines urban land use rights for 99 years that can either be renewed or require the government to pay compensation for any improvements, whereas many rural rights are under the customary regime. (Kalabamu 2000).

Adverse possession awards rights at low cost

Countries where unoccupied land is still available often have rules for "adverse possession," meaning that long-term, peaceful occupancy of a plot in good faith for a minimum amount of time confers ownership rights to the occupant. This provides a mechanism of awarding secure land tenure that is not only associated with minimal institutional requirements but also, because possession and use are required, is unlikely to be associated with negative equity consequences. Extinguishing ownership claims after a certain period eliminates the risk of past owners suddenly surfacing and claiming the land, and at the same time prevents valuable land from being left vacant for long periods at the cost of monitoring of land use by the owner. This implies a trade-off between the social objective of having land visibly utilized and the insecurity that may prevail if adverse possession is recognized after only a short period of time. Adverse possession was the main mechanism whereby most settlers in the United States acquired their land (de Soto 2000), and all 50 U.S. states have legal provisions upholding the ability of squatters to acquire ownership rights through continued possession of a property in good faith for a specified period.[9] Short horizons for recognition will increase the security of current owners' property rights and provide greater incentives to invest, but will require owners to spend more time monitoring their vacant land to prevent squatters from obtaining title. Empirical analysis of the length of time for which a squatter must occupy a property in good faith, enacted by 46 U.S. states in 1916, confirms that better title records, a more effective legal system, and higher gains from development can all be linked statistically to shorter statute lengths (Baker 2001). Thus, even though adverse possession reflects a trade-off between investment and imposing costs on current landowners, it is justified, because in most cases long-term occupants have made land-related investments, and providing them with basic protection can increase investment.

Identification of Boundaries

Defining boundaries is associated with some transaction costs, implying that the degree of precision with which boundaries will be identified will depend on the nature and use of the land in question.[10] To be unambiguous, and therefore enforceable at low cost, the boundaries of the resource, for example, a piece of land or the type of extraction that a given right allows to any user, need to be clearly defined. Precise, observable, and well-defined boundaries are easier to enforce and cost less to protect than poorly defined boundaries, implying that the way in which boundaries are defined will affect the cost of enforcement. Territorial or geographical boundaries are the most common, because they are easy to demarcate and are permanent. Note, however, that boundaries can be defined with respect to resource categories, attributes (such as specific trees), or time of use, thereby creating multiple tenures over the same parcel of land. Examples are use of the same plot of land by sedentary agriculturalists to grow a crop and by nomads who graze their livestock on the stubble or by apartment time shares. Arrangements characterized by overlapping tenures, defined according to traditional custom, are widely found in lands with low commercial value. A relatively vague definition of boundaries will be unproblematic as long as institutions to

Boundaries need to be easily identifiable

interpret the rules authoritatively are available, though this may develop into a source of conflict if either the value of the resource increases or the authority of traditional institutions is challenged.

The costs and benefits of demarcation need to be weighed

From an economic point of view, formal recording of boundaries will be efficient if the benefit from doing so, in terms of warding off challenges to resource ownership or use or facilitating transfers between users, is higher than the cost of doing so. The cost of recording rights, that is, the efficiency of the system that registers property rights and their boundaries, is an important element of these costs. Moreover, well-defined property rights will be characterized by boundaries that minimize external effects; that is, they will provide as close an overlap as possible between the unit to which property rights are assigned and the area from which the main resource value originates. This implies not only that, for some resources such as extensive pastures or noncommercial forests, the externalities may be sufficiently important to warrant some kind of group rather than fully individualized ownership, but that, even in the case of individual ownership, some mechanisms will be needed either to internalize or limit the amount of externalities generated. The factors shaping the trade-off between efficiency losses caused by incentive problems and exclusion costs caused by potential encroachment have been discussed extensively in the literature. Attempts to translate multiple tenures into systems with geographically well-identified boundaries have been difficult.

Subject of Rights

Individual assignment of land rights has many advantages

Individual assignment of property rights is the arrangement that provides the greatest incentives for efficient resource use. It is the most preferable for society if the resource over which property rights are given is of sufficiently high value to justify the costs of establishing and enforcing individual rights and if externalities associated with resource use are few and of a nature that allows addressing them through regulation. Individual ownership has emerged as the predominant form of land ownership in many cases where the benefits from continuous land use and the associated investment are high enough (Ellickson 1993). However, in even the most individualistic system, the rights enjoyed by individuals are never unrestricted, but instead limited by the need to have rights holders contribute to the broader public good. Most countries' constitutions contain a provision for a social function of land, implying that governments have the ability to expropriate land, with compensation and following a well-defined judicial process, for public purposes. In addition, individuals can come together in user groups and other formal or informal associations, to establish voluntarily norms and restrictions on owners' ability to exercise their rights. Such rules can not only help eliminate externalities, but can also provide public goods, for instance, environmental amenities and green spaces. Thus, even where land rights are individualized, they are never unrestricted.

Group rights may be desirable where there are economies of scale in managing the resources so that users have the option of improving productive efficiency or internalizing harm that co-owners might do to each other. Examples include the use of economies of scale to break seasonal labor bottlenecks (Mearns 1996) and investment in community-level infrastructure (Boserup 1965; Dong 1996).[11] In such circumstances, the costs of delineating and enforcing boundaries to individual plots are high, and even if feasible, the benefits from a transition to formal and individualized titles may not be sufficient to cover the expenses associated with their establishment and maintenance. Indeed, in a number of African countries, titles that were generated at high cost have lost their value as landowners have failed to update them. These considerations are particularly important in situations where, with limited economic development, the scope for realizing gains from land exchanges remains limited.

Similarly, in areas where risks are high and insurance markets not well developed, the guaranteed access to land that is implied in customary systems can make an important contribution to greater equity. To the extent that they have better access to private information than central bureaucracies, local communities can provide some insurance against idiosyncratic and, to a more limited extent, covariate shocks, as well as eliminate the threat of permanent asset loss. It is well known that, at low levels of development and with limited development of financial markets, communal land ownership that gives individuals use rights that they can draw upon even after a temporary absence may perform an important insurance function. It is thus not surprising to find that group ownership has been prevalent where risk is high and where factors such as remoteness, environmental hazard, or presence of external enemies imply that superior insurance mechanisms are unavailable (Ellickson 1993). Similarly, the types of property rights that emerged among more than 40 Indian communities before they came into contact with outsiders were significantly affected by the

Group rights are more appropriate if there are economies of scale and externalities, if risk coping and mutual insurance are important, and if benefits from land-related investment are low

physical environment (harsh winters) and by such community variables as regular warfare, expulsion, nomadism, and population density that affected the deadweight, governance, and exclusion costs of establishing and maintaining different access regimes (Anderson and Swimmer 1997).

A further reason for group rights is that in environments with low population density, high environmental risk, and limited access to infrastructure and markets, the benefits from individual assignment of land ownership rights may not be sufficiently high to justify the costs involved. In many of these cases, state weakness and limited outreach and administrative capacity of central government institutions will limit the ability of these institutions to effectively enforce property rights. As a consequence, even where they are not sanctioned by formal law, local institutions are bound to have a significant impact on the way in which land rights are actually implemented. In such situations, aiming to improve the way in which local institutions work may be socially advantageous and administratively less costly, and may permit covering large areas in a much shorter time, which is important if resources are scarce.

To be effective, group rights need to match resource properties and group characteristics

Given that there are many contexts where group rights will be more feasible and cost-effective than individual assignment of property rights, such group rights need to meet certain minimum criteria to be effective. While group rights define the boundaries of the community, and thus the limitations nonmembers are to respect, failure to specify rights clearly within the group may still result in suboptimal arrangements. Where this is the case, open access by group members and the associated disadvantages or disincentives for investment and sustainable use may still prevail. Specific characteristics of the management group, as well as of the resource under consideration, that are conducive to better management can be identified and provide a basis for policy advice (McKean 1996). In terms of resource characteristics, the literature on common resource tenure suggests that for rights to be defined on a group basis, a number of conditions need to be satisfied. First, the boundaries of the common property regime need to match ecosystem boundaries. Second, the award of property rights must make the community of resource users or co-owners better off than it would have been without such rights, for example, by allowing them to ward off encroachment by outsiders. Finally, the allocation of benefits from the common needs to be roughly proportional to the effort (time, money, and so on) invested. This illustrates that specific rights held under multiple tenures need not be less individualized than those under "private" property rights structures. In fact, most customary systems provide individuals with strong and inheritable rights to cropland, whereas pastures, forests, and water are often held in common.

The benefits of group rights are also enhanced if the co-owners of resource rights constitute a self-governing group with sufficient cohesion that has established accepted mechanisms for resolving internal conflict and the rules governing resource access provide for monitoring behavior and enforcing sanctions. At the same time, where deep-rooted socioeconomic differentiation of communities has taken place, there are high levels of institutional contestation, and giving group rights may not be the most preferable option. Also, rules need to be easily enforceable and ecologically conservative. The importance of easy enforcement is illustrated by the fact that in many societies rules that are not fully optimal but are easily enforceable seem to be preferred over ones that would be preferable economically but are difficult to enforce and monitor. Moreover, the stability of group rights can be greatly enhanced by a formal recognition of such rights by the state that would allow co-owners to call for protection by the police and the courts when they encountered challenges.

In cases where there are no externalities or economies of scale in resource management, group rights often tended to disappear as other mechanisms to cope with risk became available; markets for output, capital, and insurance developed; and technical progress allowed for greater diversification and reduction of the covariance of yields as well as the risk of crop failure. Improvements in the institutional environment and greater ability to access noncovariate streams of income in the nonagricultural economy are likely to decrease the cost of formal demarcation of boundaries relative to the expenses, in terms of forgone earnings, from policing informal rights. The development of financial markets will also reduce the value of the insurance offered through customary arrangements linked to land. At the same time higher land values increase the benefits from exchanging property rights among cultivators through decentralized mechanisms rather than through village authorities who may not have access to information on individual households' productive ability. This is, for example, visible in China where, until very recently, reallocation of land among producers was almost exclusively through administrative means, something that enjoyed considerable support among producers (Kung 2000). Greater opportunities for off-farm migration have led to the emergence of longer-term use rights and decentralized land transactions through

The desirability of group rights will often decrease with economic development

31

When and how property rights evolve also depend on political factors

rental markets that, by giving land to those with the highest ability, can be demonstrated to be more efficiency-enhancing and more equity-oriented than administrative assignments (Deininger and Jin, 2002).

While most of today's developed countries have undergone a process of gradual individualization of property rights to land (Boserup 1965), the evolution of property rights is neither automatic nor independent from political factors. In fact, the distribution of political power, resulting patterns of distributional conflict, inability to commit credibly to new rights, and costly decisionmaking all can either block such institutional change or lead it into undesirable directions. This is confirmed by the persistence of insecure tenure in Côte d'Ivoire and Ghana (Firmin-Sellers 2000) and blockage as well as premature imposition of more specific land rights in Imperial Ethiopia (Joireman 2001). The importance of political considerations in shaping the nature and direction of institutional change is confirmed by findings from the United States (Kantor 1998). Thus, while economic changes that increased land values and at the same time improved functioning of other markets have led to greater individualization in many cases (see, for example, Feeny 1989), this is by no means a linear process or a historical necessity. From a policy perspective, the most critical issue is to provide for sufficient flexibility to respond to local needs and to ensure that, if property rights change, such change will not eliminate rights that have been enjoyed by weaker groups.

Properties of Enforcement Institutions

Formal rights imply an ability to draw on the state's enforcement institutions, but the institutions to implement these rights need to combine legality, legitimacy, and accountability

Mechanisms of informal collective action through customary arrangements to increase individuals' tenure security and limit unsustainable use of land and dissipation of rents have evolved in many situations (de Soto 2000; Umbeck 1977), The enforcement mechanisms associated with such informal means are, however, often effective only in smaller communities; are difficult to enforce against outsiders; and may break down if individuals within the community, especially leaders, behave opportunistically as resource values rise. Thus a key difference between informal possession and a more formalized property rights system is that in the case of the latter, rights holders will be able to call on the coercive powers of the state to ensure enforcement if their rights are violated, rather than being forced to rely solely on their own efforts. In addition, informal social contracts and their property representations are not sufficiently codified and fungible to have a broad range of application outside their own geographical perimeter. The fact that informal rights cannot be traded and exchanged beyond the community is one of the reasons why, in many historical circumstances, they have been replaced by more formalized property rights once resource values have increased sufficiently to justify the cost of doing so. The main mechanisms for formalizing rights have been land registries and title documents, which not only provide protection from challenges to individuals' rights, but also make transferring these rights easier, and therefore allow the emergence of secondary financial instruments, such as mortgages, that are built on the existing rights system.

In any given situation, the ability to enforce rights depends on the ease with which rights holders can access the required institutions and obtain legally binding decisions from them and whether such decisions enjoy local legitimacy. Examples abound of cases where legislation mandating strong formal protection of property rights was of limited value as it could not be enforced at the local level, where the institutional capacity to do so was lacking. Having a legally defined right will be of little value if, in case of violation of this right, access to the courts is difficult, the case will not be heard for a long time or will not be resolved without paying bribes, or court orders in relation to a specific piece of land cannot be enforced. Indeed, investigators have identified the failure to enforce "formal" property rights in Kenya as one of the reasons for the failure of titling efforts to provide increased security of tenure (Atwood 1990; Pinckney and Kimuyu 1994). Where institutions to enforce formal property rights are either not available or do not enjoy broad legitimacy, the expected advantages are unlikely to materialize. In these cases a more advantageous option may be to build on existing systems and structures rather than try to replace them with new ones. The use of local institutions and a relatively simple system in Lithuania, as described in Box 2.1 is only one of several examples from Eastern Europe that illustrate the feasibility of a gradual approach. It illustrates the general principle that a gradual evolution of property rights that builds on local institutions is often a quicker, more cost-effective, and less conflict-prone way to securing tenure than trying to impose radical one-time change.

Evolution of Rights in Response to Changing Relative Scarcities

The precision with which resource rights are defined and the rigor with which they are enforced normally increases with the value of the resource, which is often closely related to population density. Indeed, for resources of low value, boundaries are often demarcated only loosely,

---

Box 2.1 A decentralized two-step system for registering property rights: the case of Lithuania

THE CASE OF LITHUANIA ILLUSTRATES NOT ONLY the scope for putting in place decentralized and temporary systems that can then be absorbed into a more unified framework, but also demonstrates that doing so provides tangible benefits for which owners are willing to pay. Village authorities registered ownership and use rights, establishing a temporary, person-based cadastral register of landowners at the village level. A parcel-based, integrated system under the National Agency for Cadastre will integrate these registers and eventually take their place. While initial registration is based on sketch maps with a low level of precision, more detailed surveys will be required for subsequent market transactions when the money to pay for them is available, and the hope is that this will help to make the registry self-financing. The relatively rapid progress was facilitated by the establishment of the single Department of Land Management that had jurisdiction over rural, urban, and forestland (Valetta 2000). The structure was highly decentralized, with registry offices in each municipality, and the first priority for the administrative units carrying out the technical tasks was the economic imperative of quickly transferring ownership to land rather than the utmost in technical precision. Private sector agents, including surveyors, real estate brokers, and property appraisers, helped to make progress rapid. Virtually all farmers now have an official document certifying their land ownership rights, and more than two-thirds paid for this, on average, a third of the monthly wage.

---

and resource use is governed by informal arrangements or social norms. Some minor or temporal rights, such as the right to pasturage after the harvest or right of way, are rarely formally registered, because in most circumstances the cost of doing so would exceed the value of the right. Instead, reference is made to social norms governing behavior. Similarly, given the cost involved in monitoring and writing detailed contracts regarding the specific rights to resource use transferred in any given transaction, the specifics of such contracts are left to common law or practice and custom. In fact, high-cost systems providing "full" enforcement may not always be optimal or preferable to lower-cost mechanisms at the local level. This is illustrated by mining claims in the late 19th century, where miners could either spend resources to have their claim titled or could cope with the higher enforcement costs of untitled claims by means of informal mechanisms. A general reduction in the risk of conflict led to a decline in the demand for formal documents and a greater reliance on informal mechanisms (Gerard 2001).

Sharp changes in resource values without institutional change increase the conflict potential, especially during demographic or economic transitions

The optimum type of property rights depends on the nature of the resource, its relative scarcity, the externalities that arise in its use, the cost of specifying and enforcing property rights, the state's capacity to enforce property rights, the ability to minimize external effects through regulation, and the means available within a given group to delineate and enforce rights and responsibilities internally. As none of these factors is static, the most appropriate property arrangement would be one that could respond to changing conditions in predictable ways. Once economic and social conditions change, for instance, if land values increase with higher population density or improved opportunities for trade, the value of attributes that were previously left undelineated may increase sufficiently to make delineation worthwhile (Barzel 2000). If such shifts occur rapidly and if agreed mechanisms to re-interpret past norms and contracts are unavailable, this can lead to widespread contestation and to conflict over property rights, with negative social and economic consequences.

Higher levels of resource scarcity caused, for example by population growth, will increase the value of land and can cause friction and conflict over the interpretation of traditional informal rights. To avoid these, a way to authoritatively resolve disputes about previous contracts or redefine property rights as needed in line with new economic realities will be needed.[12] This would then lead to a more precise definition of property rights in line with increased values, setting a precedent to guide the assignment and specification of property rights and contracting between parties in the future. In practice, especially in countries where the legal system is weak and multiple authorities claim to be the legitimate authorities, opportunistic behavior by the parties involved may lead to vast differences in the re-interpretation of "custom" in response to changed realities. This can give rise to prolonged claims and "institutional shopping," that is, parties pursuing disputes through different channels, for example, formal and informal authorities and legal and administrative channels, at the same time in the hope of obtaining a favorable solution (Berry 1993). Such behavior will not only increase the cost of resolving disputes but will also have an impact on the credibility of the broader legal system.

Failure to resolve disputes over land is associated with a number of negative impacts, in particular: (a) the inability to obtain a definitive solution for a long time impedes investment; (b) the transaction costs associated with legal proceedings imply that most of the increased value of the resource is dissipated rather than benefits users; and (c) the possible emergence of vested interest groups which, because they benefit from legal insecurity prevent resolution of the conflict. The last appears to be one of the reasons underlying the inability to solve conflicts in some West African countries, where court cases are drawn out for extremely long periods and where, when solutions are found, they can rarely be generalized to other cases, thereby contributing to continued

Authoritative interpretation of past norms and contracts is essential to avoid conflict over rights

insecurity (Berry 1993). Such systems are not only costly, as they imply that individuals spend large amounts of resources in a relatively unproductive way, but they also pose a danger that apparently minor conflicts about land may evolve into large-scale strife with possibly devastating social and economic consequences. This has been particularly relevant in cases where conflicts run along ethnic lines or occur between migrants and the indigenous population, as has occurred, for example, in Côte d'Ivoire (Chauveau 2000). In all these cases, mechanisms that would help to resolve conflicts quickly and early on could not only provide large economic benefits, but could also help avoid great subsequent damage.

Demand for and Impact of Secure Property Rights

Insecure land tenure is pervasive in the developing world

THE EARLIER DISCUSSION ILLUSTRATES THAT TENURE SECURITY depends on a host of both objective and subjective factors, including the clarity with which rights and obligations are defined; the quality and validity of property rights records and whether or not the state guarantees them;[13] the precision with which boundaries are demarcated; the likelihood that rights will be violated; and the ability to obtain redress by an authoritative institution in such cases, along with the reassurance that whatever measures that institution decides are deemed appropriate and can be enforced effectively. Deficiencies in any of these areas, or a mismatch between different components of the property rights system, can seriously undermine tenure security, thereby increasing the potential for conflict and undermining incentives for investment and exchange. Although there are few internationally comparable data from the rural sector, data from urban areas illustrate the magnitude of the problem of insecure tenure in a way that can be compared across regions. Figure 2.2 illustrates the widespread incidence of land-related insecurity, taking as an indicator the share of the urban population that is either squatting or living in unauthorized housing. It illustrates that, for example, in Africa more than 50 percent of the housing is in the informal sector (Angel 2000).

High levels of tenure insecurity are illustrated by an implicit or explicit demand for instruments that can increase land ownership security. For example, in Nicaragua the demand for registered certificates was significant even though households already had informal documents. Not surprisingly, this demand came mainly from the poor, who did not

Figure 2.2 Informal land occupation in urban areas, by region

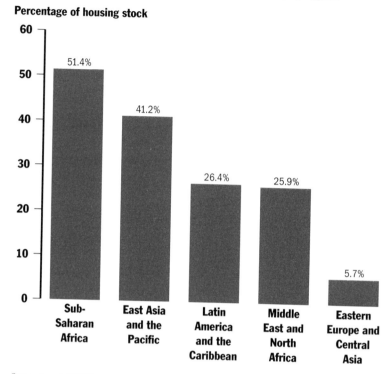

Source: Angel (2000).

have the means to increase tenure security through other channels (Deininger and Chamorro forthcoming). In Zambia, despite its low population density, almost 50 percent of farmers believe that their land tenure is insecure and would be willing to pay an average of US$40 for higher levels of land tenure security (Deininger and Olinto 1998), a finding that is confirmed by informal evidence suggesting that households have a great interest in demarcation of their plots. Qualitative surveys in urban areas similarly indicate that the priority demands of households in irregular settlements are, in descending order of importance, access to services, security of land tenure that would preclude them from being evicted, and rights to transfer or sell their dwelling unit or the land they occupy (Durand-Lasserve and Royston 2002a).

Indirect confirmation of the importance of property rights comes from the fact that in many traditional tenure systems, households undertake investments that range from marking boundaries to planting trees and building houses or sheds with the primary purpose of establishing implicit property rights to land and increasing existing levels of tenure security (Brasselle, Gaspart, and Platteau 2002; Gray and Kevane 2001; Place and Otsuka 2001). This can be seen as an indication that these households attach a high value to greater levels of tenure security. The most comprehensive evidence on this comes from Ethiopia, where tenure insecurity increases households' propensity to establish visible investments, such as trees, while at the same time decreasing their incentive to invest in activities that have a more direct and positive impact on productivity but are less directly visible, such as establishing and rehabilitating terraces (Deininger, Jin, Adenew, Gebre-Selassie, and Nega 2003).

An unitary model of the household is often inappropriate, and attention to women's control over assets is particularly relevant

Within the household, the way in which land rights are assigned or will be transferred through inheritance will affect the range of land- and non-land-related economic opportunities open to women and the spending outcomes directly under their control. Women's ability to have independent access to and to exercise control over assets is a critical determinant of their welfare and their income-earning capacity (Fafchamps and Quisumbing 1999). Past research and conceptual work were often based on a unitary model of the household; however, a growing literature indicates that this model is often inadequate and that the way in which control over land rights is assigned within the household has far-reaching implications for a wide range of outcomes (Schultz 1999). Evidence suggests that in a number of circumstances, the preferences of women and men in the same household for different types of consumption are not equal, and the ability to control assets or the benefits derived from them will have implications on the way in which household income is spent across different types of consumption items.

Equality of women's land rights to those of men is warranted from a rights-based perspective. Furthermore, a growing literature demonstrates that in Africa and Asia women's control over household assets affects consumption patterns. Households where women control greater shares of assets and land at marriage have been shown to spend more on food and on children's welfare and education (Leroy de la Brière 1996; Doss 1996; Fafchamps and Quisumbing 2002; Haddad 1997). In Honduras and Nicaragua the amount of land women own has a significant and positive impact on food expenditure as well as on children's educational attainment (Katz and Chamorro 2002). Given the importance of land in the asset portfolio of the average rural household in many developing countries, increasing women's control over land could therefore have a strong and immediate effect on the welfare of the next generation and on the level and pace at which human and physical capital are accumulated.

Increasing security of tenure does not necessarily require issuing formal individual titles, and in many circumstance more simple measures to enhance tenure security can make a big difference at much lower cost than formal titles. In fact, many of the investment effects discussed thus far can be observed even in situations where land is not fully alienable, implying that it will be important to distinguish between tenure security and transferability. Note that many studies indicate that in Africa formal land title had little or no impact on either investment or farm income (Atwood 1990; Carter and Wiebe 1990; Migot-Adholla 1993; Pinckney and Kimuyu 1994), something that is often mirrored by similar findings for urban areas (Durand-Lasserve and Royston 2002a). This strongly suggests that title is not necessarily equal to higher tenure security. One example to illustrate this comes from Cameroon, where demand for tenure security was great; however, even though formal means, which were incompatible with traditional norms, were available, households only used less expensive ways to increase tenure security that were compatible with social standards (Firmin-Sellers and Sellers 1999).[14] The most appropriate and cost-effective mechanisms to increase tenure security, and whether or not transferability will be needed, will have to be determined by applying the general principles discussed earlier to the circumstances prevailing in any given situation.

From an economic point of view, secure tenure is critical to provide incentives for households and entrepreneurs to undertake land-related investments. If their ability to keep the benefits from investments is uncertain, they are unlikely to invest or exert effort. Indeed, the desire to gain more secure property rights in situations where informal rights systems prevail induces individuals to undertaken such actions as planting trees on land they possess or setting up boundary markers as a way to increase tenure security. The need to provide more secure tenure cuts across rural and urban sectors of the economy. While early work in the urban sector has often underestimated the importance of land tenure (Werlin 1999), development practitioners now recognize that lack of secure tenure and the associated threat of eviction and poor access to basic services are important determinants of poverty in urban areas. Security of tenure has been identified as one of the most important catalysts in stabilizing communities, improving shelter conditions, reducing social exclusion, and improving access to urban services (UNCHS 1999). The United Nations Centre for Human Settlements has identified security of tenure and better governance as the two main priorities that require immediate and urgent attention, noting that there are many links between the two.

Formal title is not always necessary or sufficient for high levels of tenure security

Equity Benefits of Greater Tenure Security

Greater tenure security allows reduction of private spending on securing of property rights

Even though interventions to increase tenure security are often justified in terms of their expected impact on productivity and investment, the reduction in households' need to spend resources on defending such rights is no less important. Within communities, households' level of tenure security and the transparency and accountability of the institutions administering land rights will affect governance as well as the extent to which conflicts will arise or can be resolved without generating negative effects on social cohesion and productivity. In the context of their evolution, many customary tenure systems reward investment in visible land improvements either with more individualized rights to the land after the investment has been made or with secure rights to the flow of benefits from the investment itself, for instance, trees.

A public guarantee of tenure security reduces the amount of resources individual land owners have to spend on defending their resource, sometimes with dramatic effects. For example, in Peru formalization of land ownership in a local registry allowed households to significantly increase their participation in the formal labor market, because they were no longer required to invest in a multitude of informal activities required to maintain tenure security. Field (2002) estimates that receipt of a preliminary document increased the supply of hours worked by 17 percent, whereas full legal ownership increases labor supply by about 50 percent, or 45 hours a week per household. This finding is particularly noteworthy against the background that other welfare programs are generally associated with a decrease in labor force participation. The fact that land ownership provides an incentive-compatible safety net has long been noted in the literature (Burgess 2001). This can lead to behavioral adjustments that are not directly reflected in land prices or land transactions. For example, observers generally believe that higher levels of land tenure security in China allow households to temporarily migrate and take off-farm jobs (Yang 1997). Indeed, with greater security of land rights those households with the lowest agricultural incomes will be able to transfer their land to others, informally or formally, without fearing that they will lose the land during their temporary absence, and will thereby be able to significantly improve their living conditions (Murphy 2000).

One reason why more secure property rights can improve equity is because a higher level of tenure security through programs targeted to the poor helps to increase the value of these households' endowments.

Even if the use of land as collateral for credit is only a remote option, as it is in most of the informal settlements where the scope for foreclosure is dim and most of the residents are poor and do not have viable business projects in the first place, there may be a large need for improving tenure security to give official recognition, get an "address," and promote social stability. In addition to integrating households into the formal system, such actions can significantly reduce the transaction costs for informal lenders (Messick 1996). If the use of land as collateral is not immediately required, the information and legal requirements for land certificates can be relaxed, providing an opportunity for adopting speedier and less costly registration procedures.

Increasing tenure security can also have benefits in terms of improving local governance structures (Alden-Wily 2002). In many countries where tenure security is low, often as a consequence of past land reform, political connections are important for people to gain or maintain access to land. For example, in Mexico before the 1992 reforms, the *ejido* sector was subject to numerous restrictions on land rights, leading to clientelism, inefficient land use, and low levels of investment in rural areas and chaotic informal settlement in peri-urban areas (Gordillo, de Janvry, and Sadoulet 1998). In qualitative interviews, beneficiaries of a program to establish land rights that were both more secure and better administered highlighted that the two most important impacts of the reforms were the reduction in conflicts and the increase in transparency, along with the associated reduction of political influence in the *ejido* (World Bank 2002a).

Even though land is, in the short run, virtually indestructible, deforestation and environmental destruction undermine the long-term sustainability of the natural resource base. Conceptual models and empirical evidence indicate that more secure property rights to land will provide incentives for greater resource conservation, as illustrated in the case of Brazil, where Cattaneo (2001) identifies tenure security as a key factor in deforestation, or in Ghana, where Ahuja (1998) claims that a more pro-active policy regarding land tenure could have significant benefits in terms of natural resource management. This is supported by evidence indicating that improved forest management in practices were adopted in Nepal and Vietnam after use rights to state forests were transferred to communities and to individual farmers (Kijima, Sakuria, and Otsuka 2000; Otsuka 2002). In Panama effective property rights, even though not the only relevant factor, could significantly reduce the danger of deforestation (Nelson, Harris, and Stone

Greater tenure security can reduce environmental degradation

2001). The importance of adequate regulation is reinforced by the fact that in many contexts individuals use deforestation as a strategy to gain property rights (Angelsen 1999). Some evidence also suggests that giving more secure property rights to indigenous people will enable them to negotiate more effectively with outside interests, and will thus reduce deforestation (Godoy 1998). Environmentally appropriate land use generates externalities at the local as well as at the global level. The international community's and governments' increasing recognition of the value of such external benefits and willingness to take them into account reinforce the need for a clear definition of property rights to the lands from which these external benefits originate.

In line with earlier discussion, to reap such environmental benefits, attention to group and resource characteristics is warranted. Even in situations where full individualization of property rights is infeasible, helping communities to develop structures that overcome the coordination problems associated with the optimum use of natural resources and thereby establish effective property right regimes can enhance the sustainability of resource use, prevent environmental degradation, and promote the overall efficiency of land use (Baland 1996). For example, in Mexico the collapse of groups' collective action potential was a key factor in many cases of unsustainable use and degradation of natural resources (Key and others 1998; McCarthy, de Janvry, and Sadoulet 1997) and efforts to improve internal structures could help to achieve better resource utilization. In other instances, especially where resource characteristics demand more specific investment, as in the case of high-quality, valuable timber, groups have often chosen to assign ownership rights to individuals (Kijima, Sakurai, and Otsuka 2000). What is relevant in all of these cases is to ensure that groups have appropriate mechanisms to define and modify rules and that they are able to enjoy the benefits from such decisions.

Impact of Tenure Security on Investment and Productivity

There are three main elements of tenure security that can affect households' behavior. First, greater security against eviction, which in practice is often equivalent to longer duration of land rights, will reduce the need to spend resources on defending resource rights and the probability of getting caught up in land conflicts. This is likely to increase the demand for land-related investment. Second, greater ability to transfer land, while unlikely to affect the probability of conflict or eviction, will increase the payoff from investments linked to the land because it will allow the person who made the investment to benefit from it even if, for some unforeseen reason, he or she will not be able to personally use the land. Third, greater tenure security can enhance access to credit, thereby increasing the value of investment undertaken in situations in which limited credit supply constrains investment.

Empirical analysis of the relation between tenure security and economic outcomes needs to take account of the different elements and many graduations of tenure security. For example, open-access-property regimes provide much less security than inheritable usufructuary rights. On the other hand, long-term and fully transferable leases may, in practice, provide levels of tenure security virtually identical to those provided by titled individual ownership. Careful definition of the underlying concepts is therefore essential in any empirical study of land tenure.

In addition, empirical analysis needs to recognize the possible presence of spurious correlations between measures of tenure security and economic impacts. For example, if wealthy households have better economic opportunities but are also more likely to acquire land title, simple correlations may easily overestimate the impact of title as an indicator of tenure security. Similarly, households may be more likely to demand and acquire title to land of higher quality where the payoff from investment is higher. Failure to account for this, for example, by adjusting for land quality or household characteristics, could also lead to spurious and misguided conclusions. There are various ways to deal with this problem, such as using panel data analysis with household fixed effects or controlling for as many unobserved variables as possible. The reliability of any empirical result depends on the care taken in adjusting for these factors.

Lack of tenure security, in any of its dimensions, implies that households or entrepreneurs face a risk of losing their property rights to a plot of land (and the associated income flows) at some point in the future. As shown formally and empirically (see, for example, Besley 1995; Feder 1988), eliminating such a threat by enhancing the security provided through either informal means or formal institutions such as land titles will increase the expected benefits from productivity-enhancing,

Reducing the risk of eviction can increase land values

Figure 2.3   Impact of title status on land values, selected countries and years

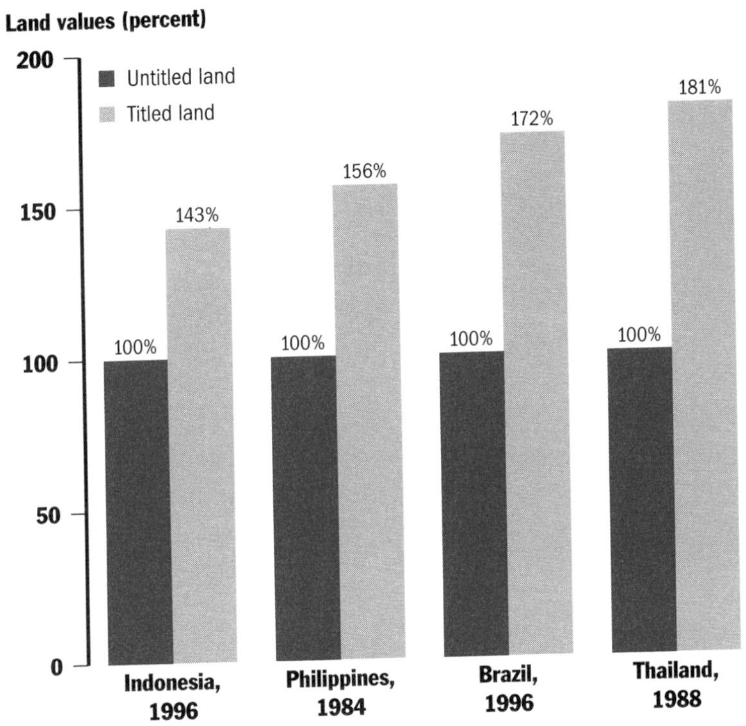

Land values (percent)

- Untitled land
- Titled land

Indonesia, 1996: 100% / 143%
Philippines, 1984: 100% / 156%
Brazil, 1996: 100% / 172%
Thailand, 1988: 100% / 181%

Source: Feder (2002).

long-term investments, and thus the owner's willingness to undertake them. Also, without secure tenure households will have fewer incentives to rent out land in the short term to other users even if doing so could have significant equity and welfare benefits. We therefore distinguish the effects of tenure security on investment and land prices before proceeding to the impact of formal land title on credit supply. Figure 2.3 summarizes the impact of secure land rights on land values in selected countries.

In Asia, higher tenure security, even if not formalized, increased investment

The importance of productivity benefits associated with more secure and individualized forms of tenure, even in a single period without any investment effects, is illustrated by the transition from collective to private cultivation that has been associated with large increases in productivity, as in the case of China (Lin 1992; McMillan 1989). In addition, the key result from a number of studies is that under formal as well as informal regimes, greater tenure security, as measured by the extent of rights possessed by the owner, significantly increases landowners' investment incentives. Especially where investments are labor-intensive but involve few cash outlays, the unambiguous conclusion is that higher levels of tenure security—even if they are not associated with high levels of transferability and are defined only at an informal level—do provide an important incentive for increased investment. Results from China, Pakistan, and Vietnam confirm the importance of tenure security for investment. Comparing plots planted with the same crop by the same household but under different tenure regimes, Jacoby, Li, and Rozelle (2002) find that farmers tend to apply more manure and labor, and to obtain significantly higher yields, on plots that are privately owned and are therefore more secure. In India, land values for titled land are, on average, about 15 percent higher than for untitled land, suggesting that possession of formal title reduces the probability of land loss (Pender and Kerr 1998).

In Thailand land ownership titles induced higher investment in farming capital (attached investments and other capital), and titled land had significantly higher market values and higher productivity per unit. Output was 14 to 25 percent higher on titled land than on untitled land of equal quality (Feder 1988). A comparison of housing prices in non-squatter residential areas and squatter areas of the city of Davao in the Philippines revealed that prices were 58 percent higher in the formal area than in the informal one and rents were 18 percent higher (Feder and Nishio 1999). Accounting for a possible impact of greater tenure security on crop choice, for example, shifting to orchards instead of growing maize, may further increase these benefits. In Vietnam, Do and Iyer (2002) provide evidence suggesting that land registration contributed to increased levels of perennial cultivation and irrigation. Higher levels of tenure security in Chinese villages have a strong and significant investment-enhancing impact, such as the application of green manure (Yao 1996). Panel data from China confirm that, controlling for other factors, land transfer rights boost agricultural investment (Carter 2002). In India investment in conservation is much lower on leased plots and on plots that are subject to sales restrictions, supporting the hypothesis that more secure land rights significantly affect household behavior (Pender and Kerr 1998). For urban settings in the Philippines, the differential in property values between dwellings of otherwise equal quality in the nonsquatter and the squatter sector was about 58 percent, and this largely benefited the poor (Jimenez 1984). In Jakarta registered land was up to 73 percent more valuable than similar land held by a weak claim (Dowell and Leaf 1992). Figure 2.4 shows the impact of title on investment in three countries.

Figure 2.4   Impact of title status on investment, selected countries and years

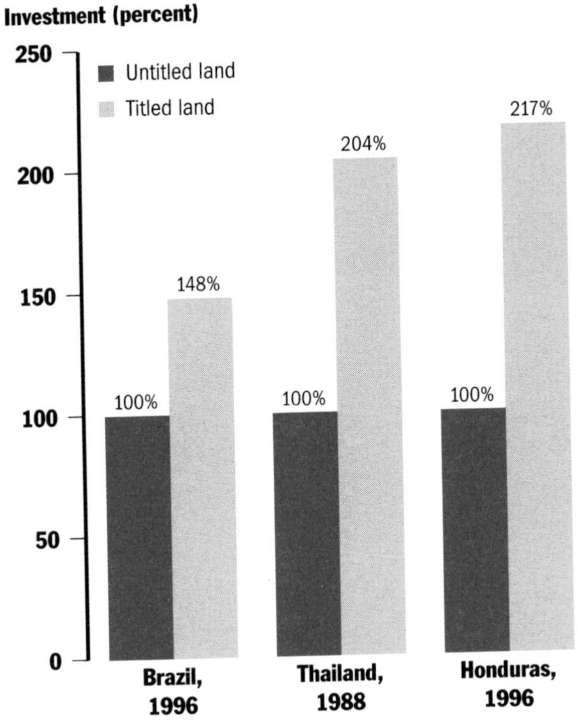

Investment (percent)

Source: Feder (2002).

In Africa, tenure security and transferability are relevant

In Ghana plots with greater transferability, interpreted as more secure tenure, increased the probability that individuals would plant trees and undertake a wide range of other investments such as drainage, irrigation, and mulching (Besley 1995). While tenure security affects farmers' investment behavior, this does not necessarily require fully individualized rights or land titles. In Niger farmers apply significantly lower amounts of manure on rented than on owned plots, suggesting that they are aware of the difference in long-term tenure security, but no significant difference is apparent between parcels held under full private ownership and those held under traditional usufruct. The conclusion is that tenure security on the latter is apparently high enough for farmers to expect to be able to reap the benefits from their medium-term investment (Gavian and Fafchamps 1996). In Malawi higher levels of tenure security under a patrilineal system have led to higher levels of tree planting, tobacco cultivation, and adoption of new technology (Otsuka 2001). In Tanzania Briggs and Mwamfupe (2000) have identified insecurity of property rights in peri-urban areas resulting from disputed ownership as a key factor underlying lower investment.

Indeed, a fundamental rule found in most customary or communal land tenure institutions is that investment in observable land improvements, such as planting trees, is rewarded with strong individual land rights (Crisologo-Mendoza and Van de Gaer 2001; Otsuka 2001; Shepherd 1991). In areas where long-term improvements such as terracing or clearing land and establishing plantations have the potential to significantly increase land productivity, a common arrangement is that tenants can either establish quasi-ownership rights to the land or significantly increase their share of the harvest, as in the case of the Republic of Yemen (Aw-Hassan 2001).[15] Similarly, in Sumatra joint ownership of land is found in areas that grow rice, which requires little investment, but an individualized system of land rights has evolved in upland areas where cinnamon is grown, implying a need for long-term investment (Suyanto, Tomich, and Otsuka 2001).

In Nicaragua, the greater security associated with registered title helped to bring the level of investment closer to the optimum and increased the value of land by almost 30 percent. Investment at the plot level is affected by the rights to the specific plot, but not by whether there is at least one titled plot (which could then be used to access credit) in the household. This suggests that, rather than improved credit access, it is the higher level of tenure security that drives the result, an interpretation reinforced by the fact that there are no significant differences in transferability between titled and untitled lands (Deininger and Chamorro forthcoming). In peri-urban Ecuador, the unconditional impact of title is to raise property values by 24 percent. Informal property rights, which communities develop over time, can to some extent substitute for formal property rights, implying that titling will have maximum effect in newly established communities where no informal rules exist yet (Lanjouw and Levy 1998). In Venezuela, from 1965 to 2000 the prices of land in informal markets were consistently between 40 to 60 percent lower than the prices for titled land (Delahaye 2001).

Analysis of the impact of higher tenure security and land titling in the Brazilian Amazon also indicates a strong impact of higher tenure security (Alston, Libecap, and Schneider 1995, 1996). For Indian reservations in the United States, Anderson and Lueck (1992) found that output on tribal and individual trust land was 85 to 90 percent and 30 to 40 percent lower, respectively, than on fee simple land. Salas (1986) provides less rigorous evidence for Costa Rica, where they estimate a positive correlation of 0.53 between farm income and title security, and Stanfield (1990) claims that titling programs have led to increases in

Formal title has a positive impact in Latin America

the value of land. More anecdotal evidence supports this: de Soto (1993) notes that in Peru investment in property increases ninefold when squatters obtain formalized title to their homes.

Land Title as a Key Determinant of Formal Credit Access

Title reduces the costs of transferring land

In addition to inducing investment, secure land ownership that can be verified and transferred at low cost is likely to increase the supply of credit from the formal credit system. The reason is that because of its immobility and virtual indestructibility, land with secure, clearly defined, and easily transferable ownership rights is ideal collateral. The provision of collateral—facilitated by the possession of formal land title—is generally a necessary condition for participation in formal credit markets for medium- and long-term credit. Titles may enhance access to informal credit markets as well, as Siamwalla (1990) observed in Thailand. Therefore, the existence of well-documented and transferable property rights and of institutional arrangements to facilitate the low-cost transfer of land can often make an important contribution to the development of financial markets. Figure 2.5 presents some of the available evidence.

The importance of the credit supply effect associated with the provision of land title is supported by evidence from Thailand (Feder 1988), where farmers' opinions and econometric evidence point toward improved credit supply as the main benefit of titling: the availability of title significantly enhanced households' credit supply in three of the four provinces. Lopez (1997) finds a similarly positive impact of title on credit access in Honduras.

For title to enhance credit access, certain preconditions need to be satisfied

The positive effect of title on the supply of credit will not emerge universally. Formal land titling and registration, as distinct from measures to increase tenure security in an informal setting, are more likely to have a strong credit market impact in situations where informal credit markets are already operational and a latent demand exists for formal credit that cannot be satisfied because of the lack of formal title. This is generally the case in countries where a certain level of per capita income has been attained, so that land is no longer the primary safety net, and if profitable investment opportunities are available for potential borrowers. Where these conditions exist, providing formal land titles can indeed contribute significantly to the emergence of financial markets. Even in these cases, measures to improve the development of credit infrastructure or access to markets may be appropriate simultaneous with titling efforts.

Figure 2.5   Impact of title status on access to credit, selected countries and years

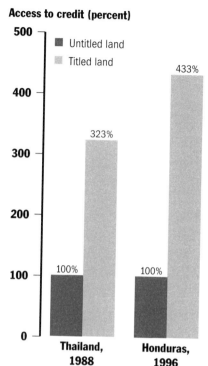

Source: Feder (2002).

By contrast, formal titles may not have an effect on access to credit in situations where (a) the option of foreclosure is not feasible, (b) the necessary financial infrastructure and/or a banking system that will lend to small producers is not available, or (c) the profitability of projects by potential users of credit is low. In addition, at low levels of income and in the absence of other mechanisms for social security, land serves as a social safety net. Foreclosing on the land of households that have defaulted on credit would deprive them of their basic means of livelihood and may not be socially desirable, which is essentially the reason for customary systems restricting the marketability of land. Even where formal law decrees that land should be fully tradable, such legislation may be impossible to implement, as was indeed the case in Kenya (Atwood 1990). Because banks are unlikely to lend under these circumstances, expected credit market effects will not materialize. In India, for example, Pender and Kerr (1999) found that formal proof of land ownership had little impact on credit supply, either because other factors strongly affected credit access by small producers or because foreclosure by banks was not an option.

The provision of credit is also normally associated with fixed transaction costs that are related to the need to screen applicants, enforced repayment, and other issues independent of the amount borrowed. The need to recoup these expenses may cause lenders to provide credit to small borrowers at significantly higher cost than to large ones, or to exclude them altogether. Thus, even where land is titled and can therefore be used as collateral, the transaction costs associated with administering such credit or with foreclosure procedures may be too high to be attractive to commercial lenders. Thus, the credit access benefits of land titling may be differentiated by wealth and accrue only to richer producers. Indeed, a study in Paraguay confirmed the existence of such a credit supply effect of title (Carter and Olinto 2003). Estimates indicated that producers with less than 20 hectares remained rationed out of the credit market and therefore did not benefit from the credit supply effect of title, implying that the credit-related benefits of titling programs accrue only to medium and large landowners. As figure 2.6 indicates, producers with a smaller landholding are more likely to be rationed in their access to capital, especially if their landholding is untitled, than producers with larger landholdings. While title is estimated to increase access to credit for all producers, the effect is sufficiently large to overcome rationing only for those with more than 20 hectares of land, implying that other mechanisms need to accompany titling for households below this threshold. Mushinski (1999) found a similar pattern of wealth-biased credit rationing in Guatemala.

Whether, in the presence of heterogeneity in endowments, small producers will benefit from policies to award title depends in part on the presence of credit markets and the ability to reduce transaction costs and policy-induced distortions that limit access to credit markets. Considerable evidence suggests that in situations in which credit markets either do not function well or entail distortions that put smaller and poorer farmers at a disadvantage, the establishment of formal and individualized property rights through titling may have an adverse impact on equity. Eliminating policy distortions and other barriers that might reduce access to credit will therefore be important before, or commensurate with, initiation of titling activities. Where titling is unlikely to increase access to formal credit even with the elimination of such distortions, and where additional interventions to increase access

Where title increases credit access, the effect may be differentiated by asset class

Figure 2.6   Impact of titling and wealth on credit access, Paraguay, 1990–95

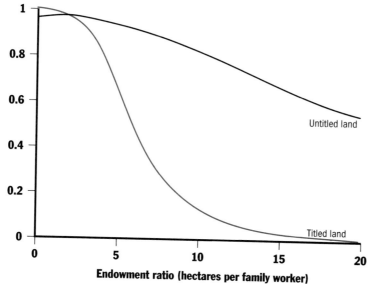

Source: Carter and Salgado (2001).

to credit by smallholders are not viable economically, lower levels of formality and precision can be used. Experience illustrates that these can be upgraded over time, as in the case of Botswana (Adams 2000).

Policy Implications

THE PRINCIPLES AND EVIDENCE DISCUSSED EARLIER IMPLY that the legal framework for land ownership should not only be comprehensive, but should also be flexible, allowing for different options depending on population density, level of economic development, and infrastructure access. Furthermore, it should explicitly recognize the rights of women and other groups that have traditionally been neglected or disadvantaged. Wherever justified and compatible with the foregoing principles, the legal framework should include formal recognition of customary rights subject to minimum standards. Even where rights are awarded to the group, they should be sufficiently specific regarding the obligations of individuals within the group and the mechanisms by which these are specified or can be changed. Finally, the institutions that administer land rights need to be backed by law, legitimate, accessible, accountable, follow clearly defined procedures, make authoritative decisions and provide information at low cost so as to not discriminate against the poor.

Definition and Demarcation of Property Rights

The foregoing discussion highlights that property rights should endure long enough to provide investment incentives and should be supported by accessible enforcement institutions that enjoy legal backing and social legitimacy; that the responsibility of individuals needs to be clear even if property rights are given to a group; and that the pertinent institutions must have the possibility of evolving flexibly in response to changing needs. Even where the ultimate right (root title) may be with a community or the state, many options are available depending on the particular situation and system. Botswana provides a good example of a gradual change in the breadth of land rights that an individual can enjoy, starting with group rights. Since 1970 the authorities have gradually strengthened individual rights, starting with the right to exclude other people's animals and to fence arable lands; allowing the allocation of land to all adult citizens, whether male or female, married or single; charging a price for transfers of developed land; and introducing common law residential leases for commercially valuable land (Adams 2000; Toulmin and Quan 2000). The critical issue is that the different systems are compatible and complement each other and that mechanisms for making the transition between different systems are well defined so that duplication and parallelism are avoided.

In customary systems, demarcation of external boundaries is critical, subject to clear membership, internal rules, conflict resolution mechanisms, and recording of transfers

Customary arrangements are dominant in most African countries and in indigenous areas of many Latin American and some Asian countries. Systems meant to closely resemble customary tenure were re-established in Mexico in the form of *ejidos* after the 1917 revolution and in China and Ethiopia in the context of collectivization. In these cases individuals' secure and normally inheritable rights to receive land, generally for individual cultivation, are based on their membership in the lineage that cleared the land. Therefore, the defining characteristic of customary tenure is that land is owned by the community rather than the individual. Exchanges through sales or rentals are limited to the community, and allowing the permanent transfer of land to outsiders formally and definitively ends the customary tenure regime. Customary systems of land ownership have evolved over long periods of time in response to location-specific conditions. In many cases they constitute a way of managing land relations that is more flexible and more adapted to location-specific conditions than would be possible under a more centralized approach (Downs and Reyna 1978; Noronha 1985). The land rights provided by such systems are often very secure, long-term, and in most cases inheritable and can be transferred within the community (Feder and Feeny 1991; Feder and Noronha 1987). Challenges will arise only once transfers with outsiders become more widespread or if internal institutions are no longer able to adequately resolve land disputes.

The literature is clear that even in cases where property rights are given to a group—that is, a clear boundary is established between members and nonmembers—whether or not an open-access regime will prevail within the group will depend on the effectiveness with which mechanisms for resource management within the group are established and managed. The widespread presence of condominium associations in industrial countries that share many characteristics with customary tenure systems illustrates that well-defined group rights are not necessarily inferior to full individual ownership and can have advantages in providing public goods. It also illustrates that in addition to defining the responsibilities of individuals within the group, mechanisms for exit and/or the transition to more individualized property rights structures need to be clearly defined if such arrangements are to be viable. As long as readily identifiable, long-term, and transferable rights to land are held by individuals within a group that satisfies the criteria outlined earlier, first providing legal recognition and regularizing groups' land ownership rights may well be a cost-effective approach to providing tenure security (Heath 1994). In many cases communities have well-established rules for assigning land rights within the group, but may face threats of encroachment or conflict from outside. If this is the case, high levels of tenure security can often be achieved at low cost by delineating rights for a group rather than for individuals. Experience suggests that such arrangements will be sustainable and equitable only if the rights and responsibilities of individuals within the group are clearly defined and if mechanisms to enforce them or to appeal infringements are in place.

In many instances conflicts arise because land transfers and the agreements surrounding them are contested, or because one of the parties involved challenges the validity of the way in which past conflicts were resolved. For this reason land transfers and agreements undertaken in connection with the resolution of conflicts should be recorded in a way that minimizes the possibility of ambiguity or re-interpretation. Providing administrative validation for arrangements and contracts, such as transfers and sales, that have been agreed on locally, provided they do not infringe on others' rights (for example, of women or holders of secondary land rights) constitutes a promising option (Lavigne Delville 2000). In fact, simple recording of sales agreements witnessed by respectable members of the community has long been used to legitimize and give social recognition to such transactions. Use of this mechanism is particularly desirable in West Africa where, because it is often migrants who are involved in land transactions, the conflict could lead to broader frictions along ethnic lines.

Recognizing occupants or formal long-term leases is an option on state lands

In situations where land users and the private sector are confident that the government will honor contracts, long-term and secure lease rights that are fully transferable can become virtually indistinguishable from private ownership. For example, in Israel most land is state-owned and leased to farmers for terms of 49 or 99 years without any negative impact on the functioning of land or credit markets (Lerman 2001). Where there are reservations or fears about the equity and productivity impact of privatizing land ownership, award of long-term leases can provide a means of achieving many or all of the benefits, or to test out the feasibility of such arrangements and then gradually expand on the basis of the experience gained in the process. For example, in China after 1978, rural land was initially given on informal lease contracts for 15 years, a period that has now been extended to 30 years. The gradual evolution of tenure security on state-owned land is illustrated in box 2.2.

Similarly, in Vietnam the 1998 Law on Land provides automatically renewable leases of 20 years for annual crops and 50 years for perennials, allows some mortgaging, and permits foreign investors to obtain leases to land under certain conditions (World Bank 2000). Obviously, as lease contracts near the end of their term, uncertainty about their continuity can reduce investment incentives. Thus, rules to ensure a fair and transparent process of contract renewal will be required. The desire to reduce transaction costs, uncertainty, and the opportunity for discretional bureaucratic interference has led many countries to stipulate automatic renewal of leases in the absence of an overriding public interest requiring termination of the contract.

Obviously, if there are doubts concerning the ability or desire of the state institutions leasing out the land to honor long-term contracts, for example by revoking leases or raising lease payments once investments that increase the value of the land have been made, the benefits from

Box 2.2   Land tenure security under state ownership

IN CHINA THE ADOPTION OF INDIVIDUAL USE rights to land under the household responsibility system in the early 1980s has contributed significantly to increased productivity and output in rural areas (Lin 1992; McMillan, Whalley, and Zhu 1989). Nonetheless, studies find that tenure security varies sharply across villages (Li, Rozelle, and Brandt 1998) and that periodic administrative reallocation of land contributes to great insecurity of property rights (Jacoby, Li, and Rozelle forthcoming). Weak property rights have been linked to environmentally unsustainable methods of cultivation, overexploitation of scarce natural resources, low investment, and decreased household welfare (Chen and Davis 1998). Furthermore, abuses of power by village authorities to effect reallocations that would provide them with personal benefits are a growing problem (Li 2002). To increase tenure security, in 1999 the Chinese government revised the 1986 Land Management Law to require that farmers receive written 30-year land use contracts and that the scope for readjustments be circumscribed or completely eliminated. This has had considerable, though regionally differentiated, impacts on farmers' perceptions (Prosterman 2001). Building on this, in 2002 the government adopted a new land law that strengthens individuals' rights, frees rental markets, protects households against arbitrary expropriation by village cadres by requiring that even small reallocations be approved by a two-thirds majority of village members, and aims to establish mechanisms to protect women against losing their land endowments (Schwarzwalder 2002).

leasing of public land will be limited or completely absent. If it is not possible to increase the credibility of government institutions and the benefits from improved ownership rights are substantial, complete privatization may be indicated. At the same time, there may be broader benefits from increasing the credibility of public institutions and making them more accountable, something that illustrates the close link between land tenure and broader legal reform.

If the value of land is sufficiently high, individual ownership rights to land are generally the option of choice. Where the magnitude of the task, the high requirements of full title, and shortage of administrative capacity render the award of fully surveyed and documented freehold title infeasible or impractical, at least in the short to medium term, intermediate options to increase the tenure security of informal urban and rural dwellers are needed. The options available include a streamlined and simplified title registration system as introduced in Peru (de Soto 2000); long-term and transferable leases as implemented in many Indian cities; or legal measures that guarantee occupancy rights and recognition of such rights, including record keeping, at the local level. These measures have often had a significant impact on increasing tenure security at a relatively low cost. Ensuring the compatibility of any simplified registration system with an

Private ownership will be key to tenure security in many cases

eventual formal titling procedure is, however, essential in order not to set up parallel systems.

Land ownership as certified by formal title will still be the option of choice where land values are sufficiently high and the administrative capacity for land administration is available. This is illustrated by the fact that many middle-income countries such as Chile, Malaysia, Mexico, Morocco, Thailand, and Tunisia have carried out large-scale tenure regularization and upgrading programs that have provided formal title with considerable success. In this context, land registration should be accessible and provide authoritative and reliable information to financial institutions and potential investors at low cost. To ensure transparency, public access to the registry needs to be enshrined in law, the administrative structure must be sufficiently deconcentrated,[16] and the physical records must be in a condition that permits such access at low cost. The agency responsible for registering land rights should also be independent from the courts and the executive.

Initial award of land documents should be systematic

As the benefit of an official registry lies in providing authoritative information on all properties in a jurisdiction, the increment in tenure security that can be offered by a legal and institutional framework that covers most of the territory and that provides a possibility for gradual upgrading as needed can outweigh the relatively low level of precision that may be necessary for cost reasons. Greater precision and detail can then be targeted to areas where land values are higher, for example, urban areas. Equity and efficiency considerations also imply that wherever possible titling programs should be systematic rather than on demand. Efficiency is increased through economies of scale, and equity is enhanced if all claims in an area are registered at the same time.[17]

Registration programs should be accompanied by publicity campaigns to ensure widespread knowledge of the rules and procedures. Often, involving communities is more cost-effective than a highly formalized way of demarcating boundaries. Furthermore, local communities have the best knowledge of the situation on the ground, and if there is a systematic requirement for them to provide consent they can object to wrong boundaries, misquoted or omitted owners, and other irregularities. This is critical to prevent the emergence of subsequent disputes that would jeopardize the security of titles and certificates awarded, reducing their value and undermining the scope for subsequent land transactions. The importance of local participation is widely acknowledged, systems that do not pay sufficient attention to this issue are either slow and ad hoc or suffer from subsequent disputes.

Even where systematic registration is being implemented, it will not be feasible at once for a whole country, thereby posing the challenge of dealing with nonpriority areas on a sporadic basis. The same is true for areas that are not included under systematic adjudication. Given that historically, ad hoc procedures of land adjudication without proper consultation have arguably been the mechanism through which traditional communities and their members have lost most of their land either to outsiders or to chiefs and community members, special attention to these situations is warranted. This will make adherence to a transparent process even more important.

Unless the authorities can make land administration institutions provide services broadly, at low cost, and in a way that inspires public confidence and trust so that owners see tangible benefits that justify their efforts to keep their property records updated, large investments in legal drafting and physical infrastructure may have little long-term effect. Indeed, institutional shortcomings can impose constraints on households' and entrepreneurs' ability to enjoy and transfer property rights that are as detrimental as ambiguous legal provisions. In fact, the case of India, where the registry essentially provides only a record of tax payments and where land disputes therefore abound (Wadhwa 2002), illustrates that a registry that does not provide authoritative and up-to-date information may be of limited use. In many cases titling programs did not achieve the expected outcomes because households failed to register follow-up transactions, thereby rapidly invalidating the value of the huge public investment. Analysis of the incentives for follow-up registration reveals that high transaction costs or transfer taxes often mean that households do not register transactions, and the authorities need to take appropriate measures to deal with this issue. Thus, to ensure sustainability, if landowners are expected to register transactions and to use the registry, their costs in time and money for doing so should be minimized.

Sustainable mechanisms for follow-up registration are required

Strengthen Women's Land Rights

Past land policy initiatives that were based on a unitary model of the household have often failed to recognize the importance of the way in which control of assets, and in particular land, is assigned within the household. This has often resulted in relative neglect of women's land rights, despite the fact that this violates basic norms of equality and evidence pointing toward the importance of women's access to assets and income for nutritional outcomes and human capital accumulation, especially for girls, as well as for women's bargaining power within the household. Irrespective of whether or not women engage in agriculture, independent asset ownership will considerably enhance their livelihood opportunities; for example, they could use land ownership to gain access to credit that would allow them to establish small enterprises or engage in other nonagricultural pursuits. Even where measures intended to enhance women's rights, such as joint titling, were introduced, results and impacts have often lagged far behind expectations, implying that greater attention to the effectiveness of interventions would be warranted.

Attention to women's land rights is particularly important if women are the main cultivators, if control of productive activities is differentiated by gender, or if adult mortality is high

In many societies women's land rights are of a secondary nature, acquired through their husbands or male relatives. As a consequence, women's ability to have independent land ownership in case of the death of their husband or divorce was limited. Divergence between ownership and control rights can have negative effects on productivity. Where the husband controls the proceeds from cultivation, this reduces women's incentives to exert efforts, and thus lowers agricultural productivity. This is particularly relevant in African countries, where women are the main agricultural cultivators, and in many Latin America and Asian countries, where men migrate or women are traditionally heavily discriminated against (Agarwal 1994; Deere and Leon 2001). In Burkina Faso the reallocation of factors of production from plots controlled by men to plots controlled by women within the same household could increase output by 6 percent (Udry 1996). Other studies highlight that bias in the allocation of land rights against women is not justified, as the literature provides no evidence of inferior efficiency by women farmers; indeed, a study from Côte d'Ivoire, for example, demonstrates that women's efficiency is not significantly different from that of men (Adesina and Djato 1997). In addition, anecdotal evidence suggests that giving women title to land will allow them to use the security this provides to access credit, possibly to start up nonfarm enterprises.

Unless women's rights are specifically protected, increases in land values caused, for example, by higher levels of population density or the emergence of export opportunities, may lead to a progressive weakening, or even the loss, of women's rights to land. In some parts of West Africa the introduction of export crops has resulted in men taking over plots previously farmed by women (Kevane and Gray 1999), similar to what occurred in Kenya (Dolan 2001). By contrast, the introduction of export crops in Ghana has increased the demand for women's labor, causing husbands to "gift" them land rights in return for labor on their husbands' cocoa plots. The resulting improved outcomes, such as spending on girls' education and health, illustrate that strengthening women's bargaining power and their control over assets clearly matters and can help improve equity (Quisumbing and Otsuka 2001). In many Indian states both laws and court rulings or prevailing practices are often strongly biased against women. Government action to address the issue has been recommended at the national level (Saxena 1999).

The devastation caused by the HIV/AIDS epidemic, together with the fact that in traditional systems widows have only indirect, and often insecure, access to land, is forcing significant adjustments. Although traditional inheritance patterns are changing in some African countries because of the significantly increased male mortality (Ntozi and Ahimbisibwe 1999), in Uganda widows suffer from significantly higher levels of land-related conflicts than others, causing losses in productivity and requiring them to spend money on trying to obtain a resolution (Deininger and Castagnini 2002). Better definition and enforcement of women's rights to land and its inheritance could therefore avoid burdening victims of such shocks with conflicts over land that are likely to further weaken their ability to effectively cope. Unless measures to effectively protect women's access to land assets are taken, general efforts to increase the security of land rights may in this context result in a higher concentration of land rights in the hands of men, with negative implications for gender equality and economic outcomes (Lastarria-Cornhiel 1997).

In most countries, traditional law implies that women's access to land is mediated through their relationships with men. Legal recognition of women's ability to have independent rights to land is thus a necessary, though by no means sufficient, first step toward increasing their control of assets. While most countries recognize gender equality before the law and outlaw discrimination against women, putting such regulations into practice requires more specific actions. In Asia women's land rights have been systematically eroded over a long time. While contestation of the main property laws has helped to improve the legal framework, shortcomings remain both in the legal basis for women's property rights and in the actual ability to implement these (Agarwal 1994). In Africa, where juxtaposition, and often conflict, between traditional patriarchal authorities and democratic institutions based on gender equality can create considerable friction, a number of countries, including Mozambique, Nigeria, and South Africa, have anchored gender

Legal recognition of women's property rights is an essential first step

---

Box 2.3   Innovative gender legislation in Latin America

IN AN ATTEMPT TO IMPROVE GENDER EQUALITY, Latin American and Asian countries have adopted a number of innovative practices. Explicit equality between men's and women's land rights is guaranteed by Nicaragua (as of 1981), Brazil (1988), Costa Rica (1990), Honduras (1991), Colombia (1994), Bolivia (1996), the Dominican Republic (1998), and Guatemala (1999). Joint adjudication and/or titling of land to couples is a requirement in Colombia (as of 1988), Costa Rica (1990), Nicaragua (1993), Peru (1997, for married couples only), the Dominican Republic (1998), Ecuador (1999), Guatemala (1999), and Brazil (2001, option since 1988) and has been proposed in El Salvador and Honduras. Furthermore, Chile, Colombia, and Nicaragua give priority and charge lower fees to female household heads in land-related interventions.

Source: Deere and Leon (2001).

---

equality in their constitutions, with a clarification that this provision supersedes any legal provision, including in customary law. The example of Uganda, where the clause pertaining to co-ownership by women was eliminated from the 1998 Land Act at the last moment, illustrates that the legal emancipation of women is often highly political and that in the absence of strong advocacy, proper attention to women's issues may be difficult to achieve (Yngstrom 2002).

Inheritance regulations often play a critical role

For many women, inheritance is an important way of accessing land. Normally the rules followed are highly culture-specific, have evolved over long periods, and continue to adapt to changes in the socioeconomic environment. Investigators have repeatedly identified lack of clarity in inheritance regulations as a major source of conflict. Where modernization will clash with traditional values, the goal should be to clarify the rules and explore the extent to which they are consistent with other values, such as gender equality, and if they are not, to examine how such consistency might be achieved at either the procedural or the legal level. The issue has become particularly important in the context of the HIV/AIDS epidemic in Africa, where the requirement to go through elaborate formal channels to effect transfers of rights in the case of inheritance has, in some cases, developed into a major burden for the poor (Fourie 2002). Legal changes to increase women's rights undertaken in Latin America (see box 2.3), and more recently in Asia, have made land legislation more gender-balanced (Deere and Leon 2001).

Although investigators have undertaken little systematic study of changes in inheritance or other legislation, empirical evidence suggests that even where legal provisions are adequate, if they clash with traditional norms their effectiveness may be limited. For example, in India women often fail to exercise their legal rights because of social pressure, and some evidence indicates that adjustments men have made to the legal provisions may make them actually worse off (Saxena, 2002). In Africa, laws in favor of women may not be effective, as those who are to benefit from them often fail to insist on their rights for fear of being accused of witchcraft or being socially stigmatized (Walker 2002). For example, even though women's rights are adequately protected in law, local institutions that male elites have traditionally dominated cannot automatically be counted on to protect and enforce these rights, as Khadiagala (2001) demonstrates for Uganda. In Eastern Europe, even though countries' constitutions mandate equality of men and women before the law, practice discriminates against the latter, for instance, by allowing the registration of property in the name of only one person, which will usually be the male household head.

All this implies that legal measures can only constitute a first step within a broader process of education and capacity building that makes women aware of their rights. To avoid or be able to counter undesirable side effects early on, the impact of legal measures needs to be closely monitored. Advocacy and awareness campaigns to draw attention to the importance of gender issues in land policy, as well as measures to make women aware of their rights and to provide them with legal aid, will be required (Gopal and Salim 1998). Even though it is rarely enough by itself, the right to inherit land can have an important role in preventing the erosion of such rights by providing new opportunities and can strengthen women's bargaining power (Gray and Kevane 2001).

One strategy to improve women's property rights that has not been fully explored is the potential for giving priority attention to women as beneficiaries of government interventions and programs. Titling programs in Latin America have developed promising approaches, including, in addition to legal changes, joint titling and explicit guarantees for women's land rights. Experience from these suggests that legal initiatives that are accompanied by dissemination campaigns are often insufficient to improve women's status. Preferential treatment of women in public programs such as titling and land reform in Latin America suggests that this provides an appropriate way to increase gender equity and has helped improve the documentary basis for women's rights, which earlier attempts

Legal change needs to be translated into local reality

had almost completely neglected (Deere and Leon 2001). Much more can be done with regard to positive discrimination in favor of women in specific projects and in rigorously evaluating the impact of gender preferences in land registration.

Build on Customary Tenures and Existing Institutions

Eliminating or replacing customary tenure is often neither necessary nor desirable

Given that customary tenure systems have evolved over a long period of time, they are often well adapted to specific conditions and needs. Even in situations where such arrangements reach their limits, building on what already exists is in many cases easier and more appropriate than trying to re-invent the wheel, which can end up creating parallel institutions with all their disadvantages. In the past, practitioners have often considered customary tenure arrangements to be an economically inferior arrangement, equivalent to collective cultivation. To facilitate economic growth and prevent the static and dynamic efficiency losses presumably associated with this form of tenure, they proposed establishing freehold title and subdividing the commons (World Bank 1975). Especially in Africa, this has helped to legitimize and continue the dualism between "modern" forms of land tenure comprising leasehold and freehold systems and "backward" forms consisting of customary arrangements that most newly independent states had inherited from their former colonial masters. In view of the limited outreach of the modern sector, which in most African countries covers at most between 2 and 10 percent of the total land area (Österberg 2002), the failure to formally recognize customary and other traditional institutions has effectively excluded the majority of land and the population using it from the rule of the law, with potentially far-reaching implications for governance.

In Africa, customary institutions administer virtually all of the land area, including some peri-urban areas with high land values where demand for land transactions and more formal property rights is rapidly increasing. Such institutions not only often have a stronger field presence than government institutions, but locals also trust them more, especially in West Africa, where colonial intervention relied more on local institutions. At the same time, the lack of legal recognition of these institutions, which *de jure* puts them outside the scope of the law, makes enforcing decisions extremely difficult for them and for those who may be negatively affected or think these authorities abuse their

Table 2.3   Status of customary tenure in new land laws, selected African countries

Country	Recognition of customary tenure	Customary rights registrable interests	Commons registrable by group	Implementation
Burkina Faso	Permissive	No	No	n.a.
Côte d'Ivoire	Partial	Yes	No	n.a.
Eritrea	No	No	No	None
Ethiopia	No	No	Yes	None
Ghana	Yes	Yes	Yes	None
Kenya	Permissive	No	No	n.a.
Lesotho	Yes	Yes	Yes	None
Malawi	Yes	No	Yes	None
Mali	Yes	Yes	No	n.a.
Mozambique	Yes	Yes	Yes	Under way
Namibia	Yes	Yes	No	None
Niger	Yes	Yes	No	n.a.
Rwanda	No	No	No	None
South Africa	Yes	Yes	Yes	None
Swaziland	Yes	Yes	Yes	None
Tanzania	Yes	Yes	Yes	None
Uganda	Yes	Yes	Yes	Minor
Zambia	Yes	No	Yes	Under way
Zanzibar[a]	No	No	Indirectly only	Pilots
Zimbabwe	Yes	Yes	Yes	None

n.a. Not appliable.

a. Archipelago of Tanzania.

Source: Based on Alden-Wiley (2002).

power to appeal or bring other action against such decisions. Formal recognition of their role could, by making such institutions more accountable, benefit everybody.

Recent reforms in other African countries have gone a long way toward recognizing customary tenure (table 2.3), thereby providing the basis for integrating it into more formal systems. In addition to the legal recognition of community rights that, for the first time, provides an opportunity to integrate the mass of land users into the formal system, a key element of these reforms is the extensive use of existing local institutions, or in some cases the establishment of new ones, to solve land disputes and provide guarantees for such rights at the local level (Toulmin and Quan 2000). Experience illustrates that legal recognition of the respective institutions is, however, only the first step that needs to be followed up by actual demarcation of land, as well as capacity building for local institutions. While the former will require attention to minor and secondary rights can have a significant impact on equity, the latter will need clear principles, procedures, and rules to prevent abuses of power and establish mechanisms of appeal. The dangers inherent in the failure to recognize customary rights and the resulting disconnect between legal stipulations and actual practice is illustrated by the case of Côte d'Ivoire. Despite a long history of participatory demarcation of community land, the 2000 Land Law failed to recognize such rights and instead mandated that all customary rights not transformed into full title within 10 years would revert back to the state. The state's limited ability to implement these provisions was questionable from the outset. At the same time, predictions that the law would create widespread tenure insecurity, conflict, and discretionary action by bureaucrats seem to have been borne out by recent hostilities in the country that were at least partly related to land issues.

To put the legal recognition of customary rights into practice, mechanisms for the demarcation and recording of the boundaries of community (or, if desired and feasible, individual) land are indispensable and have been established in a number of countries. For example, Tanzania's land policy establishes a certificate for village land and designates the elected village council as trustee for land. Individual households' plots are registered as individual customary holdings, but land is held and registered by the village. In this case the law also provides a range of options for landholding, and land previously acquired by the state can be transferred back to the village. In Mozambique the law establishes the protection of customary rights without the need for registration. The local community is given legal status, thereby eliminating the need to survey all the individual plots, but at the same time providing protection by delineating community boundaries. Foreign investors and other outsiders can acquire use rights only through consultation with communities (Tanner 2002). In Benin customary rights are recognized and will be validated in a participatory fashion. Once they have registered customary rights, individuals can apply either for land certificates or full registration, both of which can be used for credit on a cost recovery basis. Land is managed by a land management committee at the level of the commune and a village land management committee (Pescay 2002). By expanding on such innovative practices, possibly in a decentralized fashion that allows gradual upgrading over time (see box 2.4), it will be possible not only to improve security of tenure but often also to strengthen local government institutions.

Box 2.4 The scope for gradually upgrading tenure security over time

FOR THE FREEHOLD SYSTEM IN NAMIBIA TO COVER existing urban settlements would take more than 20 years, even if the required knowledge, expertise, and technical equipment were available. The lack of all these factors implies a need for a model of a land registration system that can be upgraded over time. To this end, permissions to occupy were given for the planned portions of urban areas, but these could not be mortgaged, subleased, or otherwise transferred without permission. Urban expansion increases the demand for serviced land for residential and business purposes. At the same time, the high costs involved in planning and developing land, especially with high standards of infrastructure, make land in these areas generally unaffordable for the poor. This, together with the lack of surveyors and other technical expertise, slows processes and encourages the growth of informal settlements. To cope with this a parallel registration system was developed that provides a lower form of title, called a starter title, that guarantees perpetual occupation of a site within a block without identifying the exact location of this site within the block. It also allows the possibility of transferring occupation rights according to customs or norms (by-laws) drawn up by the group occupying the site, but not the mortgaging of this right. A second title, called a landhold title, adds the ability to mortgage the land. In both cases the whole block is registered in freehold ownership by the central registry office, whereas the specific occupancy rights on the site are registered only locally at the district level. While institutional issues have slowed down implementation, observers see this as a promising option to extend tenure security quickly to large numbers of poor people in circumstances where technical and human resources are limited.

Source: Juma and Christensen (2001).

As table 2.3 illustrates, there has been considerable progress in terms of legal drafting. At the same time, the fact that some of these laws were passed some time ago without the necessary follow-up in terms of implementation, is reason for concern. Indeed, studies from Uganda indicate that the institutional vacuum created by new laws without actual institutions for enforcement can become a major source of insecurity and conflict (Deininger and Castagnini 2002; McAuslan 1998). Experience from Mexico illustrates that passage of advanced laws is ineffective unless they are backed up by adequately funded, staffed, and motivated institutions to resolve conflicts and assist communities, implying that the implementation of advanced legal provisions will require significant effort and resources to be put into dissemination and capacity building at the local level, and to ensure that mechanisms of appeal are available. In the case of Africa, integration of the customary and statutory systems remains a major challenge for policy, and more work is required to clarify both the technical and institutional options available to implement new land legislation in a context of constrained availability of human and fiscal resources (Fourie 2002).

Putting new legislation into practice poses technical and institutional challenges

Strengthen the Land Rights of Indigenous People and Herders

Governments have often underestimated the importance of land rights for marginal groups

Forests and other common property resources contribute significantly to people's welfare, especially of the poor. In Africa and Asia poor people in marginal areas often derive 30 to 40 percent of their consumption from common property resources (Cavendish 2000; Jodha 1996). The literature suggests that governments often neglected or underestimated the importance of land tenure issues in natural resource conservation and the noneconomic values associated with "marginal" lands (Heltberg 2001; Shackleton, Shackleton, and Cousins 2001). This is important, because with competing demands for land from outside, for example, for logging and mining, and with collective action problems as communities' sources of livelihood and preferences become more diverse, many of these resources are degrading, thereby jeopardizing the livelihoods of a large number of poor and marginal people (Arnold 2001).

Recent policy changes and international conventions have led to greater recognition of indigenous land rights in many countries, especially in Asia and Latin America, where a large share of the population is affected. In Latin America the indigenous population amounts to about 50 million people, or about 10.5 percent of the total population, and many more people are dependent on forest resources. Furthermore, indigenous people are highly concentrated in specific countries such as Bolivia (where 71 percent of the national population is indigenous), Guatemala (66 percent), Peru (47 percent), and Ecuador (43 percent). These four countries and Mexico (14 percent) account for almost 90 percent of Latin America's indigenous population. About 100 million people in India and some 120 million people (or 30 percent of the population) in Southeast Asia are classified as forest-dependent (Poffenberger 2002).

A growing number of countries recognize indigenous land rights in principle and allow for their internal management by the community. For example, in the Philippines the 1997 Indigenous Peoples Rights Act recognizes, promotes, and protects the rights of indigenous people and provides rights to ancestral domains, rights to transfer lands, and exemptions from property taxes. Lands that were previously administered by centralized institutions are to be turned over to the community. Similarly, in at least some Latin American countries the recognition of indigenous property rights is followed up by more far-reaching action.[18] Even where a legal framework is in place, implementation has often been slow because of gaps in the extent to which communities can actually exercise their management authority in practice. Pilot projects in Brazil, Colombia, Peru, and other countries have helped to streamline procedures for giving ownership title to indigenous communities and are currently being expanded and replicated in other countries (Hvalkof 2002).

Clearly defined property rights are particularly relevant in cases where rights granted to indigenous communities overlap with mineral or logging rights that have already been awarded to others, and where only legal clarity on their rights will enable communities to negotiate effectively with outside interests. This is illustrated in Ghana, where clear rights enable communities to negotiate with concessionaires on uses for different purposes, replanting after harvest, and specified shares of the proceeds (Amanor, Brown, and Richards 2002).

Pastoral communities are widespread in the marginal areas of the Sahel, the Middle East and North Africa, East Africa, and Central Asia. In areas characterized by sparse rainfall, the high risk of crop failure may make strategies characterized by high mobility and the associated joint ownership more rewarding than individualizing land ownership (Nugent and Sanchez 1998; Steele 2001). Strategies to manage risk in these agriculturally marginal areas depend heavily on mobility and the ability to temporarily use supplementary resources, such as crop residues, from adjacent areas or from the market. Access to such resources was in many cases unproblematic under conditions of low population density, but is becoming contested with the expansion of crop agriculture and often constitutes a source of conflict between nomadic and settled communities. Population growth and the expansion of sedentary agriculture may therefore lead to significant conflict and/or a decision by nomadic herders to shift toward sedentary agriculture themselves, as can be observed in many areas of the world (van den Brink, Bromley, and Chavas 1995). Despite the large physical areas involved, the fact that pastoralists often constitute one of the most vulnerable groups, and the potential for conflict and violence at the interface between pastoral and sedentary communities, the land tenure needs of pastoral populations have often been neglected or marginalized in the policy debate.

By its nature, most pastoral activity takes place on lands with low commercial value and incorporates mobility as a central element. In highly marginal environments, the importance of temporary access to feed resources is critical, and investigators have emphasized the importance of geographic mobility as an inherent element of a land tenure system that provides flexibility and allows the merging and shifting of rights to insure against risks (Breusers 2001; Niamir-Fuller 1999;

Overlooking the needs of pastoral communities is dangerous

Turner 1999). This is complicated by the fact that the routes followed by pastoralists often cross state boundaries and change depending on resource availability. The public good nature of the resources in question and the coordination failures in managing them have led a number of countries in Asia and North Africa to try to manage such resources through the state to reverse the degradation of rangeland and enhance the availability of feed (Leybourne and others 1993; Nordblom and Shomo 1995; Osman, Bahhady, and Murad 1994). Many observers have criticized this approach, whereby reserves to help reverse degradation and improve feed availability are opened during certain periods and are rented to herd owners afterwards, because of the high costs of fencing and guarding the reserves, the lack of financial sustainability, the creation of incentives for overstocking and the resulting negative equity effects, and the lack of any community participation.

Giving management authority to local communities is desirable, especially as pressure for settlement increases

Given the complexity of the institutional structures involved, in most situations simply introducing private property rights will be neither feasible nor cost-effective (Blewett 1995). Experience with nationalization of property rights previously held by traditional communities has been disappointing as well. It prevented tribal leaders who in the past apportioned access to and use of tribal pastures to efficiently manage their resources, leading to private land appropriation and conflicts, as in Jordan and Syria (Masri 1991; Nesheiwat, Ngaido, and Mamdoh 1998). In Ethiopia conflict ensued because traditional authorities manage access to and use of grazing resources, but are prohibited from diverting land to crop use (Swallow and Kamara 1999). Tenure insecurity increased because herders repeatedly lost their pastures to neighboring farming communities or to new migrant farmers (Ngaido 1993). Giving greater management authority to local communities is also the principle behind the *gestion du terroir* and natural resource management approaches that have been used extensively to implement community-based pastoral or integrated natural resource management projects, especially in West Africa. Although not always fully successful (Delville 2002), these approaches have highlighted the importance of local resource management and responsibility.

The negative impact of increasing scarcity of land during the lean season is compounded by increased pressure to becoming settled within pastoral communities themselves. The increase in the value of land with higher population pressures will eventually lead to increased individualization of land, implying significant changes for pastoralism (Jarvis 1991). Indeed, China's 1985 Rangeland Law emphasized individual household tenure as a necessary condition to improve incentives for sustainable rangeland management. Such contracting of grassland to households is appropriate in some areas with high human and animal population densities, such as large parts of Inner Mongolia. At the same time, in less densely populated areas pastoral tenure arrangements often continue to be based on collective access and management (Banks 2001; Ho 2000). This has led to the development of herder-driven cooperatives in Jordan that are reclaiming the management of parts of traditional pastures as grazing reserves. Many communities are adopting such an approach, and the positive results of these initiatives are being replicated elsewhere (Ngaido and McCarthy 2002).

Responding to this need, initiatives in a number of Sahelian countries, such as Burkina Faso, Mali, Mauritania, and Niger, seek to grant greater tenure security to pastoral communities, building on the positive experience with giving greater property rights and responsibility for resource management to local communities. Mauritania, for example, is introducing so-called focal-point management of lands vital to the sustainability of pastoral livestock production, together with national policy reforms to create the basis for a pastoral code that legally recognizes customary resource management practices and property rights and provides protection against encroachment by outsiders. Given that rangelands are not only fragile but, in most instances, also characterized by a legacy of mismanagement and unsettled land tenure, arriving at a sustainable policy will require recognizing the importance of ensuring access, taking account of the fragility of the land and focusing on risk management, and acknowledging the multiple-use forms and objectives of different groups of users.

Improve Functioning of Land Administration Institutions

Even if property rights are well defined by law, legal concepts need to be translated into something that can be physically identified on the ground, referred to, and transferred if desired. This creates a need for demarcation and surveys of boundaries, registration and record keeping, adjudication of rights, and resolution of conflicts. All these activities, together with other land management functions the state performs, are normally referred to as land administration (UNECE 1996). The state has an essential role to play not only in the legal definition of property rights, but also in providing the infrastructure used

Land administration translates concepts into reality

to demarcate and record property rights to enable their cost-effective enforcement. To secure property rights to land, countries will therefore have to establish institutions that carry out land administration functions. While private users will appropriate some of the benefits provided by such institutions, the reliability and comprehensiveness of the information they provide, their accessibility, and the trust they command will be critical for granting tangible tenure security to the poor.

Land administration can contribute to the achievement of broad efficiency and equity goals if a number of preconditions are satisfied. First, the institutions involved need to have clear mandates and a structure that allows them to function efficiently and free from political pressure. Second, the poor will be the first to be left out of sporadic approaches that cover part of the territory at high cost, and may even lose their rights if nontransparent processes of sporadic titling are adopted. Thus, where social and economic conditions warrant titling or other forms of land rights regularization, the danger of excluding the poor by adopting approaches that are nontransparent, fail to make the required information widely accessible, or impose high fixed or up-front costs must be taken into account. This suggests that the scope of any program should be comprehensive.[19] Regularization efforts need to be undertaken at costs that are commensurate with the benefits, thereby allowing sustainability in the long term. Finally, as a public good, the information on land ownership maintained in the registry needs to be publicly available and accessible at low cost to minimize the transaction costs for other users and to allow land and financial markets to operate at minimum cost. The cost at which these services are provided and the way in which users are charged will have a critical impact on the level of formality voluntarily chosen by landowners, and thus on the extent to which the conceptual advantages associated with well-defined and secure property rights can be realized in practice.

Cadastres and registries are key land administration instruments

Two main instruments used for land administration are a registry that handles information on land ownership and transactions and a database, called the cadastre, that contains the boundaries of parcels as defined by surveys and recorded on maps and any additional information about these parcels. The cadastre provides the basis for a number of other functions, such as land use planning, management and disposal of public lands, land valuation and taxation, provision of other public services, and generation of maps. The establishment of well-functioning land administration systems was a lengthy process in the industrial nations (de Soto 1993; Kawagoe 1999). Where these do not

Box 2.5 Key differences between deed and title registration

TWO TYPES OF REGISTRATION SYSTEMS ARE prevalent in industrial market economies: registration of deeds and registration of titles. In a deed registration system, legally recognized and protected rights to land arise upon conclusion of an agreement between the holder of the right and its acquirer. The entry of the agreement's existence and key content into the public registry is to provide public notice of the existence of a right, and challenges to property rights will be handled through civil litigation. In a title registration system, however, it is the entry of land rights into the registry that gives them legal validity, guaranteed by the state. All entries in the register are *prima facie* evidence of the actual legal status of the land. The deed registration system is used in the United States, while the title registration system is the norm throughout Europe, Australia, and most of Canada.

exist, developing a strategy that would provide a comprehensive spatial data infrastructure at low cost and in an accessible and transparent manner will be critical. Once such a data infrastructure is available and can provide a frame of reference, registries of different categories of land can often be managed at the local level, provided that ways to link the cadastres to the registry and keep the latter up to date are available. These can be quite simple, for example, information can periodically be transferred from local institutions to the center. Similarly, there is a strong trade-off between speed and the accuracy (and therefore cost) of land records. As the physical demands on a registration system can be immense, depending on the number of land parcels in a particular country, the system must be designed in such a way that it can deal with such demands quickly, efficiently, and in a sustainable way. As illustrated in box 2.5, the demands of title and deed systems differ considerably from each other in this respect. In doing so, two dangers have to be avoided. On the one hand, bureaucrats have in the past often been overambitious in the design stage but subsequently failed to deliver, or covered only very small areas. As a result, the land administration system has often failed to ensure even the basic goals of providing affordable ways to maintain tenure security and facilitate the emergence of a market. On the other hand, political imperatives of awarding a large number of titles within a short period of time should not undermine the quality and long-term sustainability of the titles awarded.

Studies of land administration systems worldwide suggest that institutional rigidities, overstaffing, corruption, and limited outreach often seriously undermine public confidence in the land registration system

There is the potential to strengthen land administration institutions, to better define their responsibilities, to improve coverage, and to enhance financial independence

71

(Adlington 2002; Sanjak and Lavadenz 2002). Many of the services public sector institutions provide, such as surveying and mapping, can be contracted out to the private sector, thereby reducing the scope for political interference and allowing the reduction of staffing levels in the public sector. To achieve this, proper regulation will be critical, something that includes the public sector's ability to enforce regulation. At the same time, the creation of private sector capacity and the feasibility of free entrance for qualified professionals needs to be maintained. In Zambia, as in many other African countries, surveyors' associations restrict entry by qualified individuals, resulting in backlogs of up to seven years for issuing titles (Moll 1996). These entry restrictions are similar to those observed in Indonesia, Malaysia, and the Philippines (Brits, Grant, and Burns 2002).

A common shortcoming in many countries is that different entities deal with rural land, urban land, and natural resources or state land. These entities may lack coordination and even compete with each other. In the Philippines the Ministry of Environment and Natural Resources, which is responsible for "protected areas," theoretically controls 72 percent of the land, but in practice much of this land is used for agricultural cultivation (World Bank 1998). Similar inconsistencies are observed in Ghana (Kasanga and Kotey 2001), Indonesia (Wallace and Poerba 2000), and Sri Lanka (Abt Associates 1999), among others. Failure to clearly assign responsibilities and define the specific type of land for which an institution is responsible will run the danger of creating overlapping mandates, which at best will increase transaction costs, and at worst will undermine tenure security and the validity of titles or land use certificates, result in resource degradation, and give rise to avoidable conflict.[20] Examples abound where lack of clarity in institutional responsibilities has resulted in the issuance of multiple titles to the same plot. This erodes confidence in the land administration system and creates a need for corrective measures that can be politically difficult and economically costly (Munoz and Lavadenz 1997) The example of El Salvador, which undertook far-reaching institutional reforms in a postconflict situation, demonstrates that in many instances, institutional reform and clarification of responsibilities are key to establishing an effective land administration system.

Earlier discussion demonstrated the desirability of comprehensive coverage and the challenges it creates in situations where the basic infrastructure for such coverage does not exist. Historical evidence suggests that distortions introduced in the process of first-time registration will be more harmful than any degree of inequality that is normally generated through the working of competitive market processes (Deininger and Binswanger 1995). In the African context, the relevance of land grabbing during initial surveys for land registration and its impact on dis-equalizing the ownership of land is well recognized (Downs and Reyna 1978). As such inequality in the distribution of assets is difficult to correct, having transparent processes for the adjudication of land in the process of awarding initial titles is of utmost importance. It should be complemented with a strong framework for quick and authoritative conflict resolution on the spot. This requires a combination of systematic campaigns in areas of high relevance with minimum measures and standards in areas where such systematic coverage is not feasible. In India the inability to provide an authoritative record of land ownership has greatly reduced the scope for privatizing high-value urban land and associated industries (Wadhwa 2002). Unclear, nontransparent, and discretionary rules for land use in urban areas in Eastern Europe, especially the separation of property rights to land and to buildings, are not only a major source of discretionary abuse of bureaucratic power, but also increase transaction costs in land markets, and therefore slow down the emergence of a financial market that is based on real estate as collateral (Butler 2002).

Low operational costs allow land administration institutions to be self-financing and ensure sustainability and some protection from political influence. This is enhanced by the ability to set fees that are sufficient to recover costs. Examples from Eastern Europe, Asia, and Latin America demonstrate that establishment of the cadastral infrastructure is a public good, the cost of which should be financed by the government with cost recovery through general taxes. By contrast, land registration can and should recover its operational costs from fees without discouraging registration and thereby contributing to the growth of an informal sector (Adlington 2002; Sanjak and Lavadenz 2002). In Thailand a program of land titling provided the basis for a substantial increase in the total amount of land revenue collected, from US$300 million in 1984 to US$1.2 billion in 1995 (Brits, Grant, and Burns 2002). High registration costs will discourage registration. This will have a disproportionate effect on the poor, who could benefit the most from a comprehensive system, but will be the first ones to be pushed into informality. This will deprive them of the benefits of land registration and will undermine the value of the entire registration system.

Conclusion

WELL-DEFINED AND ENFORCEABLE PROPERTY RIGHTS HAVE many public good characteristics. They should be long enough in duration to provide incentives for investment, based on clear and easily identifiable boundaries, enforceable at low cost, and have mechanisms in place for adjusting to a varying environment. Although public good aspects call for government intervention, land policy cannot be formulated in a historical vacuum. Rather it needs to proceed from the understanding that some laws and institutions were created with the explicit purpose of benefiting certain groups of landholders at the expense of others. Therefore, policies should attempt to overcome such inherent inequalities. Even where the needs are clearcut and do not pose major technical challenges, reforms often encounter resistance from vested interests who benefit from the status quo.

Full individual ownership with formal title is a common means of providing secure and transferable land rights once land scarcity and commercialization of the economy have reached certain advanced levels. Where this is not the case, less formal measures can often significantly enhance tenure security at much lower cost than formal titling. For example, secure long-term leases, especially if they can be transferred, can provide many of the advantages associated with full ownership rights. In other cases, individual ownership and formal title do not translate into high levels of tenure security and further measures, for example, on the institutional side, will be needed to increase people's ability to exercise effective ownership rights.

Clearly specified property rights to land that enjoy broad recognition will have important equity benefits. These equity effects come about because it is normally women, the poor, and other vulnerable groups whose rights have historically been neglected and who are least able to take costly measures to defend their land rights. Legal and institutional measures to increase their tenure security will enhance the value of their endowment and thus of their earning capacity, or, in the case of distribution of assets within the household, their bargaining power and the economic outcomes directly under their control. Numerous studies have shown that higher levels of tenure security greatly increase the incentives for land-related investment and induce better land management.

Legal reform is needed where discrimination against specific groups (women or traditional rights holders) exists, where certain categories of users or owners face a high risk of land loss or expropriation, where the status of existing property rights is not well defined or is out of alignment with reality, or where large amounts of state land cannot be transferred to users and privatized. Also, where undisputed rights exist on the ground, giving legal recognition to these can be a major advance. Giving clear rights to occupants of state land or auctioning off such lands where this does not collide with equity objectives can have large welfare and efficiency benefits. The same is true for legal recognition of women's land rights, although such recognition is at best a necessary condition that needs to be combined with legal assistance, dissemination of legal provisions, and capacity building to lead to improved land access and use by women.

Where institutions are ineffective, inaccessible, or highly discretionary, translating legal concepts into real rights and ensuring that these rights are exercised in a way that produces social benefits will require attention. This implies that interventions on the legal side need to be complemented by attention to the institutional framework governing the implementation of laws. Which framework is the most appropriate in any given setting will depend on the level and scope of broader economic development, in particular the threat of dispossession to existing owners (and the resources spent on defending property rights to land); the scope for land-related investment; and the potential for efficiency-enhancing land transfers. Mechanisms need to be chosen that are consistent with the existing institutional environment and achieve the objectives at low cost. For example, if mechanisms to allocate land at the community level work well, are transparent, and enjoy legal recognition, low-cost demarcation of community boundaries may increase equity and tenure security at much lower cost than individual demarcation and titling, something that can be left for a later stage if needed. Institutions dealing with land administration need to be transparent, accessible, and cost-effective.

In environments where the population is growing but economic opportunities remain constrained, conflict over land is likely to increase. If not effectively managed, this can mushroom into larger incidents of often ethnically motivated violence and social tension. Socially accepted and low-cost mechanisms of managing and resolving conflict to reduce its socially disruptive and investment-reducing impact and to prevent it from escalating into large-scale confrontation are likely to become increasingly important, especially in Africa. Any land administration system needs to anticipate conflict and include mechanisms for conflict resolution, especially where land is becoming increasingly scarce.

The role of the state is to promote systems that ensure security of tenure by individuals. Tenure security increases the productivity of land and the incomes of those who depend on it. While the individualization of land rights is the most efficient arrangement in many circumstances, in a number of cases, for example, for indigenous groups, herders, and marginal agriculturalists, definition of property rights at the level of the group, together with a process for adjusting the property rights system to changed circumstances where needed, can help to significantly reduce the danger of encroachment by outsiders while ensuring sufficient security to individuals. As long as groups can internally decide on individuals' resource access and other issues following basic conditions of representativeness and transparency, securing group rights can contribute to better and more sustainable land management as well as more equitable access to productive resources.

Observers are often concerned that better definition of land rights necessarily implies higher levels of transferability, and thereby creates the danger that households could lose their main source of livelihood, for instance, because of distress sales. This chapter has shown that tenure security can often be enhanced quite independently from the rights to transfer land. Indeed, many country examples demonstrate that increasing the security of property rights does not require making them transferable through sales markets to outsiders. The next chapter discusses the advantages and disadvantages of transferability in more detail.

Notes

1.   This implies that fallow land is not unused, but rather that fallowing constitutes a labor-saving method of restoring soil fertility that is in line with the relative scarcity of labor and the abundance of land at low levels of population density.

2.   The capital cost associated with slavery made it feasible only for crops with a ready export market. It was therefore used where native hunter-gatherers were too few to provide a steady labor supply, or simply moved away. For example, large farms imported slaves in the east coast of Brazil, the South African Cape, and the southeast United States, where they could produce tropical and subtropical crops, such as sugar, cotton, and tobacco, that faced no competition in European markets. By comparison, the temperate zones of the Americas (Argentina, southern Brazil, Canada, and the northeastern United States) escaped slavery because their products could not be exported competitively to temperate zones in Europe until the advent of the steamship and the railroad, at which time slavery was no longer acceptable. Large farms in areas with access to abundant labor reservoirs, such as the sugar islands of the Caribbean and Mauritius; Sri Lankan (Ceylonese)

and northeastern India (Assamese) tea plantations; and Malaysia, Sumatra, and South Africa were able to rely on indentured labor, often of different ethnic origin, instead of slaves.

3.   Table 2.1 focuses on specific measures in individual countries. It is worth noting that these were often preceded by more general land grants to rulers, for example, the papal bull of 1493 that gave the discovered and undiscovered land of Latin America to the crowns of Portugal and Spain.

4.   Even where this was done, colonial powers often adopted measures that either completely eliminated or greatly restricted the land rights that the original population had customarily enjoyed. For example, in India's *zamindari* areas, the permanent settlement of 1793 formally vested all land rights in the revenue collectors employed by the British, thereby transforming former owners into tenants at will who could be, and in many cases were, evicted upon nonpayment of the land revenue.

5.   A number of studies fail to obtain significant results in regressions of total income on land ownership (for example, Lopez and Valdez 2000). Such a result can be due to a range of factors, in particular, assumptions, including linearity, that may not necessarily hold. For Mexico, relaxation of these assumptions, together with the choice of a broader index of well-being, leads to a strong impact of land access on household welfare (Finan, Sadoulet, and de Janvry 2002). More evidence on this issue and the specific channels through which land ownership affects welfare would be highly desirable.

6.   In addition, a large body of literature suggests that inadequate institutions in a broader sense lead to policies that are not conducive to economic growth (Acemoglu and Robinson 1999; Easterly and Levine 2001).

7.   Other studies also formally analyze the problem of an elite preventing human capital accumulation by the masses (Acemoglu and Robinson 2000; Bourguignon and Verdier 2000). Thus, even though investments in human capital would be socially and individually profitable and individuals who were unconstrained in credit markets would easily be able to under-

take them (Eckstein and Zilcha 1994; Galor and Zeira 1993), poor people who do not have access to assets might be caught in poverty traps. They fail to get out of poverty not because they are unproductive or lack skills, but they never get the opportunity to use their innate ability due to credit market imperfections. In such a situation, increasing the asset endowment of the poor can lead to permanently higher levels of growth (Aghion, Caroli, and Garcia-Penalosa 1999; Bowles, Bardhan, and Gintis 2000).

8.   For example, in Egypt as early as 2200 B.C., all lands were registered at the prime minister's office. Ownership transfers had to be recorded, signed by three witnesses, and authenticated by an official seal. Similarly, in ancient China a key function of the bureaucracy was to allocate and enforce land rights. In Babylon under Hammurabi (about 1700 B.C.) and Assyria (1250–750 B.C.), records of property ownership were registered and kept by the state, and sales were recorded by deeds, often had to be conducted publicly, and had to be authenticated by witnesses or officials.

9.   Collective action by squatters in the United States was decisive in bringing about the change from competitive auctioning of land to the policy of preemption (Kanazawa 1996).

10. Whereas physical marks, such as trees, rivers, or even hills, are often considered to be sufficient for resources of relatively low value, identification of the boundaries of high-value urban plots requires much greater precision.

11. Comparisons of different settlements (Jamestown, Plymouth, Salt Lake City, and the Bermudas) suggest that while many frontier settlements started out with group ownership and production to use economies of scale in defense and other activities, the length of time during which group ownership is maintained can be related to the riskiness of the environment, the frequency of social interaction, and the hierarchical structure of decisionmaking (Ellickson 1993).

12. Where land is relatively abundant and labor is scarce, societies focus more on the ability to secure access to labor, for example, through kinship ties and class and

lineage structures, than on defining property rights to land. Given that in many cases the situation is changing gradually, this generates a need for adjustment without associated frictions.

13. While a title provides absolute tenure security in countries where the government guarantees the accuracy of entries into the registry and stands ready to pay for any errors that have been made, a title document may have little value in a setting where, possibly as a result of consecutive governments having given out titles without verifying pre-existing ownership claims, many overlapping documents are known to exist.

14. The local population used the possibilities for increasing tenure security opened up by the 1974 Lands Ordinance to place boundary markers as an inexpensive way to "formalize" existing rights at low cost without negating existing community norms. Full private title to land was obtained mainly by wealthy business people and well-connected politicians in urban centers. This illustrates not only the many gradations of tenure security, but also that the state can play a constructive role in enhancing tenure security, both by providing simple and inexpensive ways to register land and by giving communities an active role in the maintenance of such registries, for example, by having representative local bodies oversee registration and arbitrate disputes.

15. Depending on how such actions affect the probability of land loss and whether or not community rules provide compensation for such investments when a plot reverts to the community (Baland and Platteau 1998), one can envisage scenarios where communal tenure systems may increase rather than decrease the amount of land-related investment undertaken (Sjaastad and Bromley 1997).

16. While low transaction costs and broad access to land administration are extremely important, this can be achieved by deconcentrating a central government agency rather than by establishing decentralized units with independent decisionmaking power, which may lead to the absence of a national framework and of uniformity in the provision of land administration services.

17. Starting with the *ryotwari* system the British introduced in southern India around 1820, successive systematic titling programs show that conflicting claims can be dealt with through a relatively quick administrative procedure rather than through lengthy and costly legal channels. Public notice and viewing at the community level are key requirements to prevent land grabbing.

18. Of the 17 countries in Latin America with indigenous populations, only Chile, El Salvador, and Uruguay do not recognize indigenous land rights in principle, and 8 have translated the recognition in principle into concrete laws that give indigenous people either collective ownership rights or usufruct rights. To ensure that indigenous communities can effectively exercise the property rights given to them, a number of countries have to develop their legal frameworks in more detail.

19. Where warranted, systematic titling is preferable for cost reasons and because ensuring transparency is easier (Arrunada and Garoupa 2002).

20. Especially in countries with limited administrative capacity, having one agency be responsible for land administration functions may be the best option, but this is not always feasible. If this is the case, then ensuring that no gaps or overlaps between the agencies occur and that they share information and coordinate their systems is of utmost importance.

CHAPTER THREE

Land Transactions

M AKING LAND RIGHTS MORE SECURE IS A precondition for land-related investment; however, unless rights are transferable, both the magnitude and incidence of such benefits may be limited. Land transactions can play an important role by (a) providing land access to those who are productive, but who own no or little land; (b) allowing the exchange of land as the off-farm economy develops; and (c) facilitating the use of land as collateral to access credit markets where the conditions for doing so exist. The ability to transfer land also increases the incentive to undertake land-related investments.

Traditionally, much of the discussion on land markets has focused on the permanent transfer of ownership through sales. However, similar benefits can accrue from often informal transactions in land rental markets that are widespread across the world and that are less likely to be affected by, or can adjust more easily to, the market imperfections that are pervasive in rural areas of developing countries. To address these issues this chapter first discusses key factors affecting the operation of rural land markets and their potentially differential impact on land rental and land sales, then reviews empirical evidence from different regions of the world and uses this to draw some policy conclusions.

The opportunity for rights transfers will be important in many settings, both rural and urban, but the functioning of other markets, in particular, those for labor and credit, will affect the ultimate impact of land markets. As the possibility for adjusting to imperfections in these markets varies depending on whether land transfers are temporary or permanent, this chapter discusses the interaction between land with other factor markets separately for land rental and land sales markets.

For rental markets it describes the contractual options and their efficiency and equity implications, as well as evidence on the extent and impact of the operation of formal and informal rental markets in the world's main regions. Given the vast differences in the nature and level of activity in rental markets across regions, we identify the link between policy interventions and the performance of rental markets and draw conclusions for policy and research. Overall we conclude that policymakers have underestimated the potential for efficiency-enhancing transfers of land through such markets and propose a number of avenues to improve their functioning.

If sales markets are sufficiently developed so that land can be used as collateral for credit to finance investment, in addition to improving the efficiency of land allocation, low-cost mechanisms to effect land sales can also contribute to the emergence of a financial infrastructure and associated broader benefits. However, distortions in other markets or expectations about future land price increases may drive the price of land beyond its productive value, thereby making land acquisition through the sales market difficult for the poor. In addition, the transaction costs of enforcing collateral may be high, depending, among other things, on the efficiency of the land administration infrastructure. If this is the case, poor buyers, who would gain the greatest benefit from better access to land, may be disadvantaged in obtaining such access through land sales and purchase markets and, in particular, will normally not be able to rely on mortgage financing for such purchases. This illustrates that, more than for rental, the outcomes of land sales markets will depend on the extent to which other markets function, especially those for products and credit. We discuss the critical factors involved, the extent to which policy measures have been able to address them, and a number of policy implications.

Key Factors Affecting the Functioning of Rural Land Markets

IN A WORLD OF PERFECT INFORMATION, COMPLETE MARKETS AND zero transaction costs, the distribution of land ownership will affect households' welfare, but will not matter for efficiency outcomes, and everybody will operate their optimum farm size (Feder 1985). The following paragraphs illustrate how imperfections in labor and credit markets affect the performance of both land rental and land sales markets.

Labor Market Imperfections

One main reason for imperfections in rural labor markets is the cost of supervision, which arises because except in extremely limited circumstances, wage workers' true effort is not easily observable. Such imperfections imply that wage workers will have limited incentives to exert effort, and either need to be supervised at a cost or be offered contracts that provide higher incentives, such as piece rate contracts (Jensen and Meckling 1976). This issue, which has received considerable attention in the literature on industrial organization, has profound implications for the organization of production and the optimal size of the farm in numerous settings (Calvo and Wellisz 1978; Eswaran and Kotwal 1985a,b).

In agricultural production, spatial dispersion of the production process and the vagaries of nature imply a need to constantly adjust to micro-variations of the natural environment. Family members have higher incentives to provide effort than hired labor.[1] They share in output risk, and can be employed without incurring hiring or search costs. Even though owner-operated family farms may hire or exchange labor for seasonal tasks, they avoid the need to supervise permanent wage workers, implying that they enjoy a productivity advantage compared with large farms with numerous hired laborers. These attributes underlie the general superiority of family farming over large-scale wage operations.

Imperfect rural labor markets imply that land-scarce households that have to sell their labor in the market will face some transaction costs, which will imply underemployment and a marginal value of labor time below the market wage. Land-abundant households that, in a world without transaction costs and imperfect supervision capacity, would contract labor to cultivate their land, will have a marginal cost of labor well above the market wage. In this case the complete absence of land markets would force households to cultivate the land they happen to own, implying that land-abundant households would need to cultivate their land with expensive labor and land-scarce households would be trapped by underemployment in low-return, own-farm activity. The latter would be particularly disadvantageous if opportunities existed for off-farm labor market participation that would require farmers to forgo the income from renting out their land. Assuming that other factors such as ability, access to capital, and technology were equal between the two types of households, the

Supervision constraints for hired labor are particularly pronounced in agriculture and often lead to the productive superiority of owner-operated farms

ability to obtain additional land would improve the livelihood of land-scarce, labor-abundant households by allowing them to employ their underutilized labor more effectively and increasing their shadow wage.[2] Indeed, such inefficiency, especially in the employment of labor, is of considerable relevance for China, where the functioning of land markets is significantly restricted.

Capital Market Imperfections

Collateral requirements can help overcome moral hazard in credit markets

The positive impact of rental market activation on land access by the poor is diminished if access to capital depends on initial wealth, because of the need for up-front working capital to acquire inputs in addition to land and labor. Such quantity rationing in credit markets arises from the presence of asymmetric information and moral hazard (Stiglitz and Weiss 1981). In informal credit markets, credit providers use close familiarity and social control to select promising clients or projects. This implies, however, that the scope for diversifying risks across space and different types of clients is limited and means that lending entails high levels of risk, resulting in high interest rates and relatively short-term credits. Formal credit markets can overcome problems of asymmetric information by using collateral, often in the form of land. However, the costs of and political impediments to foreclosing on smallholders' land are often quite significant, implying that the transaction costs associated with providing credit to small producers may be so high as to exclude small farmers.

Thus credit market imperfections can offset the supervision cost advantage family farmers enjoy. Consequently, in the presence of credit market imperfections the supply of working capital depends on the amount of land owned. The optimal size of the operational holding varies systematically with the size of the owned holding, even if land rental markets operate perfectly. While the magnitude and direction of this effect depend on the elasticity of output with respect to effective labor and of labor effort with respect to supervision, it can overwhelm the productivity advantage of family farmers and give rise to a positive relationship between owned farm size and productivity. Working capital constraints could therefore have significant impacts on land sales, and even on rental markets. Interventions in credit markets to overcome these shortcomings are difficult and often have not had the desired effect (Brummer and Loy 2000; Kochar 1997).

Few Economies of Scale in Agricultural Production

Discussion on the "optimum" farm size for different products and locations has been considerable. Given the countervailing factors of capital and labor market imperfections, the optimum farm size is very much an empirical question. Technical economies of scale could arise from the presence of indivisible factors of production or fixed setup costs leading to an initial range of farm sizes where the average cost of production declines with farm size. In cases where other markets function reasonably well, optimal farm sizes often do not exceed the scale at which family labor is fully occupied (using seasonal hired labor for specific tasks). A large literature has demonstrated that many agricultural activities do not exhibit true economies of scale in production. Exceptions include cases of highly specialized machinery, livestock production, or plantation crops where economies of scale are transmitted from the marketing to the production stage.[3] Economies of scale associated with the processing and marketing of many agricultural products do not necessarily have important implications for the unit cost of farming operations as long as competitive markets for outputs and inputs exist. Access to such markets is sometimes arranged through cooperatives or contract growing arrangements, while production may still be most effectively organized using smaller producers (Adesina and Djato 1996; Townsend, Kirsten, and Vink 1998). Therefore one would expect to find constant or decreasing returns to scale in most empirical studies of agricultural production.

A number of studies find a negative relationship between farm size and productivity for all but the smallest farm size classes (Berry and Cline 1979; Burgess 2001; Carter 1984; Kutcher and Scandizzo 1981; Newell, Pandya, and Symons 1997; Udry 1997), and others are unable to reject the hypothesis of constant returns to scale in agricultural production (Burgess 1997; Dong and Putterman 2000; Feder and others 1992; Lanjouw 1999; Olinto 1995; Wan and Cheng 2001). Some of the observed inverse relationship can be explained by differences in land quality, as large farmers tend to cultivate less fertile land and grow crops of lower output value (Benjamin 1995; Bhalla and Roy 1988; Verma and Bromley 1987). Yet even after controlling for land quality and other differences associated with farm size, empirical studies still indicate a significant inverse correlation.

The relationship between farm size and productivity will tend to be positive in situations where credit access is more important than the ability to overcome labor market imperfections. A study of Sudan, for example, shows that yields for virtually all crops are lower for smaller farmers

Empirical studies confirm the absence of economies of scale in agricultural production

Differential credit market access can generate a relationship between farm size and productivity

and are higher for larger farmers because of the latters' ability to access capital and other inputs. In this situation the land rental market leads to land transfers from poor and labor-abundant smallholders to rich and relatively labor-scarce households (Kevane 1996). The reason is that capital market imperfections combined with reasonably functioning land and labor markets and a technology that is not too supervision intensive can make renting out land and working for a wage more attractive for small, credit-constrained households than engaging in owner cultivation without cash inputs. The inverse relationship between farm size and productivity is much weaker in Southeast Asia (David and Cordova 1994). Acute capital constraints lead to the emergence of a positive relationship between farm size and productivity in Malawi, where both land and labor are extremely scarce (Dorward 1999). Data that allow direct comparison of the efficiency of family farms with that of partnerships and large-scale collective and state farms suggest that collectives and state farms displayed lower technical efficiency than family farms and partnerships, although this difference declined over time (Brooks and Koester 1997). Family farms are not as efficient as partnerships and large-scale farms, and partnerships are superior to all other organizational forms (Mathijs and Swinnen 2001).

The foregoing discussion leads to two main conclusions. First, in settings where the production process is not capital intensive and where access to credit and capital is broadly similar across farm sizes, labor market imperfections result in the productive superiority of family farms. Second, imperfections in input, product, credit, and insurance markets will affect the functioning of land rental and sales markets, and will lead outcomes to deviate from what one would expect in a hypothetical situation of perfectly functioning markets. As a consequence, undesirable outcomes that may be observed in land rental or sales markets can be due to imperfections in other markets. Even well-intentioned regulatory interventions or administrative restrictions on land markets that do not address the underlying causes may end up worsening the situation rather than improving it. This chapter illustrates some of these issues with concrete examples from specific country and regional settings.

Implications for Land Rental Markets

ECONOMISTS GENERALLY CREDIT LAND RENTAL MARKETS WITH considerable potential to enhance productivity and equity by facilitating low-cost transfers of land to more productive producers and permitting participation in the nonfarm economy, thereby allowing consumption smoothing in response to shocks and accumulation of experience and capital. Because the structure of land rental contracts will affect productivity outcomes and theory suggests that in many situations wealth constraints by tenants may make the first-best contract (fixed rent) infeasible, a major policy concern has traditionally been to avoid the suboptimal outcomes that may arise in this context. In practice, however, any potential losses associated with share contracts have been found to be relatively small. Improving on share contracts through government intervention is difficult if not impossible, especially given the considerable flexibility for the contracting parties to adjust to imperfections in other markets. Thus while the equity outcomes achieved in land rental markets will still depend on the parties' outside options, and rental contracts are clearly less suitable as collateral for credit market transactions, the opportunities for land rental markets are quite high.

General Potential

The possibility of users exchanging land through formal or informal rental arrangements is important for a number of reasons, suggesting that in many circumstances rentals can have advantages over sales markets. For example, rental markets (a) allow flexibility in adjusting the land area used with low transaction costs; (b) require only a limited capital outlay, thereby leaving some liquidity available for productive investments rather than locking it all up in land; (c) facilitate easy reallocation of land toward more efficient users than the current owners, especially if the current owners are old, are noncultivating heirs, are urban beneficiaries of restitutions, and so on; (d) provide a stepping stone toward land ownership by the landless; and (e) help overcome, through sharecropping contracts, market failures in labor, insurance, credit, management, and supervision, thereby potentially helping secure the competitiveness of participants (de Janvry and others 2001). Indeed, rental markets operate in a variety of forms, ranging from highly informal transactions to formalized, long-term contracts.

If there are labor market imperfections or unobserved differences in ability across producers, well-functioning land rental markets can help transfer land to its best use at comparatively low transaction costs. This can improve production efficiency, and also will often enhance the distribution of income and reduce the vulnerability of poor households by

Land rental markets can enhance productivity and equity by transferring land to more productive users at low cost

offering a more stable source of livelihood than they would have by selling their labor in frequently volatile and imperfect local labor markets. Indeed, studies, some of which are discussed in greater detail later, support the notion that land rental markets transfer land to more productive producers, thereby increasing overall output in the economy. Land rental markets serve an important function in equalizing returns to nontradable factors of production, such as family labor and bullocks in India (Skoufias 1991). If the distribution of the surplus between landlord and tenant is not too skewed, rental will have a positive impact on equity.

Land rental markets facilitate less skilled producers' participation in the nonfarm economy

As opportunities in the nonfarm economy increase, land markets allow households to engage in migration, specialization, investment, and intergenerational land transfer, thereby improving productivity and participants' earnings. Households with low agricultural skills are likely to be able to obtain higher incomes from off-farm employment than from farming, and thus will be better off if they rent out some or all of their land for others to cultivate. In a growing economy land rental market activity will therefore increase over time, and if households' agricultural abilities differ, will unambiguously increase incomes for everybody (Carter, Yao, and Deininger 2002). Policy measures to facilitate the operation of such markets at low cost to effect this adjustment would therefore be justified. Where restrictions on the functioning of land markets are severe, they can become an obstacle to economic diversification. Indeed, results from Ethiopia indicate that producers who are afraid of being affected by redistribution in the future are significantly less likely to engage in off-farm work, suggesting that the way in which land markets are regulated will affect the broader rural economy and the emergence of off-farm employment (Deininger, Jin, Adenew, Gebre-Selassie, and Demeke 2003).

Land rentals help to smooth consumption in response to shocks and facilitate accumulation of experience and capital

Rental markets also provide households that have suffered unfavorable shocks another ex post option of coping with the consequences of such an event. The importance of this aspect is illustrated in the context of the HIV/AIDS crisis in Africa, which has led to households making extensive use of land rental markets both before and after the death of a household member to adjust their operational landholdings to the available family labor force, and thus increase their income over what they could have earned by their own cultivation (Drimie 2002).

Observers have long pointed to the possible existence of an agricultural ladder, whereby landless households lacking capital can start as renters or share tenants, build up knowledge and savings, and eventually become small owners. Evidence suggests that tenancy played an important role in the U.S. South after the abolition of slavery (Reid 1977). Similar movements are observed in Honduras (Boucher, Barham, and Useche 2001) and, to a more limited extent, in Nicaragua (Carter and Chamorro 2002). The difference between these countries can partly be attributed to variation in tenure security, reinforcing the notion that land transactions, and the scope they imply for households to move up the agricultural ladder and accumulate capital, are impossible without secure tenure arrangements in place. Indeed, a combination of tenure insecurity, policy distortions, and restrictions on specific rental transactions may well account for the limited evidence on mobility via the rental market in developing countries. At the same time, observers have noted that for varying reasons, land rentals often do not involve the largest landlords, and that the absence of long-term rental contracts can seriously reduce the scope for tenants to make the first step on the agricultural ladder toward eventual land ownership. This implies that policies governing the emergence and functioning of land markets will be of great importance.

Contract Choice

One issue that makes land rental of interest to policymakers is that the choice of contract will affect both efficiency and equity of the outcomes achieved through such arrangements. At the same time, the nature of rental market contracts is affected by the way in which markets for labor and capital function, the distribution of endowments, and the interventions by the government that may eliminate some contractual options or reduce or increase the transaction costs associated with them. To explain the variety of observed rental transactions this section explores the theoretical underpinnings of market development and specific forms of market transactions in land rental or sales markets and their impacts on efficiency and equity. A review of the empirical evidence on the extent to which markets function in different settings and how the differences can be explained follows. With this background one can explain why, even for countries that are similar in many respects, the extent of land market activity and the form that transactions take vary considerably as a result of policy.

Landowners who are unable or unwilling to personally cultivate their land can either employ wage laborers, with or without supervision, or rent out their land under a share contract or a fixed rent contract. Economists

The contractual options range from wage labor to sharecropping to fixed rent

have long pointed out that the size of two parameters, namely, the fixed payment and the share of the harvest to be received by either landlord or tenant, generate, at any given point in time, a continuum of contractual options that extends from pure wage labor over sharecropping to a fixed rent contract. Any rental or wage labor contract can be viewed as consisting of a fixed payment between the two parties, which can be zero, together with a sharing rule that defines how output will be divided between tenant and landowner. By affecting the incentives of the parties, the surplus to be kept by them, and the risk each of them has to bear, these two parameters will affect the efficiency and the equity outcome associated with any contract in predictable ways. They do so through their impact on the incentives for effort supply as well as on the risk that each of the contracting parties has to bear. The final impact of these on production, and thus the chosen contract, will depend on the technology and the importance of long-term investment for soil fertility and other productivity-enhancing measures.

The landlord maximizes income by choosing the number of tenants, the fixed payment, and the output share subject to the constraint that tenants achieve their (exogenously given) level of welfare in the next best option without the land. Based on this, the tenant's effort-reaction function determines the level of effort that will maximize utility in view of the constraints. Because self-employed labor has higher productivity than hired labor, for large landowners to rent out land under fixed rent contracts is more profitable than working it using hired labor in the absence of other market imperfections. If effort is unobservable, credit is rationed or insurance markets are imperfect, and tenants are risk averse, the fixed-rate tenancy contract may not be attainable or desirable and a second-best share contract would be adopted instead. Under a wage contract, workers will not bear any risk; but because they do not share in the output, they will also have minimal incentives to apply nonobservable effort. At the other end of the spectrum, a fixed rent contract will provide optimum incentives for effort supply to the tenant, but because the tenant has to pay the rent even in case of a total loss of harvest, for instance, because of flooding or drought, it may be too risky for the tenant to undertake.

The welfare impact of land rental depends on the outside options available to contracting parties

How land rental will affect the welfare of participating households will depend on the size of the surplus achieved from engaging in rental and on its distribution between landowners and tenants. A number of studies demonstrate that the number and types of outside options available to tenants, such as wage labor, will affect the outcome of the bar-

gaining between landlords and tenants as well as the efficiency of the production outcome obtained (Conning and Robinson 2002; Mookherjee
1997). This is supported by the fact that throughout history large landlords have relied on systematically reducing the availability of outside
options to obtain labor at low wages. It also implies that restrictions on
the operation of rental markets are unlikely to improve welfare outcomes
unless they change the bargaining power of one of the contracting parties. Where this is not the case, by limiting the set of contractual options
available, they may decrease overall welfare.

Effort Provision

Under conditions of certainty, and if effort is observable and enforceable, all contracts lead to equivalent outcomes and the choice of contract type does not matter (Cheung 1969). If the assumption of perfect
effort enforceability is dropped, tenants receive only a fraction of their
marginal product for all but the pure cash rental contract. Therefore
with effort unobservable and under conditions of certainty (or risk neu-
trality), the fixed rent contract clearly dominates the fixed wage and the
share contracts and will always be chosen in equilibrium. Given the
supervision costs for workers or sharecroppers, any type of contract
other than fixed rent would result in an undersupply of effort by the
tenant or worker, which would lower total production. This would
imply that the optimal course would be to offer fixed rent contracts (or
a higher share of output) to tenants who have higher skills or for tasks
and crops that are more skill intensive. In India, more experienced individuals receive tenancy or fixed term contracts and less experienced
ones receive wage contracts (Chaudhuri and Maitra 2001). Other studies show that landlords are indeed aware of tenants' level of ability (Lanjouw 1999) and that they adjust the terms of contracts to provide
higher incentives for more efficient operators and those with better capital endowments (DeSilva 2000).

**Effort supply and intensity
of input use will be
highest under fixed
rental contracts**

If fixed rent contracts are not an option, the incentive for effort supply can still be increased by the contracting parties adopting long-term
arrangements that are built on reputation effects. Sadoulet, Fukui, and
de Janvry (1994) confirm that close social relationships can increase the
incentive for tenants to provide effort. Their study compares the attributes of sharecropping contracts with kin and with nonkin and found
that nonkin sharecroppers use significantly fewer inputs and obtain less
output, but for close kin they found neither a disincentive effect nor a

**Supervision or long-term
relationships can partly
increase effort supply**

reduction in output. This suggests that embedding contractual arrangements in a long-term, personal relationship offers considerable potential to attenuate the disincentives and productivity losses that are otherwise associated with sharecropping contracts. If landlords are absentee or inexperienced in farming, they tend to choose fixed rent contracts (Jodha 1984; McCarthy, Sadoulet, and de Janvry 2001; Sharma and Dreze 1996). The time landlords spend on supervision has an opportunity cost, although recent empirical estimates suggest that this is more than compensated for by the percentage increase in tenants' effort (Ai, Arcand, and Ethier 1997; Arcand and Rambonilaza 1999).

Indivisible Endowments and Capital Market Access

Tenants' wealth and borrowing constraints limit the scope for fixed rental

With risk aversion and uncertainty, or with capital market imperfections that prevent the tenant from either borrowing to obtain working capital or to smooth consumption in case of an unfavorable shock, a share contract provides the possibility of partly insuring the tenant against fluctuations in output (Ray and Singh 2001; Shetty 1988). Under these conditions the optimal contract choice entails a trade-off between the risk properties of the fixed wage contract, where the landlord assumes all the risk and the tenant's risk is zero, and the incentive effects of the fixed rent contract, which would result in optimal effort supply by the tenant. A limit on the working capital available to the tenant (or to landlord and tenant) because of imperfections in the credit market can also lead to the adoption of a share contract as the optimal solution to the bargaining problem, where the share contract emerges as the optimum between the two extremes of too high or too low incentives (Basu 1992; Ghatak and Pandey 2000). The prevalence of share contracts in many regions around the world indicates that the circumstances under which they are a second-best solution are common.

This limited scope provides the rationale for sharecropping and interlinked contracts

Tenants may be able to meet only part of their working capital requirements in the credit market because of the limited suitability of unharvested crops as collateral and at higher interest rates than the landlord would get by offering the land as collateral. Landlords are often in a better position to provide tenants with credit and actuarially fair insurance than other financial intermediaries, because they possess information about the tenants. As the amount of credit provided will be related to tenants' expected future income, landlords can set the contractual fixed payment to zero and still be free to adjust the interest rate or accept the customary interest rate and adjust the fixed payment and share terms to realize an optimal outcome (Otsuka, Chuma, and Hayami 1992). Thus the main reason that interlinked contracts and cost-sharing arrangements are so common may be because they implicitly provide the credit or insurance tenants need in an environment where credit and insurance markets are imperfect.[4]

In a study of Tunisian sharecroppers, Laffont and Matoussi (1995) provide insights on the relationship between liquid assets and contractual parameters. The results suggest that differences in the contracting parties' working capital endowments can account for the coexistence of a variety of contracts, even in the same environment and among parties with similar risk aversion characteristics.[5] Indeed, data confirm the positive relationship between the crop share and the tenant's working capital endowment that would be predicted by theory, even with perfect monitoring of effort. Evidence shows that output increases significantly with tenants' wealth for all contract types, including share contracts, but that tenant wealth has no effect if only fixed rent contracts are considered. Similarly, the wealth of the landlord has, as expected, a negative effect on the tenant's share and a positive effect on production under the share contract, but none in other forms of contractual arrangements. Working capital, therefore, appears to be a significant explanation of the type of contract chosen and the production gains achieved on a given plot. Landlords' preference for tenants who already possess some land and draft animals, and such tenants' ability to obtain better contract terms, which is well documented in the literature (Quibria and Rashid 1986), point in the same direction. The importance of potential tenants' asset endowments is also emphasized by evidence from India, which indicates that because of wealth constraints, many potential tenants are left out of the tenancy market (Shaban 1991).

In this context, both the smallest and the largest landholders rent their land to farmers who are neither capital constrained nor suffering from the disadvantage associated with the need to supervise hired labor. This illustrates that the ability of the land rental market to bring about efficiency-enhancing transfers is constrained by potential tenants' endowment of assets and other means of production. Thus while land rental improves the allocation of resources in the presence of unequal factor endowments, potential gains are constrained by the wealth of potential participants. In addition, evidence indicates that fixed transaction costs preclude some poor households that desire only relatively minor adjustments of their operated land from entering the tenancy market. Similarly, data from India suggest the prevalence of imperfect adjustment whereby, on average, farmers realize only about 75 percent of the desired level of land transactions (Skoufias 1995).

Productivity losses associated with share tenancy are small

The foregoing discussion suggests that share tenancy will be associated with some productivity loss compared with a fixed rent contract. While numerous studies have been conducted on this topic, many of them suffer from methodological flaws. Use of appropriate methodology suggests that for India, tenancy was, on average, associated with a loss of productivity of 16 percent once adjustments for differences in land quality were made (Shaban 1991). In addition, inputs of family labor and draft animals were significantly lower on sharecropped plots than on owned parcels. The study did not find any statistically significant differences in productivity between owned plots and plots rented on a fixed rent basis, confirming that fixed rent contracts do not have any negative impact on productivity. To interpret this finding, note that it was obtained in an environment characterized by government constraints on fixed rent contracts, implying that the figure of 16 percent in productivity losses is likely to constitute an upper bound. This is consistent with the results from an exhaustive survey of the empirical literature, which finds that no strong evidence supports the hypothesis that yields under share tenancy are lower than under owner farming or fixed-rent leasehold tenancy (Hayami and Otsuka 1993).

More recent case studies provide added support for the empirical generalization that share tenancy provides a second-best arrangement that, in any given environment, is difficult to improve on unless the operation of factor and credit markets improves (Lansink, Pietola, and Backman 2002; Otsuka 2002; Quisumbing 2001; Sadoulet, Fukui, and de Janvry 1994; Sharma and Dreze 1996). Even though they cannot completely eliminate structural impediments and bring about a fully efficient allocation of land in an economy, land rental markets, including share tenancy, can go a long way toward bringing the operational distribution of holdings closer to the optimum, given existing constraints (Galassi and Cohen 1994). Given that, as noted earlier, fixed-rent contracts may be either not feasible or not optimal for many potential market participants because of wealth constraints and limited ability to bear risk, concern about the potential undesirable implications of share tenancy was probably not warranted. Even where such arrangements may result in some reduction of productivity, short of redistributing assets, devising policies that would remedy this shortcoming at a reasonable cost is extremely difficult.

Contract Length

Even if a rental contract provides tenants with adequate incentives to maximize production in any given time period, incentives to invest or to maintain soil fertility may be insufficient. Dubois (2002) illustrates the relevance of this empirically for the case of the Philippines, confirming that even in designing short-term contracts, landlords make adjustments to account for the need to maintain land quality in the long term. In a multiperiod context where tenants and landlords can develop reputation, the likelihood of a more efficient contractual arrangement is increased. In this case, the threat of losing reputation will prevent tenants from shirking or landlords from cheating if they provide essential inputs to production, and so the fixed rent contract will tend to dominate the fixed wage contract as it does when no uncertainty is present in the production environment (Otsuka, Chuma, and Hayami 1993; Roy and Serfes 2000). This is confirmed by historical data from Sicily, which demonstrate that landlords employed long-term contracts for crops that had higher maintenance needs (Bandiera 2002). In the same vein, in situations where investment is important, tenancy may be less desirable than the sale of land, because a number of reasons could prevent landlords from reaping the full benefits of land-related investments. Such a dynamic inefficiency of rental contracts is indeed confirmed empirically, even though its magnitude may be quite small (Jacoby and Mansuri 2002). Obviously, a critical precondition for long-term contracts to be entered into is that the type and nature of property rights available to the contracting parties allows them to do so.

Where investment is important, long-term contracts will be needed

Implications for Land Sales Markets

L AND SALES MARKETS PROVIDE AN OPPORTUNITY TO OBTAIN land for permanent use, which is normally associated with higher investment incentives than short-term rental. In addition, making land marketable provides a basis for using it as collateral in credit markets. The ability to formally prove land ownership at low cost and, based on this, to transact more extensively in sales markets, can be conducive to the development of formal financial markets and producers' access to formal credit even if few actual transactions are observed. At the same time, imperfections in financial and other markets may imply that land sales markets will, in cases where credit market imperfections are severe or a

Land sales markets can provide the basis for financial market development

select subset of producers benefits from distortions in other markets, not necessarily transfer land to the most productive producers.

Compared with rental markets, where contracts can be adjusted to overcome the impact of capital market imperfections, land sales markets will be affected by credit market imperfections. Furthermore, any distortions that increase the returns to land, such as subsidies, will be capitalized in land prices. This has implications for the possibility of land acquisition by the poor. A number of factors could increase the price of land above the present value of profits from agriculture. For example, in situations where financial markets do not work well or where confidence in money as a repository of value is low, land may be an important store of wealth and may be acquired for speculative purposes. Where this is the case, for poor but efficient producers to gain access to land through the purchase market may be difficult. Also, in environments where credit markets do not work well, land sales markets are more likely to lead to undesirable outcomes, therefore market imperfections or distortions in other markets could give rise to the emergence of efficiency-reducing outcomes, such as speculative purchases, distress sales, and artificially inflated land values that reduce access to land by low-income and landless buyers.

Expectations, risk preferences, and the shadow price of capital affect land prices

If all markets were perfect, the sale price of land would equal the net present value of the stream of profits that could be derived from the land, and potential buyers would be indifferent between acquiring land through rent or through purchase. However, transaction costs that are higher than in rental markets (Lence 2001), risk and portfolio considerations, limited access to credit markets, and the immobility of land all imply that the actual performance of land sales markets may be far from the theoretical ideal. In this case, higher agricultural productivity would not necessarily be translated into higher demand for land, and under certain conditions land sales markets may lead to outcomes that are not productivity enhancing. Conceptually, in addition to the expected return from cultivation, which is the same as for rental markets, the shadow price of capital, the time horizon, the discount rate, and the expectations about the future returns from agriculture and from other uses of land will affect a producer's willingness to pay for land in the sales market.

In agricultural economies where risk is high and purchasers' savings are the main source of funds for land acquisition—that is, access to credit from outside is limited and land performs an important function as a store of wealth—prices for land can fluctuate significantly over time. The reason is that because returns from agricultural production are highly covariate, demand, and therefore land prices, will be high in good crop years when savings are high, sellers are few, and potential buyers of land are many. At the same time, the need to satisfy basic subsistence constraints could give rise to a large supply of people who are forced to engage in distress sales of their land in bad years, often to individuals with incomes or assets from outside the local rural economy. Thus in areas with poorly developed insurance and capital markets land sales will likely be few and limited mainly to distress sales. Studies in Bangladesh and India confirm this hypothesis. Rosenzweig and Wolpin (1985) found that farmers in India who experienced two consecutive drought years were 150 percent more likely than other farmers to sell their land. Furthermore, individuals who had to sell off land during crises may not be able to repurchase land during subsequent periods of recovery (Bidinger and others 1991; Kranton and Swamy 1999).

During periods of macroeconomic instability nonagricultural investors may use land as an asset to hedge against inflation, and thus an inflation premium is incorporated into the real land price. If expected inflation is fully reflected in interest rates, inflation alone will not affect agricultural land prices (Feldstein 1980). The lack of other investment options can have the same effect. However, if expected inflation is not fully reflected in current or expected future interest rates, and if land is perceived to be no riskier than alternative assets, excess demand for land will increase the price of land as a speculative asset. Indeed, Falk, Lee, and Susmel (2001) and Just and Miranowski (1989) showed that inflation and changes in real returns on alternative uses of capital were the main factors in explaining changes in land prices for the United States. A simulation using the results of econometric estimation for Brazil for 1966–89 finds that 6 percent of the increase in land prices was attributable to credit subsidies and 28 percent to macroeconomic instability (inflation) (Brandão and de Rezende 1992).

With populations growing and urban demand for land increasing, people expect the price of land to appreciate, and some of this expected real appreciation is capitalized into the current land price. This is supported by Robison, Lins, and Venkataram (1985), who find that implicit rates of return to land under agriculture in predominantly agricultural states in the United States are much higher than in states where the demand for nonagricultural land is high. These returns are realized only when the property is sold, implying that in the latter the rate of return on an investment in land that is used only for agricultural production may be low.

Macroeconomic instability may lead to speculative overvaluation of land

95

Collateral value of land makes mortgage-based land acquisition difficult

Because land has collateral value, its equilibrium price at given credit costs will exceed the present discounted value of the agricultural income stream produced from the land in areas where only larger landowners have access to credit. Mortgaged land, however, cannot be used as collateral for working capital, so owners who purchase land on credit do not reap the production credit advantage, and therefore will be unable to repay the loan out of increased income from the land unless some equity is used to finance part of the transaction. Thus land sales are likely to be financed mostly out of household savings so that the purchased land can be used as collateral for credit to finance improvements and equipment. This need to purchase land out of savings tends to make the distribution of landholdings more unequal, despite the greater value of land to smaller owners arising from its insurance value and their lower labor costs. Thus both the limited availability of credit and the high cost of borrowing would prevent those who do not have accumulated savings from acquiring land. Combined with high transaction costs, these attributes also make rural land markets rather thin.[6] Speculative land price bubbles that increase the price of land over and above the net present value of the flow of services that can be derived from it are often fueled by excessive credit (Foldvary 1998). Tax preferences for larger farms or subsidies to crops typically grown by them will also drive the price of land higher than the expected agricultural profits would justify (Gunjal, Williams, and Romain 1996).

Where any of these factors drives land prices above the capitalized value of the income streams associated with such land, the poor have difficulty buying land. Even if they are provided with credit on market terms, that difficulty persists unless their productivity advantage from lower labor costs is extremely large. Because some of the imperfections and distortions are difficult to eliminate directly, for example, limited credit access by tenant farmers, reducing poverty may require giving grants to poor producers to overcome this disadvantage, especially in situations characterized by long-standing discrimination against specific groups in the population.

Credit market imperfections may lead to distress sales

Historically, distress sales have played a major role in the accumulation of land by large manorial estates in China (Shih 1992) and in early Japan (Takekoshi 1967) and by large landlord estates in Punjab (Hamid 1983). The abolition of communal tenure and the associated loss of mechanisms for diversifying risk are among the factors underlying the emergence of large estates in Central America (Brockett 1984). Cain (1981), who compares land transactions in Bangladeshi and

Indian villages with different access to risk-coping mechanisms during 1960–80, illustrates this possibility of transactions in the land sales market being driven by lack of access to credit and insurance rather than by cultivators' productive inefficiency. In villages that had access to a safety net program, the poor were able to use the land market to augment their landholdings by buying from richer farmers who sold land to undertake productivity-enhancing investments such as digging wells, purchasing pump sets, or paying for their children's education and marriages. By contrast, where such consumption smoothing devices were absent, distress sales to obtain food and medicine accounted for most activity in the land sales market. Thus whether or not households were able to buffer consumption through mechanisms other than land sales during crisis situations had a significant impact on whether markets helped to equalize or dis-equalize land endowments.

Transaction costs related to land sales can take many forms and normally include notary fees, registration fees, and survey costs, as well as any transfer fees. For example, in Russia, even though fees for notaries and registration are not excessive, fees for private surveying are equivalent to two years' of the minimum wage, constituting a significant impediment to overall market activity and reducing the ability of the less wealthy to participate (Rolfes 2002). Transfer fees that are assessed by the public sector can also significantly reduce the extent to which markets function, as in Moldova and the Philippines (Brits, Grant, and Burns 2002). Another important element of the transaction costs is the requirement, in some countries, to have any land sale approved by high political authorities, something that makes foreclosure on land owned by politically well-connected people virtually impossible (Moll 1996). This can lead to segmentation and asymmetry of land sales markets along geographic and social boundaries, a phenomenon that is indeed frequently observed in countries with a dualistic land ownership distribution and relatively undeveloped credit markets (Balcazar 1990; Carter and Zegarra 2000; Munoz 1999). In such situations land sales across farm size classes are virtually absent, but a considerable amount of land transactions occurs within farm size groups, that is, large or small farmers.

All the aforementioned factors will make land acquisition more difficult for poor households and therefore have a clear implication for the extent to which land markets can serve redistributive purposes. In many instances land markets' ability to transfer land, for instance, from inefficient and bankrupt state enterprises to private users, will still not

High transaction costs can result in segmented markets

The redistributive potential of land sales markets is often limited

only be beneficial in terms of efficiency, but will also be conducive to the emergence of a reliable and robust financial system. For this reason an efficient system of land administration that minimizes transaction costs is likely to have considerable benefits.

Well-intended government intervention may not improve outcomes

The possibility of efficiency-reducing outcomes discussed earlier implies that public intervention in land sales markets might, in principle, be justified in some situations. Clearly the most important way in which governments can help improve the functioning of land sales markets is to eliminate distortions that might bias land market outcomes; to help reduce transaction costs that would increase the barriers to participation, especially by the poor; and to improve the functioning of financial markets. Other measures governments have taken to improve sales markets outcomes have proved difficult to enforce, and their main effect has often been to increase transaction costs for participants or to drive land transactions underground, reducing the welfare of all participants. Therefore before recommending intervention, one needs to establish that such intervention can actually be effective in the given environment. Based on experience, the only interventions that appear to be justifiable are temporary land sales moratoria or limits on accumulating extremely large tracts of land in situations of rapid transition.

Empirical Evidence on Land Markets in Different Regions

FOR THE REASONS ELABORATED EARLIER, WELL-FUNCTIONING land rental markets will be most important in situations where land ownership, agro-climatic endowments, and households' skills vary widely or where economic growth, exogenous shocks, or demographic and economic transition call for a quick and flexible adjustment of holding sizes. In many circumstances both imperfections in other factor markets and government regulations imply that the actual performance and incidence of rental markets often differs widely from what would be expected on theoretical grounds. As a consequence, even in regions and settings with similar agro-ecological and economic conditions and land ownership distributions, the extent of land rental market activity often differs significantly between countries (Melmed-Sanjak and Lastarria-Cornhiel 1998). For a better appreciation of the policy issues involved, the following section reviews existing evidence on land rental and sales markets in the world's main regions.

Industrial Economies

Throughout history governments in Western European and other countries of the Organisation for Economic Cooperation and Development (OECD) have regulated tenancy in various forms, in ways that depended closely on the broader constellation of political power. Analysis of tenancy relations in several Western European countries since the late 18th century indicates that changes in land tenure regulations that improved tenants' welfare were closely related to improved parliamentary representation of tenants, high agricultural prices, fiscal crises, and the emergence of nonfarm economic opportunities that weakened the bargaining power of governments dominated by landlords (Swinnen 2002). This implies that regulation has a role to play in helping to enforce property rights and provide information that would reduce the transaction costs of land rental. At the same time, the fact that regulation of land market transactions followed rather than preceded political changes supports the notion that other economic and noneconomic factors are critical determinants of the political bargaining power wielded by individual actors and that the potential for regulation by itself to have an impact should not be overestimated.

In most industrial countries, land rental constitutes an important instrument for gaining access to land under conditions of often rapid structural change. Swinnen (2002) reports that 71 percent of farmland is rented in Belgium, 48 percent in the Netherlands, and 47 percent in France. The share of land rented in the United States increased from 35 percent in 1950 to 43 percent in 1992, much of which involves sharecropping (Dasgupta, Knight, and Love 1999). This illustrates the flexibility of land rental in an environment where security of property rights is high and long-term contracts can be enforced. It also illustrates that land rental is far from "backward" or incompatible with modern forms of operation (Allen and Lueck 1992). One of the advantages of rental rather than sales transactions in these economies is that in a dynamic economic environment, with the possibility of using other assets as collateral, many participants see few advantages in tying up large sums of capital in a land purchase and prefer to invest in other farm-specific assets (Bierlen 2000).

To increase tenants' incentives for making investments with long gestation periods, developing a regulatory and institutional environment where long-term leases can be enforced is important to ensure that rental markets can lead to optimum outcomes. Indeed, many industrial countries regulate rental markets and assist parties in various

Market regulation reduced transaction costs and increased tenants' bargaining power

Long-term contracts and information are critical to achieve optimum outcomes

ways to reduce transaction costs and contribute to broader rural development. Long-term leases and greater market transparency can be beneficial by allowing complementary investments by producers (Barry 2000). The French Society for Land Management and Rural Establishment provides access to information and legal assistance in relation to transfers of farms, both for owners and renters and across generations, to facilitate land access by the young through rental and sales. Attempts by the society to control the land sales markets through rights of preemption have not always had the desired effect (Hernandez 2001). Also the costs and institutional requirements associated with this particular model may be too high for the typical developing country where administrative capacity and transparency of the public service are limited (Feher 2001). At the same time, it illustrates that improving the availability of information, reducing transaction costs, and enhancing tenure security can help land markets to contribute to structural change in specific situations, and that local producer organizations can play an important role in helping to bring these effects about.

Eastern Europe and the Commonwealth of Independent States

Land rental was particularly important in the initial phases of the transition

The nature of land rental markets in Eastern Europe and the Commonwealth of Independent States (CIS) is fundamentally affected by the character and status of the transition process. In countries where land was restituted to former owners, short-term rental contracts were of overriding importance as an adjustment mechanism as long as formal property rights still had to be sorted out. This was the case in both urban and rural areas, and provided households that lacked either the ability or willingness to farm their land themselves, for instance, pensioners, with an opportunity to receive a stable return. In all the countries rental markets helped consolidate operational holdings (see Burger 2001 for the case of Hungary). In Moldova, for example, the emphasis on leases enhanced the ability of the land market to develop rapidly compared with, say, Estonia, which had discouraged the use of leases. More than 80 percent of the 440,000 registered private farms in Moldova operate through some type of leasing arrangement (Lerman, Csaki, and Moroz 1998).

The share of producers who lease land in Eastern European countries ranges from 2 percent in Albania with its egalitarian land distribution; between 7 and 8 percent in Bulgaria, Hungary, and Romania; and about 40 percent in the Czech and Slovak Republics. In general, rental markets contribute to the intergenerational mobility of land, that is, shift it to younger producers, in addition to transferring land to smaller producers and to those with less land but higher capital endowments. In many of the more advanced countries of Central and Eastern Europe (CEE), the share of producers who would like to buy land is significantly higher than the share of those who would like to rent more, indicating that few constraints on rental markets remain, but that sales markets do not yet function well (Deininger and Savastano 2002).

In situations where other markets are either completely absent or highly imperfect, land rental markets are unlikely to bring about a more optimal operational distribution of land. This is illustrated by the case of CIS countries such as Russia. Even though lease markets in these countries are active on paper, only a small share of households (about 7 percent) have taken their land out of a former collective to start individual farming. This implies that land is normally leased back to former collectives, which often pay next to nothing for the land they are cultivating,[7] and in some cases have stipulated contracts that are difficult for landowners to cancel (Lerman and Brooks 2001). In such a situation, regulation of lease terms may be difficult to implement and is thus unlikely to be effective.[8] The main reason for such an outcome is that privileged access to machinery, capital, and output and input markets, together with political connections, greatly increase the bargaining power of former collectives. To counter this, better functioning of markets, along with increased access to information to increase landowners' bargaining power, will be needed. This would imply more systematically informing them about their options in relation to land use and ensuring that lease terms are more transparent, that laws providing for the possibility of taking land out of former collectives can be enforced, and that widespread distortions that work against independent producers in output and input markets are eliminated (Duncan 2000; Pomfret 2000). Disseminating information, providing model lease contracts, and registering longer-term leases will reduce transaction costs and, by increasing transparency and ensuring that outcomes reached are "fair" for both parties involved, are likely to be beneficial.

Although long-term leases with clearly identified rents and rights could, in principle, provide many of the advantages of full land ownership, in practice such leases are quite insecure, as demonstrated by the situation with respect to urban land in most countries of the former Soviet Union. The various rules and regulations concerning leases are unpredictable, and in some places lease covenants appear to have developed

Short-term leases are not appropriate for public land if they are not secure and may encourage rent-seeking

into an alternative form of land use control that is associated with high levels of discretion by local governments. Even where long leases are available, the strength of property rights under a leasehold system depends on the courts and has not yet been fully tested. Refraining from use restrictions, instituting fixed or predictable rents, and allowing the transferability of leases are therefore important conditions that need to be met for lease rights to provide incentives that are equivalent to ownership. Where they can be satisfied, as is the case in a number of countries, the provision of long-term leases rather than full ownership can constitute a transitory policy to overcome political concerns associated with full ownership, with relatively minor efficiency losses. As long as local governments' ability to credibly commit to honoring long-term leases is limited, direct transfer of land into private ownership in a way that does not reduce equity may be a more desirable strategy.

The disadvantages of doing so notwithstanding, local authorities in many Eastern European countries have shown a distinct preference for leasing public land. One of the reasons for this is that in the absence of well-developed real-property tax systems, revenues from leasing are higher and more reliable than revenues from taxation. The ability to continue drawing on these revenues, together with a belief that leasing will give local governments greater economic control, are central to the reluctance to move ahead with privatizing public land and enterprises. Tenants prefer leasing because it allows them to avoid up-front purchase prices, which are frequently well above market rates, and there may be many ways for them to avoid payment of full rents. However, given that leases are likely to be much less secure than transfer of ownership, they are likely to reduce investment incentives, especially as local governments may raise rental rates once land has been developed. This is important, especially in systems where the state has a monopoly on land allocation and where governance is weak and corruption is rampant.

Where land is highly fragmented, the transaction costs of rental will be high

In some CEE countries, the high transaction costs associated with land rental have emerged as a constraint in two respects. First, to the extent that landholdings are highly fragmented, assembling a contiguous holding of land large enough to facilitate viable cultivation with machinery requires entrepreneurs to negotiate with numerous small landowners, something that is not only associated with high transaction costs, but also increases the incentives for any of the landowners to engage in opportunistic behavior by threatening to withdraw their piece of the land in an effort to extract a high surplus. Second, for those renting land to make investments in complementary capital, longer-term contracts are needed. Where these have not emerged, for example, because many owners did not want to commit for the longer term because of the significant uncertainty about the future course of land markets, investment has been impeded. As a result, in some CEE countries there are now more producers who state that they would like to buy land than producers who would like to rent (Deininger and Savastano 2002). This highlights the importance of full clarification of ownership rights to land and the elimination of other obstacles that distort land prices to facilitate the emergence of a financial market that could help support sales transactions.

Such constraints are particularly relevant where insecurity related to the impact of European Union (EU) accession on farm prices, as well as demand for land by foreigners, has thus far limited the potential for sales markets to become active, and the level of activity in these markets remains limited (Mathijs and Swinnen 2001), These insecurities will also affect the cost of other types of interventions to speed the process of consolidation of operational land holdings, which experts often consider to be critical for future productive development of the region.

For private farmers in most Central European countries the highly fragmented land ownership structure, the relatively high transaction costs of renting, and the fact that many urban landowners have no intention of going into farming implies that the potential for land sales markets is high. For example, in Bulgaria 2 million landowners hold 20 million plots, that is, an average of 10 each, with an average size of 0.23 hectare (Kopeva 2002). While the lack of the necessary infrastructure (clear title, cadastre, registries, and so on) to facilitate land sales continues to be a constraint, governments in most of the countries are implementing programs to address this issue. High transaction costs, including government-imposed transfer fees, are, however, a serious obstacle to market development.

In many Eastern European countries the purchase price of land is significantly above the capitalized value of agricultural profits (Deininger and Sarris 2002) because of government restrictions that drive up land prices, as well as speculation about the benefits of joining the EU and the demand by foreigners that might materialize with EU accession in both Eastern and Central European countries. Although peri-urban land markets and some mortgage lending are starting to develop in a number of Eastern European, and even CIS, countries, activity in sales markets for agricultural land remains low (Deininger and Savastano 2002).

An uncertain economic outlook reduces the extent of sales market activity

Even where productive land does not seem to have been overvalued, as in Moldova, the use of land as collateral is extremely limited, and providing access to credit, including finance for land purchases, through cooperatives or the use of movable collateral often provides a more immediate option (Chiriac 2002). In CIS countries that have not yet physically demarcated individual land plots in former collectives and where mortgaging agricultural land remains prohibited, land market activity is obviously even lower, and is restricted to peri-urban areas—for example, in 2000 fewer than 1,500 land mortgages were recorded in the whole of Russia (Overchuk 2002).

Inability to physically identify plots hinders market development

While the privatization of agricultural land has reduced the Russian government's ability to interfere in production decisions, much needs to be done to improve agricultural productivity and use its potential for stimulating rural growth. Ill-functioning land sales markets make the transfer of land resources to more efficient producers difficult. The authorities often viewed the distribution of land shares to members of former collectives as a transitional tool on the road to reformulated large farms, rather than as a step toward creating smaller farm units and did not draw up parcel boundaries. Market transactions are limited, because holders of land shares prefer to rent to the reconstituted collectives to derive a continuing income, and even if they did sell their shares, few savings instruments are available in which they could invest the proceeds.

A danger of speculative concentration may justify high land ownership limits

In the typical transition environment, where risk is high, access to input and output markets is imperfect, and information on legal options is limited, politically and economically powerful former managers of collective farm enterprises have often been able to induce the new owners to re-invest their land shares in a reformulated collective. Unless provisions for their protection are in place, bankruptcy of the collective would imply that the owners of land shares would lose their assets, which by passing land into the ownership of creditors could re-create a highly concentrated land ownership structure, with all the associated negative impacts on equity and efficiency. The fact that in Russia some large conglomerates have acquired millions of hectares of land for speculative purposes, largely because they expect it to be valuable for mineral extraction, suggests that such concerns can be of empirical relevance (Uzun 2002). To prevent such speculative acquisition at prices that are well beyond the actual value of the land, it will be important to inform landowners about their rights and educate them about the value of land in the longer term. As long as such knowledge remains limited, high limits on land ownership (in the thousands of hectares) may also be justified.

Box 3.1 The scope and flexibility of land rental contracts in West Africa

GHANA'S COCOA SECTOR CAN ILLUSTRATE HOW markets and the contracts used in them evolve dynamically in response to increasing land scarcity. In the early 19th century a share contract (the *abusa*) emerged as a way to attract migrants who were interested in establishing plantations, but did not have enough capital to buy land. Migrants received land on which they established a cocoa farm and gave one-third of the developed area or one-third of the yield back to the original owners of the land. By the 1960s more than 95 percent of the land was cultivated by migrants who had acquired land in this way. With increasing land scarcity, the practice became less common, the terms of the contract shifted in favor of landowners to a 50 percent share contract (the *abunu),* and the increasing formalization of contracts ensued. Contracts are now signed in front of witnesses, who receive a fee, and are perceived as more secure than within-family access to land, where elders can behave opportunistically or even disinherit their family members. Agro-industry has also developed similarly structured outgrower arrangements with share tenants.

Source: Amanor and Diderutuah (2001).

Africa

Evidence from Africa highlights that country- or region-specific constraints on land market activity that are associated with government intervention have a significant impact on land rental market activity. In West Africa, where colonial administrations never seriously questioned land ownership by indigenous communities and instead aimed to integrate local populations into commercial production, rental markets have a long tradition and have evolved in a dynamic way in response to environmental conditions. Complex mechanisms to transfer land and tree rights for varying periods have been common since the 19th century and are often linked to recipients making long-term investments, as in the humid areas of Benin, Cameroon, Côte d'Ivoire, Ghana, Nigeria, and Sierra Leone (Adesina and Chianu 2002; Amanor and Diderutuah 2001; Chauveau 2000; Edja 2001; Manyong and Houndekon 2000). The case of Ghana (see box 3.1) illustrates the flexibility of contractual arrangements and their adjustment to changed factor scarcities.

At the same time high levels of population growth with limited development of the off-farm economy have led to increased scarcity of land, higher rental rates, and a tendency for rental transactions to become more widespread and formalized, often with the use of formal witnesses. In many cases this has led the young to contest land transactions conducted by their parents, especially if these involved immigrants or ethnic

Rental markets are active in West Africa

105

minorities. This suggests that in addition to more rapid nonfarm development to help alleviate the land constraint, clarifying and formalizing contracts could have benefits in terms of land productivity and conflict avoidance and resolution.

Government intervention undermines rental in some East and South African countries

In Southern Africa, by contrast, rentals are rare, partly because of relative land abundance, but mostly because of the earlier rigid division of the land into native reserves, which were used mainly for semisubsistence producers, and areas reserved for whites, which depended on migrant workers (Otsuka 2001; Place 1995; Zeller, Diagne, and Kisyombe 1997). While many of the regulations that had historically precluded the development of a land rental market have been eliminated, land reform policies and the passage of strong tenancy protection laws in some African countries continue to affect the development of the market. In Ethiopia, a land policy that makes land rights conditional on residence in the community discourages off-farm activities and migration. In the absence of investment and technological advances, the adoption of which may be affected by insecure tenure and the inability to use the land as collateral, such a tenure regime has been claimed to run the danger of leaving agriculture in a Malthusian trap (Rahmato 1997).

In other countries of Eastern Africa, both land sales and rentals appear to be relatively active and appear to contribute to the equalization of operational or even ownership holdings of land, as confirmed for the case of Uganda (Baland and Platteau 1998; Carter and Wiebe 1990; Place 1995; Platteau 1996). Evidence from Uganda also suggests that activity in rental markets has increased sharply with economic liberalization and the associated growth of opportunities in the nonfarm economy; indeed, the share of households renting land increased from 13 percent in 1992 to 36 percent in 1999 (Deininger and Mpuga 2002).

Most empirical studies imply that in line with theory, land rental helps to improve efficiency and transfers land to those with low land endowments. Data from Sudan suggest that land rental markets transfer land to smaller producers (Kevane 1996). In western Ghana, Estudillo, Quisumbing, and Otsuka (2001) show that tenancy transactions have equalized the operational land distribution. Case study evidence also suggests that such temporary land transfers have a positive impact on equity, being generally pro-poor and beneficial for women (Place 2002). Despite this positive outcome, a number of countries still fail to formally recognize land rental transactions (Delville 2002). Others link the ability to maintain land rights to residence in a village or to continued cultivation. This neither enhances efficiency nor is in line with traditional practice whereby households could migrate out and still retain their land allocation rights. In Uganda, by transferring land to more productive producers, rental markets facilitate greater allocative efficiency in rural areas (Deininger and Mpuga 2002). Moreover, evidence from Ethiopia suggests that restrictions on land rental not only reduce the opportunity for more productive use of land, but may also constitute an effective obstacle to the development of the nonfarm sector, as farmers who had taken on nonfarm jobs perceived a significantly higher risk of losing land through redistribution than those who engaged in self-cultivation (Deininger, Jin, Adenew, Gebre-Selassie, and Demeke 2003).

Evidence suggests that higher levels of population density, commercialization of agriculture, and migration increase activity in African land sales markets. Observers have looked at market transactions in Ghana, Nigeria, Sudan, Tanzania, and elsewhere (Feder and Noronha 1987). In central Uganda, 58 percent of landholders reported that they had purchased land as early as the 1950s (Barrows and Roth 1990), and land sales markets seem to have been quite active ever since (Place 1995; Roth, Bruce, and Smith 1994). In Ghana the proportion of land acquired through purchase from individuals, which averages between 4 and 5 percent, reached 18.8 percent in migrant villages (Quisumbing and Otsuka 2001). In South Africa, even though markets remain thin, some purchases by formerly disadvantaged households are emerging (Lyne and Darroch 1997).

Sales market activity varies widely, even in the same country

While this suggests that informal land sales markets are fairly active in some African countries, little analysis is available on either how market prices compare with capitalized values from agricultural production or how such markets affect the productivity of land use. Evidence from Uganda suggests that actual purchase prices for land, while lower than cultivators' self-assessed land values, are high compared with profits from agricultural production, implying that land carries some premium as a store of wealth. This would limit the scope for acquisition of land by poor but efficient producers, a hypothesis that is supported by the fact that productivity is not a significant determinant of participation in land sales markets. At the same time, the fact that rental markets are active implies that there is little negative impact on either productivity or land access overall (Deininger and Mpuga 2002). More evidence on the links between land rights, migration, and off-farm participation would be desirable.

While the activity of land sales markets is highest in peri-urban areas, evidence from this sector also illustrates that legal and institutional restrictions often prevent the formalization of transactions. The fact that land sales are often authenticated by written sales agreements

Informality of sales can lead to conflict

that are witnessed by a number of people, including local notables, local government officials, and sometimes even lawyers (Kironde 2002), clearly demonstrates a desire for greater formalization of transactions. Instead of forcing them into informality, something that will both increase the likelihood of them being disputed in the future and reduce the price that sellers will be able to obtain, governments should take appropriate steps to recognize informal transactions. Recognition of such transfers may be a low-cost way to prevent future conflict, especially in peri-urban environments, where because of population growth or in-migration, land prices are often increasing rapidly.

Asia

Government regulation accounts for large differences in land rental activity

In addition to traditional factors such as population density, the ownership distribution of land, and the emergence of nonfarm opportunities, the regulation of tenancy in some Asian countries but not others appears to have given rise to considerable differences in tenancy rates. In the 1990s the proportion of tenant households (including pure tenants and owner-tenants) was high in Bangladesh, Pakistan, and the Philippines; modest in Indonesia; and low in India and Thailand. While a relatively egalitarian distribution of land, together with the availability of forestlands that until recently could be used to expand cultivation, appear to account for this low rate in countries like Thailand, the reason for low tenancy rates in India is likely to be related to land reform regulations that prohibit tenancy (Radhakrishnan 1990; Ray 1996; Thimmaiah 2001; Thorat 1997). Even if some tenancy has moved into informality, this could have important welfare effects (Deshpande 2002). In Bangladesh (Hossain 1978) and India (Pant 1983; Skoufias 1995) small farmers rent from large ones, although other studies report tenancy contracts within farm size classes in India (Sarap 1998; Sharma and Dreze 1996; Swamy 1988).

Rental markets can develop rapidly and generally benefit the poor

Land rental markets have started to emerge in Asian countries that have recently liberalized land tenure arrangements, such as China and Vietnam. In China, where until recently rental was not needed because of frequent land reallocations, the share of households participating in land rental arrangements increased significantly from 2.3 percent in 1995 to 9.4 percent in 2000. Moreover, 22.4 percent of households indicate that at the current market rate they would be willing to rent (Deininger and Jin 2002), suggesting that with economic development and greater emergence of off-farm opportunities, the potential for further increases in rental market activity is considerable. This can be advantageous not only for productivity, but can also help consolidate the high levels of fragmentation currently characterizing the Chinese countryside. A similar increase in the incidence of land rentals over time is apparent in Vietnam in an environment that started from a highly egalitarian allocation of land. In 1992 only 3.8 percent of rural households participated in land rental, compared with 15.8 percent in 1998, with more productive households being significantly more likely to rent (Deininger and Jin 2003).

In an environment of rapid economic change, allowing markets to reallocate land across households with differential endowments or abilities can help attain significant gains in efficiency and equity (Benjamin, Brandt, and Rozelle 2000). Figure 3.1, which provides a nonparametric regression (including 5 percent confidence bands) of actual and desired rentals in China against holding size and a measure of households' productive efficiency or ability, illustrates not only that the rental market shifts land to more productive and land-poor producers, but also that a considerable unsatisfied demand for land rental exists. The latter can be seen by comparing the thick line, which refers to actual land market participation, to hypothetical participation at existing prices. This suggests that reducing the constraints imposed on land rental would allow markets to contribute to greater equalization of endowments across households, thereby improving productivity and income distribution and increasing the welfare of those concerned.

Because of differences in ability across households that village officials cannot observe, decentralized land markets will be better suited to achieve the associated efficiency and equity gains than administrative mechanisms. As the differences in skills across households normally become more important with economic growth and the emergence of off-farm opportunities, for a society to shift from an allocation of operated, as distinct from owned, land that is completely egalitarian to a situation where operational holding sizes are determined by supply and demand at the local level will become increasingly advantageous. Indeed, rental markets have developed quite rapidly following the implementation of more secure property rights and the elimination of local restrictions on rental. Compared with administrative allocation by village cadres who have only limited opportunities to observe ability, land rental markets allow more productive households to gain access to land and thereby increase output by about 12 percent, holding other things constant (Deininger and Jin 2002). This suggests that in an

Figure 3.1   Actual and desired rental land, China

As a function of land endowment
Mu (1 mu = 0.067 hectare)

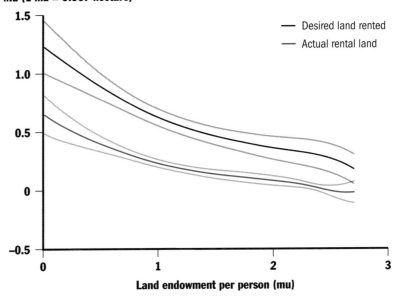

Land endowment per person (mu)

As a function of household agricultural ability
Mu (1 mu = 0.067 hectare)

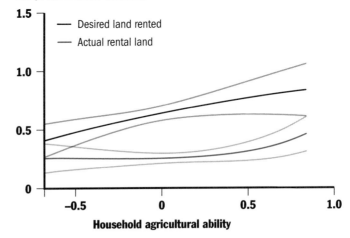

Household agricultural ability

Note: Bootstrapped confidence bands are given for each line.
Source: Deininger and Jin (2002).

environment where land ownership is distributed in an egalitarian fashion, decentralized land rental markets permit realizing much greater productivity gains than would be possible under administrative reallocation of land without the danger of negatively affecting equity. This seems to be one of the reasons why countries such as China and Vietnam are increasingly restricting the scope of administrative reallocation and loosening restrictions on land rental as the nonfarm economy develops (Turner, Brandt, and Rozelle 1998).

In a number of Asian countries, such as Cambodia, China, and the Lao People's Democratic Republic, the state or the collective still owns the land, and insecurity of rights often implies that formal sales markets do not exist, although observers report many informal, short-term transactions. An analysis of the impact of sales of land use rights in Vietnam reveals moderate levels of activity in the sales market depending on the region. Although buyers were generally characterized by higher productivity, there is some evidence of distress sales in the sense that households that experienced significant income loss were more likely to sell land. However, better functioning of credit markets was found to attenuate this effect, implying that liberalizing land sales markets will be less problematic in areas where access to rural finance is assured (Deininger and Jin 2003). Contrary to this, in Sumatra, Suyanto, Tomich, and Otsuka (2001) find that land sales transactions contribute to greater inequality of landholdings compared with rentals, which help equalize operational holdings.

Latin America

Given the high inequalities in land ownership, one would expect the scope for efficiency- and equity-enhancing land rental transactions in Latin America to be large. Contrary to that expectation, rental activity in many countries is actually quite limited, something that can be explained to result from informational imperfections and the ensuing high transaction costs, as well as the impact of past restrictions on rental markets that have weakened landowners' perception of the security of their property rights. The impact of rental restrictions has been significant. For example, in Colombia the amount of formally rented land decreased from 2.3 million hectares in 1960 to 1.1 million hectares in 1988 following the imposition of rent ceiling legislation (Jaramillo 2001), and much the same occurred in Brazil. Land rental restrictions also led to widespread tenant evictions in many Latin American countries. While in many cases the restrictions have been

A legacy of rental market restrictions affects market activity

111

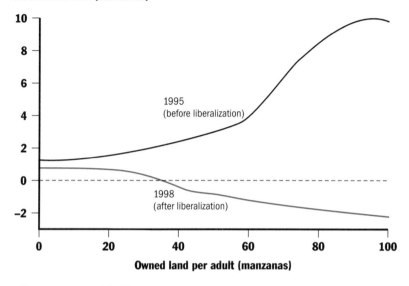

Figure 3.2 Land rental before and after agricultural market liberalization, Nicaragua

Net rental of land (manzanas)

1995
(before liberalization)

1998
(after liberalization)

Owned land per adult (manzanas)

Note: 1 manzanas = 0.699 hectare.
Source: Deininger and Chamorro (forthcoming).

repealed, participation in rental markets continues to remain limited. In 1998, more than a decade after the rental restrictions had been lifted, tenancy rates in Colombia were still only about 11 percent, way below their 1960s' level, highlighting that restoring confidence in the property rights system takes time (Deininger and Gonzalez 2002).

In Nicaragua 22 percent of producers participated in rental markets in 1998/99. Even though the areas involved were small and contracts were typically short term, a comparison with 1995 data indicates that the elimination of subsidies has considerably improved the rental market's tendency to shift land to land-poor producers (Deininger, Zegarra, and Lavadenz forthcoming). This impact of economic policies on rental market outcomes is illustrated graphically in figure 3.2 using nonparametric regressions and shows that before economic liberalization in 1998, rental markets shifted land from small to large farmers, whereas the opposite was true after disproportionate protection for large farmers had been eliminated in the context of macroeconomic liberalization.

Case studies from a number of other Latin American countries show that the main factors limiting land rental transactions are weak property rights and the lack of reliable conflict resolution mechanisms (Bastiaan and Plata 2002; Jaramillo 1998; Zegarra Méndez 1999). The ensuing insecurity implies that landowners are reluctant to rent out for fear that tenants will establish a claim to the land. Hence rentals are few, informal, short term, and often limited to closely related people to facilitate enforcement. The legacy of intervention, together with the external shocks and financial crises experienced during the 1990s, may explain why, even though a distinct effect of land market liberalization on rental activity can be observed, the magnitude of this effect has been less than might have been expected at the outset (Barham, Carter, and Deininger 2003).

Given that one of the main preoccupations of government policies in Latin America has been to provide poor but productive producers with land, a comparison of the results of decentralized rental with those of centralized land reform efforts is of interest. In the case of Colombia, Deininger and Gonzalez (2002) show that rental markets have been much more effective than government-sponsored land reforms in bringing land to productive and poor producers, similar to what was observed in the case of China (Deininger and Jin, 2002). This implies that land reform efforts may benefit from making greater use of land rental markets, or even from taking specific measures to increase activity and improve the outcomes from the operation of these markets.

Land rental can provide land to productive but poor producers

While land purchase prices vary widely, recent macroeconomic liberalization and the associated elimination of special privileges for large producers have helped to lower land prices considerably, thereby reducing incentives for speculative land acquisition and bringing prices more in line with profits from agricultural cultivation. For example, in Brazil land prices dropped by up to 70 percent in the early 1990s (Bastiaan and Plata 2002), making it easier to acquire land for productive purposes. Much the same occurred in Colombia, where the overall level of land purchase prices is now more in line with productive returns (Lavadenz and Deininger 2002). Although lower land prices would be expected to increase the demand for land sales transactions, low international commodity prices imply a need for those acquiring such lands to make additional investments to allow a shift to other crops. The undertaking of such investment may be prevented by the lack of the necessary marketing infrastructure and technology or the absence of, or high transaction costs associated with, rural credit.

Land sales markets in Latin America are relatively active, with average annual turnovers of 5 percent in Colombia, 2 to 3.5 percent in Venezuela,[9] 1.4 to 2 percent in Ecuador, and 1 percent in Honduras (Jaramillo 2001). However, even in situations where activity is high,

Even where they are active, sales markets are often segmented

markets are often found to be highly segmented implying that sales involve either from large to large or from small to small producers but rarely across different farm size groups. Such segmentation of land sales markets is also observed in Nicaragua (Carter and Chamorro 2002). It is in part due to the cost of subdivision and high transaction costs, and in part due to lack of long-term financing for the poor associated with the continent's dualistic land ownership structure (Barham, Carter, and Sigelko 1995).

Land markets' limited capacity to help equalize land ownership in an environment characterized by highly unequal land access is illustrated by the ambiguous impact of export booms in crops where smallholders have some comparative advantage. In Guatemala, an export boom in winter vegetable products induced a transfer of land from larger farms to smaller farms. Farms that began with relatively large holdings (3 hectares) did not increase their landholdings significantly after the boom period, while those households that had less than 1 hectare prior to the boom and who began producing boom crops expanded their landholdings significantly (Barham, Carter, and Sigelko 1995). By contrast, in Paraguay an agricultural export boom led to sharply increasing real land prices and increased land access by the largest-farm-size class, presumably because of its better access to credit and markets. Outside the boom area, small farmers were little affected, and in some cases even continued to accumulate land (Carter and Galeano 1995).

This suggests that the purchase market does not operate as a mechanism of land access for labor-abundant, capital-constrained households, but that agents that are not capital constrained can translate relative technical efficiency into effective demand for more land (Carter and Salgado 2001). The importance of capital constraints as a determinant of outcomes observed in land sales markets is also illustrated by mobility analysis of small producers who benefited from Chile's land reform. While upward mobility by these households is extremely limited, the analysis shows substantial upward mobility by a new class of well-financed, often nonagricultural professionals and business people who purchased land from the original beneficiaries (Carter, Barham, and Mesbah 1996), which has led some to characterize Chile's agricultural export boom as exclusionary (Jarvis 1989; Ortega 1988). This interpretation is supported by the fact that only 20 to 30 percent of those who sold their farms did so because of a lack of interest in farming or because of old age (Echenique and Rolando 1991). Observers noted similar patterns of land concentration triggered by export booms in several Central American countries in the 1970s and 1980s.

Policy Implications

THE FOREGOING EVIDENCE INDICATES THAT LAND RENTAL markets have considerable potential to improve productive outcomes, suggesting that failure to harness their potential could forgo large equity and productivity benefits. To realize these benefits governments need to ensure that tenure security is high enough and to explore options for eliminating unjustified restrictions on the operation of land rental markets. While limitations on land sales markets may be based on a stronger conceptual foundation, efforts to implement such restrictions have almost invariably weakened property rights, implying that their unintended negative consequences have often far outweighed the positive impacts they were intended to achieve, especially as such restrictions may often be evaded. Because activity in land sales markets is normally low or highly localized in most developing countries, getting credit markets to function well is more effective than centrally imposed limits on land transactions, with the exception of loose restrictions on land ownership in situations of rapid change.

Land Rental Markets

Tenure security is a key precondition for the operation of land rental markets. Indeed, the level of tenure security and of trust in the long-term security of land rights seem to be key elements in explaining the large variation in the incidence of rentals across countries. However, the literature has not paid sufficient attention to this issue. Where land tenure is not secure, landlords who rent out will run the risk of not being able to claim their land back, implying that tenure security is especially crucial for the emergence of long-term contracts. Evidence from Western European and other industrial countries suggests that with secure long-term rights and long-term rental contracts, many entrepreneurs with limited capital endowments may actually prefer to rent than to buy land.

In Vietnam the provision of secure, long-term land rights, even at an informal level, increased the volume of rental transactions benefiting poor but productive households (Deininger and Jin 2003). In the Dominican Republic insecure property rights not only reduce the level of activity in the rental market, but also induce market segmentation, that is, rentals are restricted to pre-existing social networks (Macours 2002). In Nicaragua, Deininger and Chamorro (forthcoming) show that insecure tenure

Tenure security is a critical precondition for rental markets to function

reduces participation on the supply side of the land rental market. In Thailand, Brits, Grant, and Burns (2002) report increases in the incidence of land transactions after titling. In Ethiopia the fact that any land that is not self-cultivated by the owner for two seasons can be confiscated is a major impediment to the emergence of a rental market and off-farm migration (Deininger, Jin, Adenew, Gebre-Selassie, and Demeke 2003). Government intervention that undermines landowners' rights to land can thus reduce the extent of rental market activity.

Secure tenure is particularly important for long-term contracts and investment incentives

Unless secure long-term contracts are available, the incentive for either tenants (who may be the only ones with the labor and information available to do so) or for landlords (who may have the needed capital) to make investments in land may be severely limited. The ability to adjust for this type of market failure without long-term contracts that can be enforced in a credible way is limited. The existence of long-term rentals in many parts of the world implies that rental contracts can be adjusted to avoid disincentives to land-related investment. At the same time, in situations where past policies undermined either the security of tenure or producers' ability to enter into unrestricted rental contracts, restoring trust and providing the level of tenure security needed for long-term rentals may not be feasible in the short term. Where, as a consequence, long-term and secure rental contracts are not an option, land rentals may need to be complemented with other mechanisms to facilitate the socially most desirable level of land transfers across producers.

Because of concerns about the loss of efficiency that could result from sharecropping or a view that tenancy is an exploitative relationship, governments in many countries tried to either limit sharecropping or regulate rental in a way that would improve the welfare of tenants. While motivated by considerations of social justice, such interventions had implications for productivity that often affected their ability to contribute to social goals as well. Furthermore, to improve the equity outcomes from rental markets in urban and rural areas, governments have often imposed rent controls or ceilings on the amount of rent landlords can charge, all aimed to increase the security of tenure enjoyed by tenants.[10] In many cases this led to large-scale self-cultivation by landlords or the adoption of wage labor contracts, both modes of production that are inferior to tenancy in terms of production incentives and outcomes (Ray 1999). Indeed, studies show that implementing tenant protection and rent ceilings effectively is not easy and that where implementation is incomplete, they can easily reduce land access and thus equity, contrary to the professed goals. For example, estimates indicate that the introduction of tenancy legislation in India was associated with the eviction of more than 100 million tenants, which caused the rural poor to loose access to about 30 percent of the total operated area (Appu 1997). Furthermore, by threatening landowners who lease out with the loss of their land, the legislation has driven tenancy underground, thereby reducing the opportunity for greater land access through rental markets and greatly reducing informal tenants' bargaining position and their ability to enforce contract terms.

Realizing that rent controls without tenant protection will simply lead to widespread evictions, many Indian states have introduced more comprehensive tenancy reforms that combine low limits on rents with protection of tenants against eviction. The intent was to improve cultivators' status and welfare, and the reforms contain three main elements: (a) the imposition of rent ceilings; (b) the award of permanent rights to tenants, subject to landowners' rights to retention; and (c) the transfer of ownership rights to tenants on lands not claimed by landowners. Such reforms met with considerable resistance by landlords and were therefore difficult and costly to implement. Indeed, of all the Indian states only West Bengal, after a communist victory in state elections in 1973, mounted an effective campaign for tenant registration. Analysis suggests that the impact of doing so was positive and that agricultural productivity increased (Banerjee, Gertler, and Ghatak 2002). Tenants' ability to subsequently acquire limited amounts of land through the regular sales markets reportedly also increased slightly (Rawal 2001). For India as a whole, tenancy reforms affected poverty reduction, but not productivity growth (Besley and Burgess 2000), suggesting that a productivity impact requires significantly more than just passage of a law. This is in line with land reform experience in Japan and Korea, where similar tenancy reforms were rapidly implemented.

Conceptual arguments also indicate that while rent controls can transfer some resources to tenants, they tend to make everybody worse off by restricting the supply of land available to the rental market, undermining tenure security, and reducing investment (Basu and Emerson 2000). Examples from a number of countries support the argument that rent controls are normally an inefficient way to transfer resources for a number of reasons. First, implementing tenancy laws is costly in terms of economic resources and administrative capacity. Second, rent ceilings will invariably reduce landlords' investment incentives and possibly their willingness to rent out, implying losses in productivity. Finally, the benefits from rental legislation are largely confined to current tenants, and the

Effective implementation can lead to productivity gains, but rent controls are unlikely to be an efficient way of transferring resources

imposition of tenancy regulation will decrease the supply of land rentals and access to land or housing by those who did not have a contract at the time when the legislation was promulgated, that is, the landless and the extremely poor. In South Africa, tenancy protection laws that were passed as an interim measure until more comprehensive land reform would be implemented could, in the absence of such reform, well end up undermining options for land access by the poor. In Asia, the negative long-term effect on land rental market activity is often exacerbated by the prohibition of subleasing by tenants who benefited from tenancy reforms or their heirs.

Rent controls reduce investment and the functioning of rental markets

Moreover, rent or price regulation often obstructs the functioning of land markets at the urban periphery, forcing large numbers of migrants who are continuing to come to the cities into slums and informal settlements, where they have to subsist without access to needed services and often at high prices. This deprives them of incentives for housing-related investment and may limit their ability to obtain credit to improve their livelihoods and provide employment for others. Efforts to promote equity by using rent or price regulation have proven to be ineffective and costly, and where warranted other channels, such as targeted subsidies, would have been more effective (Renaud 1999). Although there are many instances where tenancy continues to be widely practiced despite its legal prohibition, the de facto illegal nature of the tenancy relationship might provide landlords with additional leverage that they can use to bargain down the reward to tenants. The unofficial nature also prevents including tenants in structures that are often essential to ensure governance and sustainable resource use at the local level, for example, water users' associations. Even in India considerable discussion is now under way about eliminating rent ceilings to facilitate greater access to land by the poor (Saxena 2002). More in-depth study of specific steps in particular settings is warranted, including the possibility of small farmers renting out to large landlords (a phenomenon known as "reverse tenancy") and its implications.

The foregoing discussion and the strong evidence suggesting that short-term land rentals will contribute significantly to efficiency and equity imply that land rental restrictions have no merit. Legal or other restrictions on the functioning of rental markets that continue to be in place in many countries—for example, China, Ethiopia, and India—will have a negative impact on agricultural productivity and households' welfare; will discourage investment, off-farm employment, and migration; and will increase the insecurity of land rights. Similarly, sharecropping has long been recognized as a second-best solution under given constraints. Ample evidence indicates that eliminating this contractual option leads would-be renters to rely on wage labor, which is both less efficient and less equitable, and that abolishing restrictions on rental markets would be desirable. While some evidence suggests that rent ceilings and tenancy restrictions can transfer resources to the poor in the short term, both theoretical and empirical analysis suggests that the long-term impact will not be advantageous to the poor. At the same time basic preconditions, such as the security of property rights, the ability to enforce contracts at low cost, and the availability of the necessary information, are key to facilitate the longer-term contracts that will be needed to cope with structural change. To a large extent, the magnitude of the impact of tenancy on equity and investment in the longer term will depend on these factors. The only relevant policy questions are how to sequence the elimination of rent ceilings and other restrictions on tenancy in a way that minimizes disruptions, ensures that sitting tenants will be compensated for any investments they have made, and avoids negative equity impacts.

In addition to eliminating distortions and undertaking measures to improve the functioning of other factor markets in rural areas, steps to reduce the transaction costs associated with land transfers, for example, through better land records or standard contract formats (which the individual parties can adopt or not as they choose) and default regulation of tenancies, provide an opportunity to improve the level of activity in land rental markets.

Tenancy has long been viewed as an important transitional stage that allows peasants to accumulate capital and gain agricultural experience, therefore eliminating sharecropping as a rung on the agrarian ladder, will not contribute to equity in the long run. The unavailability of sharecropping as a contractual option is also likely to be associated with considerable inefficiency in production, especially where risk and credit market constraints impede the functioning of fixed rent markets. Bans on sharecropping or the imposition of a low ceiling on landlords' share therefore have no merit and may lead to large efficiency losses. Collier (1989), for example, estimates static efficiency losses of more than 10 percent associated with the unavailability of share contracts in Kenya. In view of the theoretical analysis and empirical evidence that suggest that outlawing sharecropping will be neither feasible nor cost-effective, only a few governments continue to openly advocate such a far-reaching measure. At the same time restrictions on rental in more general terms still continue to be widespread.

The benefits of eliminating rental restrictions could be large

The elimination of restrictions on land rental in Mexico's *ejido* sector illustrates not only that regulation can have far-reaching impacts even in cases where in practice it is widely neglected, but also that in pursuing this goal, legal and institutional changes need to go hand in hand (Deininger, Bresciani, and others 2002). As in the case of India, many of the restrictions imposed on land leasing in Mexico were widely circumvented in practice. Nonetheless, since the large-scale transfer of land into *ejido* tenure in the 1920s and 1930s, restrictions on the ability to rent out or sublease *ejido* land appear to have led to disproportional concentration of poverty in *ejidos* (Gonzalez and Velez 1995). Comparison with the private sector, where no such restrictions existed, suggests that rental market restrictions were associated with reduced land market activity; land underutilization; limited opportunities for the poor to access land; lower incentives for investment; and increased susceptibility of households to threats and extortion by local authorities who, in theory, had the right to withdraw the land allocation of anybody who engaged in land rental (Zepeda 2000). As illustrated in box 3.2, recent reforms that eliminated these restrictions not only had a discernible impact on governance at the local level, but also had a significant and positive impact on activity in rental markets and household welfare (World Bank 2002a).

Land Sales Markets

The discussion thus far implies that even if land sales are not restricted, land sales markets are likely to be much less active than land rental markets virtually everywhere in the world because of higher transaction costs, difficulties in accessing long-term capital to finance land purchases, and insecurity about future economic developments that would significantly affect land prices. On the supply side some evidence indicates that in an environment with limited insurance markets, exogenous shocks can lead to distress sales of land. On the demand side distortions in product markets, together with imperfections in credit and financial markets, will have an immediate impact on the way in which land sales markets function and, in a number of cases, for example, Colombia Nicaragua, and Uganda, seem to be important enough to imply that sales markets can be less productivity enhancing than rental markets.

Not surprisingly, in view of the manifold obstacles that may affect the functioning of land sales markets, these markets have attracted even more attention and government intervention than rental markets. This

Government restrictions on land sales have rarely achieved desired outcomes cost-effectively

Box 3.2   The impact of eliminating restrictions on land rental

THE 1992 *EJIDO* REFORM IN MEXICO ILLUSTRATES two issues. First, it shows that group rights can be perfectly consistent with secure land tenure by individuals, and that if adopted with a view toward making institutions more accountable, they can have a significant impact on governance. Second, it illustrates that even without full ownership rights, efforts to improve the functioning of markets can significantly increase land market activity thereby increasing access to land by more efficient producers as well as participation in the off-farm economy.

The legal changes to recognize group tenure consisted of three main elements. First, the legal status of the *ejido* was enhanced by recognizing the legal personality of *ejidos* and vesting the general assembly of all members with the ability to regulate internal matters, including establishing joint ventures with the private sector and regularizing land ownership within the *ejido*. To ensure that these sensitive questions could be tackled without the political interference that had traditionally charac-

terized the *ejido* sector, a procedural framework was established, including rules for decisionmaking. A second element was the liberalization of land markets. Land rental transactions were completely freed, while land sales were allowed within the *ejido*. Finally, and most important, *ejidos* could undergo a voluntary program of land regularization that, in a participatory process, helped to establish and demarcate the boundaries of community land. With a 75 percent majority the *ejido* assembly could decide which of the community lands should be parceled out to individuals and which should be held in common property, or whether landowners in the *ejido* should be allowed to make the transition toward a private property regime. In all cases households receive certificates that document their share of the land. Studies show that this increased transparency led to increases in rental market activity and household welfare and to improved governance without the sell-off that many of the program's initial critics had feared.

Source: World Bank (2002a).

section briefly discusses the different forms such interventions have taken and their impact. The conditions under which land sales markets would cause significantly negative effects are, however, likely to be quite localized and time specific. Restrictions on land sales markets that may be perceived as appropriate in one location or at one point in time may be highly inadequate in other situations or at other times. Experience worldwide supports the view that blanket restrictions on the functioning of markets are likely to be evaded and may have undesirable side effects. Indeed, few of the restrictions that countries have imposed have had lasting positive effects, and most of them were either difficult or impossible to enforce and have had many unintended and negative consequences, including the growth of bureaucracies to enforce them. Two possible exceptions might be justified in specific situations where the external environment is changing rapidly. One is the imposition of high land ownership ceilings. The other is that if transparent mechanisms for decisionmaking are available and local communities bear the costs of their decisions, they may be given the authority to restrict the transferability of land as is the case in most customary systems. The expectation is that with changing economic circumstances, restrictions will be relaxed. Where transparent mechanisms are unlikely to prevail, the preferred policy should be to forgo restrictions.

Transferability Restrictions

Restrictions on the transferability of land reduce credit access

Governments have frequently imposed restrictions on the transferability of land through the sales market on beneficiaries of land reform or settlers on formerly state-owned land to prevent them from selling or mortgaging their land. Such a restriction could be justified as a temporary measure to prevent the beneficiaries of a land reform program from selling their land based on inadequate information or in response to temporary imperfections in product and financial markets. Even temporary restrictions on land mortgages can be counterproductive, however, as they would deprive beneficiaries from accessing credit during the establishment phase when they need it the most. The literature has reported cases where farmers were forced to resort to less efficient arrangements, such as usufruct mortgaging and use of wage labor, to gain access to credit (Hayami and Otsuka 1993). Investigators have also noted this problem in Korea (King 1977) and in the Philippines (Chuma, Otsuka, and Hayami 1990), where restrictions on land market activity have limited investment. Land received under land reform in Chile was freely transferable, and Jarvis (1985) views this as one of the key ingredients of its success. Precluding land reform beneficiaries from sales in the medium term would reduce efficiency by preventing adjustments in response to differential beneficiary abilities, and could, if combined with rental restrictions, cause large tracts of land to be underutilized. The danger of beneficiaries' undervaluing their land could be reduced through other means, and the goal of preventing small landowners from selling out in response to temporary shocks would be better served by ensuring that they have access to output and credit markets and to technical assistance, and by providing safety nets during disasters to avoid distress sales.

Restrictions on land sales markets can increase the costs associated with certain actions, but if the rewards from circumventing them are high enough, will not eliminate them. For example, owners who have no desire to farm tend to disregard the temporary prohibition of land

---

**Box 3.3   Dangers of land privatization in an environment
with multiple market imperfections**

IN SOME CIS COUNTRIES, MANAGERS OF FARM enterprises took advantage of the rural population's complete lack of asset management experience to entice the new shareholders to sell their land shares. In this way, large segments of the rural population turned over their main asset, and land was concentrated in the hands of a small number of farm bosses. In Kazakhstan the government could probably have avoided this negative effect by temporarily restricting the buying and selling of land and instead limiting transferability to short-term, or perhaps medium-term, lease transactions. Such an approach to the transferability of land would allow rural people to postpone irrevocable decisions to a later stage, when the economic situation has normalized and individuals have become more cognizant of the implications of land transactions.

Source: Csaki, Feder, and Lerman (2002).

---

sales in Nicaragua and circumvent it by long-term rentals with the promise to sell, which because of the associated insecurity leads to much lower land prices (Strasma 2000).

A number of countries have combined initial privatization of land with a moratorium on land sales to prevent the possibility that, after decades of collectivism, new landowners' exposure to land sales markets may cause them to dispose of their assets without being aware of their true value, leading to negative social consequences and concentration of land in the hands of speculators. The example of some CIS countries suggests that such concerns may not be completely unfounded (see box 3.3). Moratoriums may be justified as a way of allowing new landowners to acquire better knowledge of their assets and prevent quick sell-offs at unrealistic prices in an environment where markets work imperfectly.[11] In Albania this restriction has been combined with a right of first refusal, whereby before consummating a land sale to an outsider, neighbors or village members must be given the opportunity to acquire the land at the same price for some period. This has few adverse consequences and can help allay communities' fears of being bought out by outsiders.

General imposition of restrictions on the transferability of land by sale is unlikely to be enforceable or beneficial. In many situations such restrictions will have little impact in practice because of the absence of land or credit markets. Where appropriate institutions for intragroup decisionmaking are available (Libecap 1986), permitting the community to limit sales and giving it the right to decide whether to eventually allow sales to outsiders may be an acceptable compromise between equity and efficiency concerns (Barrows and Roth 1990). Restrictions on the marketability of land are common in many developing countries, and many customary or communal systems prohibit the sale of land to outsiders. Some countries, such as Bolivia, have a minimum holding size that cannot be mortgaged or alienated. While these regulations impose some losses in terms of foregone credit market access, they can also help to reduce undesirable social externalities from driving some people into destitution (Andolfatto 2002). As long as they are the product of a conscious choice by the group and the group has clear and transparent mechanisms for changing the land tenure regime, they are unlikely to be harmful. As traditional social ties loosen or the efficiency loss from the sales restriction becomes too high, groups are likely to allow sales to outsiders in some form. The recent constitutional reform of the land rights system in Mexico allows for free sales and rental within all *ejidos* and for decisionmaking by majority vote on whether to eliminate the restriction on sales to outsiders. An initial evaluation of the reforms suggests that with appropriate technical assistance communities are clearly able to make such decisions (World Bank 2002a).

Land Ownership Ceilings

Low land ownership ceilings have been ineffective in facilitating the breakup of large farms and can significantly reduce investment

Countries have often imposed land ownership ceilings to facilitate the breakup of large farms and the associated sales of land to small producers or to prevent socially destabilizing accumulation of land. Even where such measures had a strong economic and social justification and where conditions for implementing them were favorable, ownership ceilings had only a marginal impact on land redistribution. For example, in West Bengal, where tenancy reform was implemented with considerable success, Appu (1997) estimates that only 6 percent of above-ceiling lands were redistributed to the poor. Observers agree that the main reasons for such failure were political, including an inability (or unwillingness) to act quickly, which facilitated spurious subdivision of holdings on paper by landlords, and exceptions for high-value crops, such as sugar or bananas, which generates considerable latitude for arbitrariness and corruption. Since the imposition of ceiling laws in most Asian countries, population growth and subdivision of land through bequest have further reduced the ability to use land ceilings as a means of making land available to the market.

In some countries, for example, the Philippines, existing land ownership ceilings restrict the functioning of land markets. As these apply to natural persons as well as to financial institutions, this not only eliminates banks' incentive to foreclose on properties that have been mort-gaged for irrecoverable debts, but also reduces the ability to use land as collateral for existing loans, and may therefore contribute significantly to the low level of rural investment observed in this country (Deininger, Maertens, and others 2002). Application of ownership ceilings to plan-tation crops has been linked to reduced investment and employment generation by landowners who were above the ceiling, as well as by new investors who were able to get access to the land they required only through long-term leases from a large number of smallholders (Hayami and Kikuchi 2000). Similar restrictions on land are present in Sri Lanka, and observers claim that they have reduced land values by 50 percent, thereby significantly reducing the value of the asset endowment of the poor (Abt Associates 1999). Even where ceilings might have been effec-tive when they were imposed, subdivision of land in the interim, either as a consequence of population growth and inheritance or to evade the ceilings, has greatly reduced their potential effectiveness. In addition, given the significant cost of implementation, land taxation may be a mechanism to improve the utilization of land or make land available to the market in a less costly and distortive manner.

Some studies attribute a role to land ceilings in preventing new, large consolidations after land reform (Cain 1981; Mahmood 1990), for example, in Japan and Korea. Even though ceiling legislation is unlikely to have been the only factor, this argument seems to have some merit, and ceilings above, say, 1,000 hectares, that are clearly aimed at dis-couraging speculation following land reform or farm restructuring may be justifiable if the issues related to enforcement can be tackled.

High ceilings may help to limit speculative land concentration

Land Price and Ownership Limits

To avoid the exploitation of landowners with limited information, a number of countries fix minimum and maximum prices for land. For example, some Eastern European countries have established "norma-tive" prices for land that were either to guide activity in land sales mar-kets or to specify a legally binding price range. While guidance on land prices, preferably differentiated by region and some broad land use classes, can be useful to provide information to market participants, a binding price range is unlikely to be effective, and in practice has been widely neglected, especially as normative prices were often set an unre-alistic levels. While it is doubtful that such legislation has prevented land sales with prices above the ceiling, it is likely to have reduced the

Land price ceilings are unlikely to be effective

price received by those transacting. A government role in disseminating information on land prices can be justified as a public good to increase transparency in the market. However, establishing a set price, especially if it is independent of quality characteristics, is neither justifiable nor easy to implement, and many countries seem to have been abandoned it as impractical (Csaki, Valdes, and Fock 1998).

Land ownership by foreigners is often highly charged politically

Many countries, including industrial nations, either prohibit foreigners from owning land (for example, Bulgaria, Indonesia, the Philippines, Romania, Switzerland, and Tanzania) or only permit such land ownership under strict conditions (Hodgson, Cullinan, and Campbell 1999). Even in developing countries, where because of shallow domestic capital markets the benefits from abandoning such legislation could be considerable, the issue is often politically charged and trying to eliminate such restrictions could result in a divisive political debate that distracts attention from more urgent issues. Where this is the case, long-term leases that are open to foreigners may be a more practical and preferable option. Restrictions that limit the right to own land to physical persons out of fear of promoting a concentration of land in the hands of anonymous corporations, as adopted in a number of Eastern European countries such as Estonia, Lithuania, and Moldova, have in practice proven to be more harmful by limiting incentives for legal entities to invest in land improvement. Some of these countries have now abandoned the restrictions following the realization that corporate forms of land ownership, especially joint ventures, can provide much needed access to capital.

Land Consolidation and Minimum Farm Size Restrictions

Land fragmentation can result from inheritance or land redistribution

Fragmentation of agricultural land has two main sources. One, which has been of great historical relevance, is the successive division of small farms into smaller and smaller plots through inheritance in a situation where nonagricultural employment was limited. Over long periods of time, social norms that either require equal division of land among all heirs or the undivided passage of the family's land to only one of them have had a significant impact on the rural landscape in many European countries (Platteau and Baland 2001). A second source of fragmentation is the type of land redistribution policy adopted in the course of decollectivization and farm restructuring. In many instances, providing new landowners with a large number of plots of different quality was politically more appealing than facing the tradeoffs associated with giving larger parcels with relatively homogenous soil quality (Tran 1998).

This implies that in those CIS countries that privatized and distributed land, but also in China and Vietnam, individual households can hold a large number of land parcels, often in odd shapes, something that has often been claimed to be detrimental to efficient cultivation.

Another instrument that governments have used to improve the structure of agricultural landholdings or to prevent further fragmentation has been the imposition of minimum farm size limits or restrictions on subdivision. Similar to what was observed in the case of maximum farm size limits, where economic conditions often prompted households to act in a certain manner irrespective of government regulations, such restrictions have rarely prevented undesirable outcomes entirely, but by making them illegal have forced households into informality. For example, Mexico prohibits subdivision upon inheritance to prevent fragmentation, but this provision is widely neglected in practice. Rather than helping to improve the agrarian structure, this provision clogs up the judicial system: about half the conflicts before the agrarian courts involve inheritance disputes (World Bank 2002a). Minimum farm size legislation was similarly ineffective in Morocco, and led to many disputes. In Brazil, Graziano da Silva (2001) identified minimum farm size legislation as a factor impeding the growth of the nonagricultural economy by making the pursuit of part-time farming economically less rewarding. In all these cases, creating the conditions for rental and sales markets to function better seems to be preferable.

Minimum farm size limits or subdivision restrictions are ineffective in preventing fragmentation

Excessive fragmentation of agricultural parcels can harm agricultural productivity in a number of ways. It increases the amount of land needed for paths and roads; adds to the time needed to get to plots; requires additional spending on fencing and boundary demarcation; increases the difficulties of management, supervision, and pest control; and makes investments in irrigation, drainage, and soil conservation, as well as the use of certain machinery, more difficult. However, farmers may seek some fragmentation of plots to diversify crop locations and manage risks, overcome seasonal labor bottlenecks, and match soil types with crops to overcome inefficiencies in land, labor, credit, and food markets (Blarel and others 1992; Fenoaltea 1976; McCloskey 1975). To decide whether concern about such fragmentation is warranted, an understanding of the causes underlying this phenomenon, the magnitude of the losses it may impose, and the availability of policy options that could deal with the problem at a reasonable cost is necessary. With the emergence of a dynamic nonfarm economy, mechanized farming becomes desirable and the losses from fragmentation may assume greater relevance. Experience

The disadvantages of fragmentation increase with the level of mechanization

127

in industrial countries shows that fragmentation becomes a serious constraint requiring intervention once it impedes the ability to use machinery on a large scale in areas with a rapidly decreasing agricultural population (Bentley 1987). In France, for example, Simons (1987) finds returns of up to 40 percent for consolidation.

Empirical evidence suggests that the costs of fragmentation are relatively modest in unmechanized, semisubsistence agriculture, where rental markets can often be relied on to bring about a structure of operational holdings that is more in line with economic needs. For example, Heston and Kumar (1983) suggest that in Asia, instances where fragmentation had historically involved high losses in output are rare, a conclusion that is supported by more recent evidence from Pakistan, where benefits from consolidation are considered to be small (Ali, Parikh, and Shah 1996). To date the quantitative evidence from studies exploring the productivity impact of fragmentation in China is not particularly positive, even though levels of fragmentation are extremely high, with average farm sizes below one hectare split, on average, into nine plots (Wenfang and Makeham 1992). To consolidate land, in 1988 the city of Pingdu in Shandong province adopted the "two-field system," which consolidated parcels that were then auctioned off among farmers. Analysis suggests that the program reached some of its goals: the average number of plots held by participants decreased from 7.6 to 3.4 and their technical efficiency was 6.7 percent higher than that of nonparticipants (Chen and Brown 2001). Nevertheless, a poor record of implementation led to conflict and resistance, and in 1998 to the abandonment of the program. Households prefer to be able to rent out land on an individual basis and, in doing so, also seem to be able to capture most of the effects that were hoped for from a more centralized form of consolidation (Lin, Cai, and Li 1997). Other studies from China, which show that consolidation could lead to output gains of up to 15 percent, also recommend relying on voluntary and decentralized market processes rather than on administrative solutions (Wan and Cheng 2001).

Market-based solutions should be exploited before embarking on specific consolidation programs

Numerous countries have used the fact that the cost of negotiation may be too high for individuals to bear voluntarily as a justification for one-time interventions that combine inducements and restrictions to bring about consolidation of operational holdings. Such programs can be justified only in situations where, once consolidated, holdings are unlikely to be fragmented once again, a condition that is normally satisfied only at higher income levels or if fragmentation was the outcome of an involuntary process. The fact that consolidation programs often incorporate development of rural infrastructure in an effort to improve conditions for nonagricultural employment in rural areas has often added to their complexity and costs, as well as the time taken to complete such actions. In considering interventions to promote consolidation, an important initial step is to ensure that the opportunity for decentralized options to achieve consolidation of operational holdings through unconstrained rental and sales markets has been exhausted, and that the institutional infrastructure to implement interventions in a transparent fashion is available. Most developing countries have not yet met these conditions (Giovarelli 2002).[12] Even in some Eastern European countries where, because of the mechanisms adopted to redistribute land, the benefits from consolidating operational holdings could indeed be high, the economic viability of consolidation programs remains to be demonstrated, and careful evaluation of ongoing experiences would be highly desirable and would be needed before more widespread adoption of specific approaches can be recommended.

Conclusion

THE METHODOLOGICAL DISCUSSION DEMONSTRATES THAT for a number of reasons, land markets cannot be viewed independently from the broader social, institutional, and economic framework. Subsidies will be capitalized in land values, therefore economic distortions will affect households' propensity to acquire land. In addition, imperfections in other markets will have differential impacts on specific types of households and therefore affect land market outcomes. Furthermore, institutional factors that affect the costs associated with land market transactions are a key determinant of the level of land market activity and its capacity to enhance equity. Neglect of institutional issues by policymakers forces participants to adopt informal arrangements and generally provides advantages to those with greater endowments and better access to information, and may not be advantageous to the poor. A differentiated approach to land market policy that is aware of the trade-offs and the opportunities as well as the limitations of government policies is therefore most likely to be appropriate.

In the past policymakers have often underestimated the potential for land rentals to contribute to greater productivity and increase the welfare of the poor. Evidence suggests that land rentals can provide access to land in a low-cost fashion as a response to exogenous shocks, off-farm employment, and changing opportunities and interests, or even in situations where the final ownership status of land is still being clarified. The extent and direction of rental market activity, and by implication its impact on productivity and equity, will be affected by the functioning of other markets, the outside opportunities available to potential tenants, and the security of property rights. Imperfections and distortions in other markets, as well as wealth constraints, will affect the impact of land rental on productivity, but in most situations rental markets, including sharecropping arrangements, improve the allocation of land and enhance equity. Where property rights are not secure or are perceived to be insecure, landowners will not be willing to rent out under longer-term contracts, even though such contracts may be desirable to facilitate structural change and the associated investment decisions. Finally, the impact of rental markets on equity will depend on how the surplus is shared between landlords and tenants, something that depends on the alternative opportunities open to the latter. Even though the transaction costs associated with land rentals are normally lower than those in sales markets, making information on land ownership, contractual forms, and prices more widely available offers opportunities to reduce them.

Scope for land rentals is often underestimated, and the potential difficulties associated with land sales often have been neglected

While permanent land transfers normally provide higher incentives for long-term investment, land sales markets are normally associated with higher transaction costs than land rental markets. In addition, acquiring land through purchase requires a considerable outlay of cash, which may be out of reach for households that do not have access to nonagricultural income, especially where long-term mortgage credit for land acquisition is unavailable. In situations where markets for credit and insurance are imperfect, the supply of land in the sales market may be mainly through distress sales. Distortions that favor larger farmers, as well as the tendency of land prices to exceed the capitalized value of agricultural incomes from land, imply that even in situations where small farmers have a strong productive advantage, the contribution of land sales markets to bringing about a farm size distribution that is more efficient and more equitable may be limited.

Restrictions on land sales market continue to be widespread, though difficult to implement

Governments worldwide have adopted a large array of discretionary measures in relation to land sales, even though in principle economic incentives, for instance, through land taxation, are likely to be much preferable to rigid regulations.[13] These measures have rarely achieved their desired impacts, suggesting that even where a case for restrictions or other types of government interventions may exist, any judgment on their merit has to include an assessment of implementation capacity. In many cases where centralized restrictions on land sales markets may be justified, enforcement difficulties have generated distortions whose impact was worse than that the restrictions had set out to remedy. With the possible exception of loosely defined restrictions on maximum farm sizes, universal limitations on sales markets are therefore unlikely to be effective, but may lead to the emergence of large bureaucracies that develop a self-interest in maintaining these restrictions. Given these difficulties, and the large variations in conditions in any given country, a more decentralized approach may be preferable. Indeed, cohesive communities have often imposed restrictions on the transferability of land to outsiders at certain stages of their development out of a concern to maintain social harmony and prevent landlessness. Policy should ensure that the mechanisms for reaching such a transition are transparent and representative, and that changes in such rules are feasible when they no longer serve the interests of the majority of community members.

A final conclusion from the evidence presented is that it is unrealistic to assume that restrictions on the functioning of markets will lead to significant and quick redistribution of land and other productive assets to the poor. Where a strong social, political, and economic case for such redistribution exists, other mechanisms will need to be adopted. There is considerable potential for such mechanisms to draw on market outcomes in more imaginative ways than in the past, for example, to facilitate targeting and the acquisition of managerial experience by potential beneficiaries. Relying on markets alone will, however, not be sufficient.

Land markets will not equalize a highly skewed land ownership distribution

Notes

1. Empirical evidence confirms that family labor is more productive than hired labor and that the intensity of supervision by family members affects the performance of hired labor (Frisvold 1994).

2. A similar argument about the excess value of land access could be applied to any household that had an abundance of another imperfectly traded factor, such as farming skill.

3. However, the supervision advantages of owner-operators have, in many cases, motivated large processors to contract production out to smallholders under outgrower or contract farming schemes that often pro-

vide credit in kind as well as technical assistance (Glover 1990).

4. The traditional interpretation that these interlinkages are devices landlords use to bring the second-best outcome closer to the first-best outcome by increasing tenants' supply of effort (Braverman and Stiglitz 1982) requires strong assumptions that are generally not satisfied in developing countries (Otsuka, Chuma, and Hayami 1992).

5. If risk were a major factor in choosing the optimal type of contract, one would observe significant variation in crop shares according to the riskiness of the

crops grown on particular plots. This has not been observed empirically, however.

6. Rural land sales are relatively few, even in industrial countries. The percentage of farmland transferred, on average, each year is 3 percent of the total in the United States, 1.5 percent in the formal sector in South Africa, 1 to 1.5 percent in the United Kingdom, and 0.5 percent in Ireland and Kenya (Moll 1988). The literature highlights the difficulty of land acquisition through borrowing by would-be smallholders despite their productivity advantage (Binswanger and Elgin 1988; Carter and Mesbah 1993). At the same time, even in developing countries urban land markets can have much higher levels of transactions (Brits, Grant, and Burns 2002).

7. This is often facilitated by regulations that limit the amount of rent to be paid or specify a minimum lease period.

8. Some countries adopt minimum lease terms to facilitate the stability of land sizes, for example, nine years in France, while others impose maximum lease terms to discourage land re-concentration, for example, three years in Vietnam.

9. Activity varies considerably across regions. Annual turnover of land amounts to as much as 12 percent in recently colonized areas, but is about 2.5 to 3 percent for private lands and only 1.5 to 2 percent for lands that had been subject to agrarian reform (Delahaye 2001).

10. The literature includes considerable discussion of urban rent ceilings, which are widespread in rural areas not only in South Asia and Southeast Asia (Malpezzi, Chun, and Green 1998). In Eastern Europe, similar legislation often limits the rent that can be charged to the land tax that has to be paid to the government, a measure that would tend to undermine the functioning of rental markets. Note that in Western Europe tenure legislation has historically been imposed to advance equity goals; however, even in this case, preventing over-regulation has been difficult (Ravenscroft, Gibbard, and Markwell 1998).

11. The experience of the mass privatizations supports this argument. Many recipients of mass privatization vouchers in Russia in the early 1990s rushed to sell them to speculators and professional investors. They did not recognize the long-term value of the new asset and precipitously converted it into something familiar—cash. These early voucher sellers understood the implication of their irrevocable decision only much later, when gradual normalization had led to steep increases in the value of the privatized companies' stock, which they could have owned had they only avoided selling the vouchers.

12. In many instances consolidation programs have been linked to infrastructure or other projects to provide public goods to rural areas. Providing these benefits independently from measures aiming at simultaneous land consolidation may often be more feasible and much simpler.

13. While part of this can be explained by problems with implementing land taxes, it may also be related to the fact that direct interventions offer greater options for bureaucratic discretion.

CHAPTER FOUR

Fostering Socially Desirable Land Use

T HE PREVIOUS CHAPTERS DEMONSTRATED THAT even basic institutions such as land rights and land markets will be unable to operate without receiving support from the state in the form of public goods and a conducive policy environment, and that in environments where other factor markets do not work well, unfettered operation of land markets by themselves is unlikely to bring about a socially optimal outcome. This chapter reviews what this implies in terms of the government's role to either establish the framework that will allow markets to function, to go beyond markets to ensure that social and equity concerns are satisfied, or to regulate markets so that externalities and other market failures are adequately accounted for. All these areas imply an important role for governments.

The chapter begins by reviewing the progress of and the remaining challenges for the tremendous restructuring of the farming sector in Eastern Europe and the CIS to lead to productivity-enhancing outcomes. Then, based on historical and more recent experience with land reform, it identifies and discusses a number of implications of productivity-enhancing land reforms. Next the chapter turns to conflict over land, based either on historical grievances or on increasing scarcity of productive land combined with limited off-farm opportunities, which is becoming increasingly relevant in many developing countries. Finally, it examines how governments can contribute to more effective land use by privatizing land where no rationale for government ownership exists, by taxing land to encourage its productive use and provide resources for the delivery of public goods and the functioning of local governments, and by land use regulations that maximize social benefits.

Restructuring the Farm Sector in CEE and CIS Countries

OVER THE LAST DECADE, THE RURAL SECTOR IN VIRTUALLY all the countries of Eastern Europe and the Commonwealth of Independent States (CIS) has undergone dramatic change in the context of the shift from a collective to a more individualized structure of land ownership characterized by greater responsiveness to market forces. In the countries affected by this transition, the main challenge is to establish the basic legal and institutional framework for the development of a diversified and productive rural sector, including the scope for well-functioning markets for outputs and inputs, land, and other factors of production. This section provides a background to the reforms, reviews progress in their implementation, and highlights challenges that transition countries may need to confront in the future to ensure that the expected improvements in productivity and household welfare materialize.

Background and the Reform Process

Beliefs in the productive superiority of collective farms were mistaken

Prior to 1989 all these Central and Eastern European (CEE) and CIS countries were characterized by large-scale collective farming. Collectivization was imposed based on a belief in the superiority of large industrial farms and their apparent economies of scale and to gain access to capital, overcome imperfections in input and output markets, and provide other services to members in times of need. The evidence does not support the belief in the existence of economies of scale in agricultural production except for marketing and input access. In virtually all cases of collective agriculture, productive performance was dismal. Collectives in China, Cuba, Ethiopia, Nicaragua, Peru, and Vietnam suffered from incentive problems, absenteeism, underinvestment, tendencies toward discriminatory employment of nonmembers, and low productivity, even if compared with a smallholder sector that was discriminated against (Deininger 1995). In Nicaragua and Peru individualization ensued as soon as the possibility of doing so arose (Melmed-Sanjak and Carter 1991; Merlet and Pommier 2000), as also occurred in Ethiopia, where collectives were disbanded in the early 1990s (Rahmato 1993). The transition from collective to private models of cultivation has often been associated with large increases in productivity, as in China after the 1978 introduction of the household responsibility system (Lin 1992; McMillan, Whalley, and Zhu

1989) and in Vietnam after the reforms of the early 1980s (Ravallion and van de Walle 2001; Tran 1998). Land reform and restructuring of the rural sector have therefore become a key part of the transformation of the rural sector in all CEE and CIS countries.

Individual countries' responses to the challenge of transforming the land ownership structure and the consequences for productivity and household welfare differ widely. The adoption of vastly different processes has led to the emergence of variation in farming structures, productivity, development of rural factor markets, and poverty outcomes. The processes chosen to privatize land and restructure the agriculture sector were affected by such factors as the distribution of land ownership before collectivization, the status of ownership after collectivization, the length of communist rule, and the ethnicity of precollectivization owners (Lerman 2001; Macours and Swinnen 2000a). Collective structures were economically unviable long before the political changes of the 1990s. Nonetheless, they were more than just a means of production, in particular, they provided workers with a wide variety of social services. The fact that many employee-shareholders remain in collective structures rather than exercising their right to leave with land and property shares can be explained not only by the adverse economic environment and the risk this implies for private individual farming (Amelina 2000), but also by the fear of losing access to social services. Thus policies will have to take account of the fact that farm restructuring is not only about productivity, but also about ensuring the availability of key social services to the rural population and the provision of safety nets to accompany the process of structural reform.

Given the difficulty of establishing the legal and regulatory infrastructure for well-functioning markets, the initial impact of restructuring on production was almost universally negative. Price liberalization and subsidy cuts together caused a decline in relative prices for agriculture, contributing to almost half of the observed decline in agricultural output and to the necessary adjustment in the overall size of the agriculture sector. The uncertainty associated with transition and with climatic factors caused an average output fall of around 10 percent each, and the disruption associated with privatization, farm restructuring, and the need to adjust both factors of production and techniques account for the remainder of the drop in output (Macours and Swinnen 2000b). The breakup of large farms into small units was not necessarily a major source of output decline, as illustrated by the performance of Albania, which despite breaking up its collective sector achieved the highest rate of output growth of all the CEE and CIS countries following transition (Cungu and Swinnen 1999).

Farm restructuring poses economic and social challenges

135

Modalities of Restructuring

Restitution was adopted mainly in CEE countries

The CEE countries all allow full private ownership of all types of land and have generally privatized land by restituting it to its former owners in the form of physical plots (table 4.1). The exceptions are Hungary and Romania, which pursued mixed strategies whereby land was restituted to former owners, but a portion of it was also distributed to agricultural workers in the interests of social equity.[1] Poland is selling off state-owned land, while Albania has pursued a strategy based on full redistribution of land to cultivators.

The availability of old ownership records and the presence of a clear legal basis for assessing their validity has generally made restitution easier to implement than in countries where records were destroyed or where the legal basis remains unclear, such as Nicaragua. Nevertheless, the processes have often been lengthy and complicated.[2] For example, in Estonia, in marked contrast to the rapid privatization of assets, land restitution is a slow and cumbersome process. About 75 percent of land remains under state ownership and is leased out on short-term leases, something that is not conducive to bringing about the structural transformation needed (Csaki, Valdes, and Fock 1998). Bulgaria has amended its restitution law at least 20 times since its promulgation in 1991 (Giovarelli and others 2002), and in Russia, from the first draft to the actual passage of a law on agricultural land turnover took more than six years (Overchuk 2002). Also Davidova and others (2001) cite the continuing uncertainty about land claims associated with the restitution process as a main reason for the insufficient development of land sales markets and of the supply of credit to rural areas. The fact that restitution is difficult is consistent with experience from other countries such as South Africa, where only a recent radical simplification of the process has helped speed it up and ensure that uncertainty regarding land ownership is resolved quickly.

The ensuing fragmentation of land ownership increases the importance of land markets

In a hypothetical situation with perfect functioning of land rental and sales markets, the restitution of land to its former owners in many of the CEE countries, which was adopted mainly for political reasons, should not affect productive outcomes. Instead, one would expect entrepreneurs to initially rent and eventually possibly buy the land they require to advance their activities. However, many of the factors discussed earlier, in particular, insecurity about land rights because of changing legal frameworks and because of bureaucratic inertia and discretion even in cases where the legal provisions were clear, have initially

Table 4.1 Nature of land rights, selected CEE and CIS countries

Region and country	Potential private ownership	Privatization strategy	Allocation strategy	Transferability
CEE				
Albania	All land	Distribution	Plots	Buy and sell, leasing
Bulgaria	All land	Restitution	Plots	Buy and sell, leasing
Czech Republic	All land	Restitution	Plots	Buy and sell, leasing
Estonia	All land	Restitution	Plots	Buy and sell, leasing
Hungary	All land	Restitution and distribution	Plots	Buy and sell, leasing
Latvia	All land	Restitution	Plots	Buy and sell, leasing
Lithuania	All land	Restitution	Plots	Buy and sell, leasing
Poland	All land	Sale of state land	None	Buy and sell, leasing
Romania	All land	Restitution and distribution	Plots	Buy and sell, leasing
Slovakia	All land	Restitution	Plots	Buy and sell, leasing
CIS				
Armenia	All land	Distribution	Plots	Buy and sell, leasing
Azerbaijan	All land	Distribution	Plots (from shares)	Buy and sell, leasing
Belarus	Household plots only	None	None	Use rights nontransferable; buy and sell dubious
Georgia	All land	Distribution	Plots	Buy and sell, leasing
Kazakhstan	Household plots only	None	Shares	Use rights transferable, buy and sell of plots dubious
Kyrgyz Republic	All land	Distribution and conversion	Shares	Five year moratorium
Moldova	All land	Distribution	Plots (from shares)	Buy and sell, leasing
Russia	All land	Distribution	Shares	Leasing, buy and sell dubious
Tajikistan	None	None	Shares	Use rights transferable
Turkmenistan	All land	None, virgin land	Intra-farm leasehold	Use rights nontransferable
Ukraine	All land	Distribution	Shares	Leasing, buy and sell dubious
Uzbekistan	None	None	Intra-farm leasehold	Use rights nontransferable

Source: Adapted from Csaki, Feder, and Lerman (2002).

limited the scope for such markets in a number of countries. At the same time clear differences are beginning to emerge across countries in the extent to which markets function.

Redistribution was adopted mainly in the CIS

CIS countries are characterized by greater variation than CEE countries concerning the recognition of private ownership rights (table 4.1), the process of farmland privatization, and the transferability of such land. Some countries, such as Armenia, Azerbaijan, Georgia, the Kyrgyz Republic, Moldova, Russia, Turkmenistan, and Ukraine, allow citizens to hold private property rights to all types of land. Others, for example, Tajikistan and Uzbekistan, do not recognize private ownership rights, while Belarus and Kazakhstan recognize rights to household plots only.[3] In addition to providing an important safety net, these plots have historically accounted for more than one-third of recorded production.

Table 4.2 shows the tremendous transformation, at least in quantitative terms, that within a decade increased the share of land operated individually in CEE from 21 percent in 1990 to 78 percent in 2000, transferring a total of about 33 million hectares from collective to individual ownership and management. Albania, Latvia, and Slovenia transferred significantly more than 90 percent of their agricultural areas, whereas other countries are still left with significant levels of state ownership. The corresponding figures are lower for CIS countries, where individually operated land increased from 4 percent in 1990 to 22 percent in 2000. Even in this group, only Belarus, Russia, and Turkmenistan had less than one-fifth of their land area under individual control in 2000, and given their physical size, the absolute amount of land transferred into private operation was large by any historical measure (Deininger 2002). Despite the partial character of the reforms, the total amount of land transferred into private ownership in the CIS countries during the last decade is larger than Mexico's land reform, which lasted almost a century (1917-92) and transferred about 100 million hectares to the "social sector." It was also larger than Brazil's 30-year land reform effort, which transferred about 11 million hectares, much of it in frontier areas, and the successful land reform in Japan, which involved the transfer of 2 million hectares, compared with 0.5 and 0.2 million hectares, respectively, in Korea and Taiwan (China).

Land redistribution provided a safety net during transition

The experience with land privatization followed two different modalities. The first was practiced by "radical reformers" such as Armenia, Georgia, Moldova, and to some extent Azerbaijan and the Kyrgyz Republic, where land was distributed very broadly. In many of these settings land makes an important contribution to households' subsis-

Table 4.2 Share of land held privately, selected CEE and CIS countries, 1990 and 2000

Region and country	Agricultural area (millions of hectares)	Percentage of individually owned land		Land transferred to private ownership (millions of hectares)
		1990	2000	
CEE				
Albania	1.1	4	100	1.08
Slovenia	0.5	92	96	0.02
Poland	18.4	77	82[a]	0.92
Romania	14.8	12	67[a]	8.14
Hungary	5.9	6	54[a]	2.83
Bulgaria	6.2	13	96	5.15
Czech Republic	4.3	5	80	3.23
Slovak Republic	4.9	5	99	4.61
Latvia	2.4	5	95	2.16
Lithuania	3.5	9	67	2.03
Estonia	4.5	6	65	2.66
Average CEE	66.6	21	78	32.82
CIS				
Armenia	1.4	4	7	0.94
Georgia	3.0	7	26+25[b]	1.32
Ukraine	43.0	7	26	7.98
Moldova	2.3	9	84	1.73
Belarus	9.4	7	17	0.94
Russia	195.0	2	13	21.45
Kyrgyz Republic	11.0	1	23	2.42
Kazakhstan	222.0	—	29	63.94
Azerbaijan	4.4	3	33	1.32
Tajikistan	1.1	2	38	0.40
Uzbeckistan	26.7	2	28	6.94
Turkmenistan	40.3	—	16	6.37
Average CIS	558.6	4	22	115.73

— Neglible (0.2).
a. Figure refers to 1997.
b. Refers to leasing by households and by private enterprises.
Sources: Csaki and Kray (2001); Csaki and Nucifora (2002).

tence, and the broad distribution has often been credited with helping to avoid destitution during the transition. In the future, as the broader economy develops, the challenge will be to link these producers to markets and to provide mechanisms for voluntary consolidation. Under a second modality, followed by a much larger group of countries, land has been privatized by giving households land shares that entitle them to a parcel of land that is not physically identified and that in most cases continues to be leased back to new structures established on the basis of the old collective farm enterprise and often closely resemble the latter.

Land shares allowed quick privatization, but often did not lead to the restructuring of productive units

Because shares do not correspond to actual land parcels, privatization often made little difference to the way enterprises were actually run (Lerman 2001). Whether and how such shares can be transformed into actual parcels differs by country, but is critical for the extent to which privatization will result in actual changes in production practices and the operational structure. Moreover, in cases where land shares have been contributed to the capital of the restructured collective enterprises, the danger is that if an enterprise becomes bankrupt, land share owners may lose all their assets to new, large-scale landowners, often the former collective farm managers, who enjoy preferential access to markets (Csaki and Nucifora 2002). This is the case in some countries that issued notional land use rights and asset ownership certificates to farm workers, who either had to convert their land share rights into land parcels to start private farms or contribute them to the capital of the collective enterprise. Not surprisingly, in view of prevailing market imperfections and extremely risky environments, most farmers opted for the latter.

Russia illustrates the process as well as the outcomes. Out of an estimated total of 195 million hectares of agricultural land, by 2000 the state had transferred 126 million hectares, or 65 percent of the total, into private ownership. Of these 126 million hectares, 118 million hectares (an area comparable to the size of continental Western Europe) were privatized by issuing land shares to some 12 million agricultural workers, retired agricultural workers, teachers, health care professionals, and other "social sphere" workers, while the remaining land was privatized through land transfers for the creation of private farms and for use as household plots. However, most of this land is held by agricultural enterprises that, in practice, operate in a way that is similar to their predecessor collectives. Farms that are truly privately operated account for only 6 to 7 percent of the agricultural land (with household plots making up another 6 percent). Similarly, in Ukraine 84 percent of the landowners rented their land share certificates to the farms from which the certificates were issued (Rolfes 2002). This implies that in many CIS countries, little actual restructuring of the productive structure has yet been accomplished.

The impact on economic performance has therefore been limited

The decline in output that characterized the initial phase of transition has been reversed in most CEE, and even CIS, countries. In addition to increases in total output, there are clear signs of expansion by more profitable farm enterprises and contraction of loss-making farm enterprises

(Uzun 2002; Yanbykh 2002). Nevertheless, much remains to be done to improve productivity in the rural sector. With hindsight, initial beliefs that privatization would lead to the rapid establishment of a family farming structure were too simplistic and unrealistic given the slow progress in improving the functioning of other rural markets (Gardner and Serova 2002). While the restrictions on land rights and their transferability made it more difficult for individuals to take the risk of establishing private farms, they were only one among many factors. This does not imply that restructured collectives or corporate large farms will remain the mainstay of the rural structure, and large farms may eventually give way to a diversified farm sector that entails family farms as well as corporate farms and partnerships.

Challenges Ahead

Land shares were often used as a way to "privatize" land in an egalitarian way with minimal political resistance. However, the continued inability to link land shares to actual parcels in many countries has made it difficult for holders of these shares to use the parcels directly or to make any decisions about their management. Field studies show that resistance from local bureaucracies and opposition from the management of large agricultural enterprises, together with the difficulty of obtaining startup capital or access to machinery, make claiming land difficult even in situations where the legal possibility of taking land shares out of the collective is well defined. While any procedures chosen to link land shares with actual parcels will have to take the specifics of the local situation into account, a number of countries have developed and tested procedures that could serve as a model for others.

The earlier discussion implies that to achieve optimal social and productive outcomes, well-functioning markets for credit and other factors of production are critical; however, such markets do not emerge automatically, but require a high level of institutional and legal infrastructure that is still lacking in many of the transition countries. Experience shows that implementing a program of land reform that will not only redistribute land, but will also improve participants' welfare, requires paying attention to a host of other factors. Given the complexity of the task and the differences across countries, and even situations within countries, carefully evaluating the emerging experience and trying to use the lessons to provide a framework that can make an effective contribution to beneficiary welfare will be critical, rather than insisting on a patent approach for ideological reasons. Even in CEE, large areas remain under state ownership. Reducing transaction costs, including complex bureaucratic proceedings; imposing hard budget constraints and bankruptcy proceedings; and establishing mortgage legislation could help deal with this problem and improve both efficiency and access to land and help develop the financial sector.

One implication is that the opportunity for increasing agricultural productivity and rural welfare will depend not only on improving the functioning of land, but also on other factor markets in rural areas. Progress in this regard is not only uneven across countries, but strongly affects the extent to which land market liberalization can either be achieved or can contribute to rural growth. For example, in Uzbekistan the fact that controls on output and input decisions remained strong and that outputs were heavily taxed clearly limited the incentives of private producers to exit collectives, and thus whatever gains could have been realized from the limited privatization of land rights (Pomfret 2000).

In addition to measures such as improving governance and accountability at the local level and providing infrastructure, creating an environment where service cooperatives, as distinct from production collectives, could provide access to markets, credit, information, bargaining, and insurance, despite farmers' suspicions of "collective" institutions, would be important. Farmers' associations are widespread in Romania and other CEE countries. In Azerbaijan farmers seek out opportunities to establish farmers' associations for marketing (Csaki and Nucifora 2002). Creating an array of service cooperatives and providing startup capital and links to extension services, market information, and credit could offer considerable opportunities in such an environment, as has been demonstrated in a number of countries (Lerman, Csaki, and Moroz 1998).

Unless an appropriate policy framework is in place, encouraging land transfers may have negative equity and efficiency consequences. Countries where the land rights that private farms can obtain are inferior to those granted to state farms, or where the leases given to landowners are too short to provide investment incentives and carry numerous restrictions limiting the security of tenure enjoyed by individuals, will have to undertake further legal reforms (Duncan 2000; Lerman and Brooks 2001; Pomfret 2000). In this context, privatizing land in the form of paper shares can, at best, only be a first step in a process of structural transformation that would include attention to markets for other factors. Even in situations where, as in Russia, large differences in productivity across different types of farms have emerged (Yanbykh 2002), transferring land from less to more productive users or splitting up the land base into either private farms or smaller successor enterprises is difficult or impossible. Improving the transferability of land, especially in rental markets, and enhancing the incentives to foreclose on bankrupt farms could help speed up the restructuring in these cases (Csaki and Lerman 2000).

Enhancing Land Access through Land Reform

EARLIER DISCUSSION POINTED OUT THAT THE EXTREMELY unequal and often inefficient distribution of land ownership observed in many developing countries was in most cases the outcomes of power relationships and distortionary policies rather than market forces. The analysis of these phenomena also indicates that in many of these situations one cannot expect markets alone to lead to land redistribution at the rate that would be required to maximize efficiency and welfare outcomes. This can provide a justification for support to land redistribution both on grounds of productive efficiency and of the wider social impact of extreme inequality in the distribution of productive assets. This section reviews the justification for such intervention and highlights some of the key issues that need to be addressed before reviewing the status of land reform in different regions and drawing some conclusions for policy.

Historical Evidence

As noted earlier, rapid transition from landlord estates to family farms has led to stable systems of production relations, because the organization of production remained essentially the same family farm system. By contrast, the reform of hacienda systems, that is, systems where tenants had a small household plot for subsistence but worked on the landlord's home farm for most of the time, has been difficult to the point that observers have declared the "game of Latin American land reform" to be lost (de Janvry and Sadoulet 1989). In most of these systems large landowners responded to the threat of land reform by reducing their reliance on hired workers or tenants who could have made claims to

Hacienda and landlord systems differ significantly from each other

Table 4.3   Extent and characteristics of land reforms, selected economies and years

Country	Area		Beneficiary households		Average area per household (hectares)	Period
	Total area (thousands of hectares)	Percentage of arable land	Number (thousands)	Percentage of rural households		
Africa						
Egypt	390	15.4	438	10.0	0.89	1952–78
Kenya	403	1.6	34	1.6	11.85	1961–70
Zimbabwe	2,371	11.9	40	3.1	59.28	1980–87
Asia						
Japan	2,000	33.3	4,300	60.9	0.47	1946–49
Korea, Rep. of	577	27.3	1,646	45.5	0.35	1948–58
Philippines	1,092	10.8	1,511	24.2	0.72	1940–85
Taiwan, China	235	26.9	383	62.5	0.61	1949–53
Central America						
El Salvador	401	27.9	95	16.8	4.22	1932–89
Mexico	13,375	13.5	3,044	67.5	4.39	1915–76
Nicaragua	3,186	47.1	172	56.7	18.52	1978–87
South America						
Bolivia	9,792	32.3	237	47.5	41.32	1953–70
Brazil	13,100	11.3	266	5.4	49.32	1964–94
Chile	9,517	60.1	58	12.7	164.09	1973
Peru	8,599	28.1	375	30.8	22.93	1969–79

Sources: Eckstein and Horton (1978); El Ghonemy (1990); Grindle (1990); Hall (1990); Hayami, Quisumbing, and Adriano (1990); McClintock (1981); Powelson and Stock (1987); Prosterman, Temple, and Hanstad (1990); Scott (1976).

land ownership under a possible reform program (Diaz 2000; Horowitz 1993). They either resorted to extensive livestock production and ranching or, aided by significant credit subsidies, shifted to highly mechanized self-cultivation (Binswanger, Deininger, and Feder 1995). Former workers often joined the ranks of the landless, and in many cases the reforms made them worse off rather than better off. Table 4.3 presents a historical summary of land reforms.

Experience in Asia, but also in Africa and, to a lesser extent, in Latin America, illustrates that land reform can significantly improve household well-being. Land reforms in Japan, Korea, and Taiwan (China), all of which were accomplished under external pressure, have helped improve welfare, and often also productivity. Korea's land reform is anchored in its constitution, which imposes a land ownership ceiling of about 2.7 hectares per individual. In this context, large amounts of land were sold to tenants under favorable conditions, with average prices of about 1.5 times the yield, significantly lower than earlier market prices of about 5 times the crop yield. The land reform process took more than 10 years to complete, and in many aspects the state acted as an arbiter between landlords and tenants (Jeon and Kim 2000). Similarly in India, abolition of the land rights of rent collecting intermediaries is widely judged to have been highly successful, in contrast to the more limited success of land ceilings and tenancy legislation (Appu 1997).

In Kenya immediately after independence, the so-called million acre scheme distributed about 300,000 hectares of formerly white-owned large estates to small farmers, with positive economic results (Scott 1976). Even though the program gathered momentum, for example, by farmers forming groups to purchase larger farms, the government discontinued it, partly for political reasons (Kinsey and Binswanger 1993). Following independence in the early 1980s, Zimbabwe initiated a land reform program that redistributed about 250,000 hectares of land. Participation in the land reform program improved households' ability to accumulate assets, as well as their crop income, and reduced overall inequality (Gunning and others 2000). The first phase of land reform in the Philippines, based on a 1972 law, benefited about 0.5 million households. Aided by the availability of green revolution technology, this measure led to significant improvements in household welfare (Otsuka 1991). Effects in terms of investment and human capital accumulation have been estimated as significant, positive, and long term (Deininger, Maertens, and others 2002). Evaluation of the implementation of a subsequent law highlights that more progress has been made than often thought (Borras 2001), even though some beneficiaries still lack the complementary resources needed to make the land productive (Hirtz 1998).

Given the inequality of its land distribution, Latin America has a long history of land reform. Extensive land reforms in Bolivia, Guatemala (reversed in 1954), Mexico, and Peru have all been the outcomes of political struggles for the restitution of ancestral territories and the recognition of political rights. Encouraged by support from the general political climate in the early 1960s, which saw a smallholder structure as an effective bulwark against communism, land reforms moved ahead in Brazil, Chile (partly reversed in 1973), Colombia, Ecuador, and the Republica Bolivariana de Venezúela. In many cases, reforms had an explicit antifeudal purpose, seeking to displace the traditional agrarian elites and to eliminate labor relations based on peonage and servitude. In Nicaragua land reform occurred in the context of

Land reform can have a positive long-term impact, but success often remained elusive

145

a revolutionary change of government in 1979, although the impact on household welfare was limited because of the adoption of collective structures (Enriquez 1992). Various waves of land reform were carried out in El Salvador, where as in Guatemala, land was the subject of a long political struggle and played a key role in peace negotiations to settle armed conflict (Seligson 1995). In Chile a more egalitarian land distribution that was the outcome of the political turmoil of the 1970s was judged to have permanently changed the nature of Chilean agriculture, set off a boom in investment, and greatly activated land markets, thereby having a significant impact on the agrarian structure (Jarvis 1985).

Many reforms, especially in Latin America, remained incomplete

Traditional Latin American land reforms have often focused on access to land as opposed to a focus on broader household welfare and competitiveness of beneficiaries. Not surprisingly, because of a failure to provide beneficiaries with the prerequisites for making the best use of their land in a competitive environment, their record of solving the problem of rural poverty has been poor (de Janvry and others 2001). Another shortcoming of past land reforms in Latin America has been their tendency to substitute frontier settlement for a true effort at land redistribution in the interior of the country. The way in which land reform was undertaken in these contexts has been empirically linked to increased deforestation (Fearnside 2001). In addition, the implementation of some land reforms entailed perverse incentives. For example, where invasion of land can lead to expropriation, in some circumstances landowners and groups of individuals who are not the target group of the program may collude to bring about an expropriation, leading to increased violence (Alston, Libecap, and Mueller 1999b, 2000). Clearly countries should avoid setting up such perverse incentives.

Historical experience shows that giving access to land has been easier than securing the competitiveness of beneficiaries, and that by failing to do so a number of reforms remained incomplete (Warriner 1969). As a consequence, second-generation issues related to securing the competitiveness of reform beneficiaries, and in some cases even their tenure security, remain to be addressed. As illustrated in box 4.1 for the case of Colombia, the relative lack of success has led to considerable changes in land reform policies over time in many countries.

Reforms were often guided by short-term political objectives or an "agrarian" focus on full-time farming, with too little emphasis placed on productivity aspects, and consequently a limited impact on poverty

In most cases, the primary motivation for undertaking land reforms has been political rather than economic (Herring 1999). Past land reforms in many countries often aimed at calming social unrest and allaying political pressures by peasant organizations rather than increasing productivity.[4] Governments initiated many land reform programs in

Box 4.1 Changes in land reform policy in Colombia

LAND REFORM HAS BEEN ON THE POLICY AGENDA in Colombia since 1936, when a weak law to protect tenants and redistribute idle land proved ineffective and was unable to prevent violent conflict (Grusczynski and Jaramillo 2002). In 1961 the government set up a land reform agency, the National Institute for Agrarian Reform and Frontier Settlement (*Instituto Nacional de Colonizacion y Reforma Agraria*), to deal with the issue. However, the focus was on frontier settlement rather than on redistribution, and the continued existence of a distorted policy regime, together with a tendency toward re-concentration of land fueled by drug money, implied that land reform had only a limited impact: the Gini coefficient for land ownership shifted from 0.84 in the 1960s to 0.81 in the 1990s. Following macroeconomic liberalization and associated decreases in land prices, a law aiming

to replace the centralist approach with one where those in need of land would be able to obtain a grant (worth up to 70 percent of the purchase price up to a specified limit) that would enable them to acquire land in a decentralized manner from landlords willing to sell was passed in 1994, but unwieldy regulation and the fact that financing was limited to land purchases implied that, in practice, the process was little different from that in effect before (Rojas 2001). The inability of many of the farms established to repay their debts has led to sharp cutbacks in financing for land reform, the lion's share of which is now spent on the operational costs of *INCORA* rather than on investment, suggesting that any future attempts at land reform will have to pay attention to institutional issues (Lavadenz and Deininger 2002).

Africa and Latin America in response to political pressure (or to divert attention from other problems) rather than as part of a long-term rural development strategy. As a consequence reforms were often designed ad hoc and were out of line with actual needs and capacities, and commitment to them faltered once social emergencies subsided (Barraclough 1970). Moreover, individuals targeted to benefit from these programs were often the politically most vocal and well connected rather than those with the best ability to make productive use of the land or the most deserving poor (Alston, Libecap, and Mueller 2000; Deininger and Gonzalez 2002; Fearnside 2001). The political nature of land reform programs implies that even in situations where such programs can lead to significant improvements in productivity and household welfare, as in the case of Brazil, which has recently stepped up its efforts (see box 4.2), countries are unlikely to undertake them unless a strong political movement campaigns effectively for their implementation (Teofilo 2002).

Another element that has often reduced the impact of land reforms while increasing the cost of their implementation was the desire to award land plots large enough that beneficiaries could derive a livelihood from agriculture only. This was inefficient not only because it

---

Box 4.2 Brazil: land reform to combat poverty in a middle-income country

WITH A LAND DISTRIBUTION AMONG THE MOST unequal in the world, Brazil is characterized by a high level of landlessness and a politically vocal demand for land reform. Recent studies estimate the number of households that are candidates for land reform at 2.5 million. A land reform institute established in 1964, the National Institute for Colonization and Agrarian Reform, distributed 10 million hectares to about 300,000 families and colonized about 14 million hectares for some 75,000 beneficiary families in its first 30 years of its existence. Greatly increased funding and political resolve meant that since 1995 more households have benefited from land reform than in the previous 30 years. Overall, 584,000 households received a total of 18.7 million hectares of land. At the same time, and partly because of macroeconomic adjustment and the elimination of agricultural protection, which decreased land prices, the cost per household more than halved between 1995 and 2000 (Teofilo 2002).

As the constitution prohibits the expropriation of lands below a minimum size, the government has initiated a model of community-based land reform, whereby households receive grant resources for investments on land acquired through voluntary negotiation. While the program was politically controversial and its impact has not yet been properly evaluated, preliminary evidence suggests that where it was well targeted to the poor and implemented with the involvement and support of local nongovernmental organizations, it acquired land at low prices, significantly lower than those in the market or paid as compensation for expropriation of comparable land (Teofilo 2002), helped to expand the range of land and beneficiaries, and improved the welfare of participating households (Buainain and others 2002). The challenge is to guarantee the continued competitiveness of land reform beneficiaries within a policy framework aimed at development of rural areas.

---

neglected the diversity of livelihood options among the poor and the scope for beneficiaries to gradually expand their operations, but also because in many cases other constraints, for example, on the ability to obtain working capital, prevented beneficiaries from making full use of the land they received. Recent evidence that suggests that access to relatively small amounts of land, in some cases not even owned land, can provide significant welfare benefits (Finan, Sadoulet, and de Janvry 2002) supports this view, suggesting that awarding smaller plots could, in some settings, act as a catalyst and have considerable welfare benefits. In some Latin American countries, the land reform institutes that were in most cases established during the 1960s still implicitly or explicitly follow the full-time farmer paradigm, suggesting that significant institutional change, and much closer collaboration with local governments, will be required if the remaining reform agenda is to be tackled in a way that can be justified from an economic as well as a social point of view.[5]

While reform of landlord estates will benefit former tenants, all of whom already have experience with managing a farm, selecting land as well as beneficiaries is more difficult in situations where highly mechanized farms or previously underutilized lands are to be distributed to landless people. The desire to achieve quick results tempts reformers to redistribute land that already comes with productive infrastructure. The example of the Philippines illustrates that even in cases where land reform is justified, having a mechanism that selects truly underutilized lands, with minimum side effects for lands that are well utilized, is critical, because the productivity increase and thus the economic and social benefits to be derived from redistributing well-functioning plantations to former workers are likely to be extremely limited (Hayami, Quisumbing, and Adriano 1990). In many cases where this was done, lease-back arrangements soon emerged, whereby land reform beneficiaries immediately rented back their land to the former plantation owners under long-term contracts of 30 to 50 years, and neither productivity nor household welfare improved. Even where beneficiaries tried to establish their own cooperative or collective arrangements for cultivation, the outcome was often conflict among beneficiaries and de-capitalization of the farms, not dissimilar to what Peru experienced in highly mechanized sugar plantations in the 1970s (McClintock 1981).

In view of the significant wealth transfer involved, selecting beneficiaries through administrative agencies and de-linking land reform from other activities can lead to corruption. Establishing clear rules at the local level, encouraging participation by civil society, and emphasizing a systematic program of training and preparation will be critical (Deininger 1999). Land reform should also avoid the temptation to focus only on beneficiaries, and not neglect those, such as farm workers, who may lose their jobs but not receive land and therefore be negatively affected. For example, in Zimbabwe workers on farms that were subjected to redistribution constitute one of society's most vulnerable groups. Land reform that does not include provisions for this group may lead to further deterioration of their welfare and may well imply that the overall equity impact of reforms will be negative (Moyo, Rutherford, and Amanor-Wilks 2000). This is particularly relevant in the African context, where the challenge for land reform to provide the basis for a vibrant and productive rural sector is large and accomplishments thus far have lagged significantly behind expectations (see box 4.3).

Box 4.3   Challenges of land reform in South Africa

THE CASE OF SOUTH AFRICA ILLUSTRATES THAT land reform is one of a number of ways to increase access to land and productive assets by the poor. Based on a history of dispossession of its black population, livelihood opportunities in the country's rural areas are distributed in a dualistic fashion, and the rural economy depends on migrants' remittances and government handouts. To hasten development of the sector's productive potential, as of 1994 the country implemented a program of agricultural liberalization. This was complemented by a land reform program resting on the three pillars of tenure reform, restitution, and redistribution, given that markets will not help to redress the inherited bias in the asset distribution.

Tenure reform aims to increase tenure security for about 6 million households: 3.9 million in former homelands, 0.8 million permanent farm workers, and 1.3 million households in informal and squatter housing in and around urban areas. Restitution provides specific compensation to victims of forced "black spot removals," that is, wholesale eviction of black farmers located in white areas undertaken since 1913. More than 90 percent of the cases lodged come from urban areas, and progress was slow until the process was simplified in 2000. The aim of the program of redistributive land reform was to provide opportunities for the large number of black households wanting to gain access to land, but that lacked formal documentation. Originally the program provided a grant of up to about US$2,500 per household equal to the maximum subsidy under the National Housing Program. While this amount was not expected to be sufficient to establish an independent agricultural operation, it was designed to provide startup funds for an agricultural enterprise and has since been replaced by a more flexible scheme. Targets for land redistribution were extremely ambitious: the government aimed to transfer 30 percent of the country's 99.07 million hectares to about 3 million people between 1994 and 1999. After three years of operation, only about 200,000 hectares of land had been transferred to about 20,000 households, partly because of structural limitations (Zimmerman 2000).

Although some viable farm enterprises seem to have been established (Deininger and May 2000), much of the potential of land reform remains unrealized (Cliffe 2000; Hall 1998). In some cases bureaucratic processes and other restrictions have made it difficult for beneficiaries to enter into labor-intensive and high-return activities (Hamman and Ewert 1999). Indeed, households participating in government-assisted land reform projects perceive themselves as having lower levels of tenure security than formerly disadvantaged households who acquired land through private transactions outside the government program (Graham and Darroch 2001), and more land appears to have been redistributed to formerly disadvantaged groups through the market than through government land reform (Lyne and Darroch 1997). To increase decentralization and integrate the program into the broader rural development agenda, the government has modified the program to increase the role of beneficiaries, local governments, communities, and the private sector, thereby improving implementation.

Key Issues for Land Reform Programs

The fact that, as illustrated in previous chapters, the poor will often be unable to access land through the purchase market, implies that market forces are unlikely to be able to correct highly unequal and often inefficient distributions of land ownership (Carter and Zimmerman 2000).

Moreover, rental markets suffer from dynamic inefficiencies with regard to investment by either landlords or tenants (Jacoby and Mansuri 2002). In this case, land reform could have a role in helping countries not only to overcome the legacy of the past, but also to establish a basis for higher growth, distributed in a more egalitarian fashion, in the future. Increasing awareness of the importance of more egalitarian land distribution has led to renewed interest in redistributive land reform as a way to achieve sustained poverty reduction and improved productivity. Before the 1990s, the ideological and political constraints associated with the Cold War strongly affected the nature and impact of redistributive land reform. Since then, programs to adjust and eliminate agricultural subsidization have created a better basis for the productive operation of smallholder farms growing high-value crops. Domestic political tensions have caused land reform to re-emerge as an important issue in many countries where land remains highly unequally distributed, as well as in postconflict countries where access to land was often a central demand that led to the conflict.

At the same time, policymakers need to be aware that land reform is not a magic solution, and that a number of factors may affect the scope for successful implementation. Distortions that would increase land values should be eliminated and mechanisms to strengthen tenure security and improve access to land through (rental) markets need to be exhausted, or at least addressed simultaneously with any land reform program. Failure to do so will either make land reform unsustainable or increase its cost to a point where replicability will be compromised. Also, beneficiaries who want to participate in land reform will need to make a conscious choice for this type of program, especially in view of the experience of past programs that all too often put people on the land who would have preferred to receive other assets instead.

Beneficiaries' ability to make productive use of land acquired during land reform will depend on a change in the pattern of land utilization, clear delineation of responsibility for production outcomes, and the construction of complementary infrastructure suitable for smallholder agriculture. In many cases the lack of capital prevented beneficiaries from significantly increasing the efficiency of production, and in the case of redistributing well-run plantations may even have reduced productive efficiency (Hayami, Quisumbing, and Adriano 1990). Even if they are workers of the former farm, beneficiaries are generally unaccustomed to making independent entrepreneurial decisions, a constraint that is particularly important if realizing the benefits of land

Land reform can be justified on efficiency and equity grounds as one strategy for providing access to productive assets

Access to nonland assets and working capital is essential

151

reform requires significant modifications to cropping patterns or marketing arrangements. In the many cases where the farms acquired for land reform were not farmed at full capacity, were run down and decapitalized, or were highly mechanized, the neglect of simple works, such as clearing pastures, erecting fencing, and constructing basic infrastructure, or of the need for some startup capital, can often be linked to beneficiary failure and eventual desertion. Similarly, programs that were limited to the mere transfer of land to existing workers without being concerned about complementary investment, training, technical assistance, and provision of resources beyond the mere land were generally associated with limited equity and efficiency benefits.

Access to assets needs to be complemented by credit and output market access, transparent and participatory selection of beneficiaries, and fiscal viability

Without access to credit markets, land reform beneficiaries may well be worse off than they were before, when their landlords provided them with inputs, and possibly even with credit for smoothing consumption. A large-scale land reform program in Ireland actually worsened access to credit by limiting the ability of new landowners to mortgage land while at the same time cutting off the informal credit they had previously obtained from their landlords (Guinnane and Miller 1997). Severely restricted access to credit together with insecure property rights have led to widespread selling of land by former land reform beneficiaries in Nicaragua, often at prices below the productive value of the land (Jonakin 1996), as well as in Brazil (Alston, Libecap, and Mueller 1999a); Chile, where many land reform beneficiaries sold their endowments within a decade (Jarvis 1985); and the Philippines (Hayami 2000).

As many land reform programs award comparatively large grants to beneficiaries, there is considerable scope for moral hazard in beneficiary selection. To avoid this, nongovernmental organizations (NGOs) and farmers' organizations have an important role in helping to make land reform effective in transforming political as well as economic realities (Barraclough 1999; El Ghonemy 1999). Considerations of beneficiaries' ability to deal with risk will also be critical for land reform efforts. In the presence of credit market imperfections, the redistribution of property rights will improve incentives for work and investment, but lack of access to credit may constrain beneficiaries' ability to improve productivity and increase investment (Bardhan, Bowles, and Gintis 2000). Mechanisms to facilitate access to credit, possibly through micro-lenders (Carter and May 1999), will therefore be extremely important in land reform programs and may have been given too little attention in the past. In some cases arrangements whereby a financial intermediary supervises production, provides input credit in kind, and helps organize marketing have helped reform beneficiaries overcome obstacles posed by market imperfections, at least during the establishment phase (Deininger 1999). NGOs and grassroots movements can fulfill an important role in providing access to markets, technology, and other inputs critical to the success of land reform beneficiaries (de Janvry, Sadoulet, and Wolford 2002). As the record of government institutions in providing such services has not been encouraging (Molina 2002), strengthening and building on existing organizations to help with the initial establishment of land reform beneficiaries has many advantages.

A main reason why governments have favored land reform over other redistribution strategies has been the belief that with a constitutional provision for expropriating underutilized land, it would be a relatively cheap option. They have often used nonindexed government bonds as a means of compensation, thereby further reducing the real value of payments for land. However, governments' ability to acquire land at below market costs has been rather mixed, and they only seem to have acquired land at much below market prices in Japan, Korea, and Taiwan (China). In many cases governments ended up paying compensation above what could reasonably have been considered a fair market price following landowners' appeals to sympathetic courts. Lack of funding was a key reason for terminating land reform programs, especially where the continued existence of implicit and explicit distortions, for example, protection and the use of land as a tax shelter, drove land prices above the capitalized value of agricultural profits, which implied that compensation to landlords was overgenerous. In addition to increasing the fiscal cost of land reform, such distortions also reduce its sustainability, as they encourage land reform beneficiaries to sell out to large farmers, thereby contributing to the re-concentration of holdings. In addition to eliminating distortions, approaches that would make large rural landowners pay for at least part of the land reform efforts, for instance, through a land tax, may be worthy of greater attention. The use of land taxes to finance land acquisition could greatly increase the viability of such reforms at the macro level.

Implications

In practice, governments have applied a number of models to implement redistributive land reform. These include expropriating land, mostly with compensation; privatizing state land; auctioning off land owned by bankrupt enterprises; or providing potential buyers with a grant that can be financed out of general revenue, a more decentralized mechanism than the others. Specific programs differ from each other in broad parameters, such as overall cost, targeting to poor producers, and incentive structure, and in the extent to which they are achieving their goals. Common issues that, according to evaluations, have compromised the scope for poverty reduction inherent in these programs, include the following:

- A failure to pay sufficient attention to capacity building and training before beneficiaries gain access to land not only creates misperceptions about the nature and scope of a land reform program, but generally also results in the selection of beneficiaries who are better off or have pre-existing knowledge, thereby limiting efforts to reach out to the poor.

- A failure to carry out ex ante assessment of the viability of the activities to be undertaken by beneficiaries reduces the economic sustainability of land reform projects, lowering their potential to a point where the welfare impact of land reform is so limited that beneficiaries might desert their lands. This would also include an assessment of the extent to which access to land can be a way to lift rural households out of poverty.

- The desire to gain access to productive resources or bureaucratic inertia in the process of identifying land may prevent prudent assessment of the potential of the land received or of the obligations incurred by those obtaining the land. Unless this is done, large amounts of resources may be transferred to landlords or bureaucrats instead of to beneficiaries who, in addition, may assume unsustainable burdens.

As the example of Brazil illustrates (see box 4.2), a key precondition for land reform to be feasible and effective in improving beneficiaries' livelihoods is that such programs fit into a broader policy aimed at reducing poverty and establishing a favorable environment for the development of productive smallholder agriculture by beneficiaries. If these are in place, several instruments are likely to complement each other, for instance, expropriation with compensation, negotiated land reform, devolution of government land, and regular land sales as well as rental markets, with different modalities being suitable for different target groups (de Janvry and Sadoulet 2002). When land reform is appropriate, governments should carry it out transparently, in a nondistorting fashion, and as quickly as possible so as to avoid the possibility that regulations adopted to facilitate the implementation of land reform will negatively affect other avenues for accessing land. Irrespective of the political and institutional constraints that can hamper the implementation of effective land reform, interventions to advance redistributive reform should have a number of characteristics, namely:

- The land reform programs need to be integrated into a broader strategy for rural development to, among other things, provide an indication of the dimension of such a program and the role of land compared with nonland assets, and cannot be abstracted from the broader macroeconomic context.[6] Land reform cannot be limited to providing land, but needs to put households on a viable trajectory of development. This normally requires a strong element of training and capacity building, as well as provisions for complementary investment to make the land productive.
- The design of programs should be based on clear and transparent rules and provide incentives to maximize productivity gains, for example, by selecting underutilized lands or employing labor-intensive modes of land use. Landlords should be paid fair compensation, but not more.
- A multiplicity of paths to access land will need to underpin land reform, including, in addition to state-sponsored land transfers, progressive land taxation to increase the supply of underutilized land, divestiture of suitable state land, foreclosure of mortgaged land, and rental and sales markets. Unless these are implemented quickly and decisively, many of the measures—especially the imposition of low land ceilings, rent controls, and tenancy legislation in an attempt to increase the supply of land or to reduce prices—have been largely ineffective, and if they persist will have negative long-term consequences.
- The rights given to beneficiaries need to be secure and unconditional.[7] To allow access to credit and the possible movement of beneficiaries' children out of agriculture, beneficiaries should be allowed to rent or sell their land, perhaps after some initial period to give them enough time to become more familiar with the productive potential of their farms.
- A level playing field, that is, an undistorted policy environment supportive of smallholder agriculture, is critical if land reform interventions are to be sustainable.[8] This implies that in many cases interventions to increase land access need to be accompanied

by policy changes and institutional strengthening for provision of complementary services and access to markets and technology.

- The implementation of any land reform program should be decentralized, with potential beneficiaries and communities taking the lead to help beneficiaries access social infrastructure; diversify against risks; and allow them to take advantage of other infrastructure, such as markets, technology, and credit. Efforts at land reform should complement existing mechanisms for land access, for instance, rental markets and programs in other areas.

- The provision of some grant financing will be needed for land acquisition, complementary investments, and working capital. Such grants should be justified with respect to the benefits to society arising from the intervention, that is, increased social peace and productivity. They should be explicitly targeted toward the poor, and should ideally be provided in a form that facilitates access to credit and output markets in the future.

- The government has a role in providing training and technical assistance before and after the transfer of land to beneficiaries, in addition to providing targeted support in the form of grants or loans on a scale that is sufficient to establish economically viable undertakings, while at the same time striving to accommodate a maximum number of beneficiaries. Both types of support should be explicitly targeted toward the poor in a transparent way that precludes capture by powerful local elites.

- The rule of law, in particular, existing property rights that have been acquired in good faith in systems where property rights are privately held, need to be respected. Expropriation without fair compensation would not only have deleterious effects on the economy as a whole, but could also generate a wave of subsequent restitution claims that, in addition to being expensive to settle in financial terms, would create social conflict that is difficult to overcome. Taxation of land would be a more effective way to increase supply.

These principles apply across a wide range of different approaches to land reform, which suggests that countries have to confront the underlying issues irrespective of the specific land reform model used. Also, there is considerable opportunity for learning from past mistakes. To make such learning possible, rigorous, participatory, and transparent evaluation that is undertaken with the express purpose of providing feedback to the process of implementation will be needed.

Reducing the Incidence and Impact of Land-Related Conflict

EARLIER DISCUSSION HAS ILLUSTRATED THAT LAND CONFLICTS originating either in historical inequities or in increased land scarcity can have far-reaching impacts on social peace. Such conflicts are more likely to arise where (a) there is a history of large-scale, historical expropriation of land rights; (b) land becomes more valuable either because of technical and economic change or as a result of increased scarcity of productive land brought about by population growth; and (c) economic opportunities are lacking in other sectors of the economy and/or the state is in fiscal crisis. History provides many examples where the deprivation of land rights as a feature of more generalized inequality in access to economic opportunities and low economic growth have caused seemingly minor social or political conflicts to escalate into large-scale conflicts with devastating economic and social consequences. At times this has led to disintegration of the state, for example, in Burundi, Côte d'Ivoire, El Salvador, Guatemala, Rwanda, and Zimbabwe. This section discusses how land policy can help to deal with the issues arising in postconflict situations and how, by helping to reduce the conflict potential, it can prevent small-scale conflict from expanding into generalized violence. Given the limited attention this topic has received in past research, this section is more exploratory than others, aiming to draw attention to the issue rather than presenting firm and established policy conclusions.

Dealing with Postconflict Issues

In many countries, protracted and violent struggles have significantly reduced the performance of the agriculture sector and of the economy as a whole. Many analysts have emphasized the important role of peasant discontent in incidents of regional and national violence (Goldstone 1991; Huizer 1972; Kriger 1992; Migdal 1974; Moore 1966; Rueschemeyer, Huber, and Stephens 1992; Scott 1976; Skocpol 1979; Wickham-Crowley 1991). The losses caused by such conflicts are difficult to measure, but some notion of their magnitude can be gauged from their duration, which often lasts over several decades, as in the case of Colombia, where land has been a focal point for violence since the late 1930s, and from the intensity of conflict if it erupts. The example of Colombia,

Many historical conflicts have their roots in struggles over land

157

Box 4.4   The many facets of land conflict throughout history

IN GUATEMALA, COMMUNAL LANDS WERE IN EFFECT expropriated in 1879 by a law giving proprietors three months to register land titles, after which the land would be declared abandoned. Most of the "abandoned" land was then allocated to large coffee growers. Redistribution attempts in 1951-54 were reversed following a military coup in 1954, when virtually all the land that had been subject to land reform was returned to its previous owners and farms expropriated from foreigners were allocated in parcels averaging more than 3,000 hectares (Brockett 1984). Since then Guatemala has seen a repeated pattern of suppression and radicalization of resistance. The peace accords require land distribution as a critical element of the postconflict strategy, but progress thus far has been limited and has not always led to the expected improvements in productivity.

Smallholder land was similarly appropriated in El Salvador. A 1856 decree stated that all communal land not at least two-thirds planted with coffee would be considered underutilized or idle and would revert to the state. Communal land tenure was abolished in 1888. Sporadic revolts and countermeasures followed. Areas with severe land pressure emerged as centers of the revolt of 1932, during which thousands of peasants were killed (Mason 1986). Guerrillas promising land and other agricultural reform gained considerable support in

rural areas, and violence continued to escalate until 1979, when reform-minded officers engineered a coup and introduced land reform. Narrow eligibility rules sharply limited the number of beneficiaries of land reforms, and more than a decade of civil war ensued. The 1992 peace accord mandates additional land reform.

Colombia also demonstrates the perils of land-related tensions. Conflicts over land between tenants and large-scale farmers at the frontier escalated from isolated local attacks in the early 1920s to more coordinated tenant actions by the late 1920s. While the government considered various kinds of reform legislation during the 1930s, the law finally passed in 1936 vested rights in previously public lands with large landlords rather than with the tenants cultivating the land (Gruszcynski and Jaramillo 2002). A series of tenant evictions followed, leading to a quarter of a century of violence (1940-65). Land reform legislation in 1961 and 1968 regularized previous land invasions, but did nothing to improve the operational distribution of landholdings, and far fewer peasants benefited from the reforms than had previously been evicted (de Janvry and Sadoulet 1989; Zamosc 1989). Peasant land invasions intensified during the early 1970s, leading to the declaration of a state of emergency after 1974. The conflict has not yet been resolved.

together with many others, also demonstrates that the temporal link between unequal access to land and open conflict is often not immediate. Indeed, unequal land distribution often becomes a rallying cry in situations of economic hardship that are only indirectly related to land. Thus even though land-related grievances are often not the sole source of uprisings and violent conflict, failure to address them can significantly increase the potential for conflict in situations where, as in the case of South Africa and Zimbabwe, some groups have historically been deprived of their land rights (see box 4.4).

Especially where land was an important factor leading up to conflict, attention to land issues in postconflict situations is critical. Specific land-related aspects of such situations include (a) the need to use land to provide a livelihood for demobilized soldiers and displaced populations; (b) the presence of large numbers of refugees who may have been driven from their lands and whose documents to prove ownership have been destroyed or lost; (c) a particularly severe situation for female-headed households and widows, who typically account for 20 to 25 percent of all households in postconflict situations, and for orphans, whose land access is particularly insecure not only because they lack formal documents, but also because they originally accessed land only indirectly, for example, through the head of the household; (d) a breakdown of traditional village structures and the often well-balanced systems of informal secondary land and resource rights that were associated with them; (e) a rapid increase in the frequency and extent of land disputes, which often constitute about two-thirds of the civil case-load of a judiciary that is unable to cope with the demands, a situation that is often complicated by the direct involvement of the military or representatives of other state organs; and (f) a contamination with land mines and difficulties in physical movement.

Given the historical precedents, dealing effectively with land issues has often been a pressing need in the immediate postconflict period. The ability to deal with the requirements quickly and effectively has often made a major contribution to postconflict recovery. In Mozambique the government could only achieve the quick resettlement of about 5 million people after the peace agreement, because instead of drawing up elaborate plans, it relied on local institutions to mediate and resolve the conflicts that emerged. Once this had been accomplished, the right to occupancy by rural families, as well as a strong role of local institutions, was enshrined in the new Land Law, which was subjected to elaborate public discussion and debate involving 200 NGOs and 50,000 individuals (Negrao 2002). Locals and outsiders recognize that the new Land Law made a major contribution to social and economic stability (Tanner 2002). Similarly in Ethiopia, the ability to redistribute land quickly made an important contribution to the rapid reintegration of demobilized soldiers into the economy (Ayalew, Dercon, and Krishnan 2000). Recognition of land rights acquired through mere occupation and rapid resettlement of displaced people were critical in Cambodia, where calls for land users to register their claims resulted in the lodging of almost 6 million initial claims, and

Comprehensive resolution of land conflicts can help in postconflict recovery

159

Failing to resolve widespread land conflicts can affect long-term economic performance and social peace

observers have repeatedly identified the ability to deal with these quickly as an important element of postwar reconstruction (Zimmermann 2002).

By contrast, the case of Nicaragua illustrates that failure to resolve property claims quickly can affect productivity and investment in the long term. In this case, since 1990 property rights to land have been a hotly contested issue in the transition from a revolutionary state to a democratic market economy. Inability to arrive at an agreement on property rights issues has led to the establishment of a legal and institutional framework that instead of being conducive to conflict resolution, contributes to the multiplication of conflicts and their persistence over time (Everingham 2001). The macroeconomic consequences in terms of the cost to the government of compensating expropriated holders of property rights (estimated at between US$1.5 billion and US$2 billion) and to the private sector through the reduction of investment caused by insecure property rights are considerable. In addition, the need for the poor, in particular, the beneficiaries of the Sandinista land reform, to spend scarce resources to defend their property rights has a decidedly negative impact on equity.

In countries where protracted confrontations and social violence over property rights threaten to undermine unconsolidated democratic institutions, attention to establishing a legal basis for clarifying land rights that is unambiguous and simple to implement will be essential. This will often include strong provisions for adverse possession, as in the case of Cambodia. In this context, many of the desirable elements of legal and institutional reform, as well as land regularization in general, will be relevant, although they will have to be implemented in a more speedy fashion than in traditional programs of institutional reform and land titling.

Avoiding a Buildup of "Low-Level" Conflicts

The empirical literature is unambiguous in highlighting that unresolved conflicts prevent investment and that establishing institutions to resolve these quickly can, especially in peri-urban areas, help unlock considerable amounts of investment (Kasanga and Kotey 2001; Merlet and Pommier 2000). While rigorous quantification is scant, a recent study from Uganda finds that unresolved conflict reduced output on a plot of land by more than 30 percent (Deininger and Castagnini 2002). Figure 4.1 illustrates this difference in productivity between plots with

Figure 4.1 Productivity of plots with and without conflict, Uganda, 2001

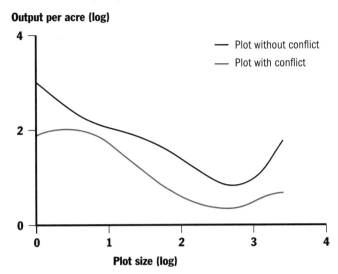

Note: Nonparametric regressions of productivity. The difference in output is statistically significant throughout. Bootstrapped confidence bands have been omitted.
Source: Deininger and Castagnini (2002).

and without conflict using nonparametric regression. As it affected women and widows disproportionately, such land conflict was detrimental to equity. Furthermore, recent changes in the legal status of women's land rights and the local implementation structure appear to have increased rather than reduced the likelihood of conflict.

High levels of population growth with limited opportunities for non-agricultural employment and the resulting competition for land and threat of landlessness can give rise to serious land conflicts and accompanying social tensions and violence, both across and within communities and within households. These demographic and economic changes create multiple sources of conflict around land, including (a) land scarcity and the associated appreciation of land resources; (b) emergence of monetized land transactions in situations where previously land was inalienable; (c) opportunistic re-interpretation of earlier contracts, especially if they involved outsiders; (d) clashes between traditional and modern authorities with at least partly overlapping responsibilities and often different norms and clienteles, which cause them to issue verdicts that contradict each other; (e) grievances over appropriation of land by

Land conflicts are more likely to arise during demographic and economic transitions

161

certain groups or outside powers, including the declaration of environmentally protected areas that have a long history of utilization by communities; and (f) state land policy that eliminates all community ownership of land, questions foreign ownership, or establishes new legal and administrative provisions with little consultation, and therefore often with only a narrow basis for implementation and a lack of understanding by officials.

The wide variety of circumstances in which conflicts can arise is illustrated by case study evidence pointing to conflict between different types of land use such as farmers and herders, between locals and migrants, and between generations within families. Conflict within families often starts to erupt in relation to inheritance-related land transfers. In West Africa the younger generation, especially those unable to find nonagricultural employment, often competes for land with the descendants of migrants and questions their parents' giving away land cheaply to "foreigners," an issue that can easily spill over into intercommunity relations, with a potentially far-reaching impact. Unless broad growth occurs in the economy, such conflicts may be difficult to avoid. To deal with them appropriately, three elements appear to be crucial, namely: (a) the development of an incentive structure that rewards settlement of conflicts and insistence on informal resolution as a first step, (b) the ability to give legal validity to agreements reached as a result of such informal settlements, and (c) a system of conflict monitoring and information dissemination to help establish norms of acceptable behavior that would help affected individuals resolve conflicts among themselves.

Minor land-related conflicts can easily escalate

The absence of mechanisms for informal negotiation and arbitration and the lack of institutional capacity to decisively resolve conflicts within, but especially across, communities in a way that is perceived as fair generate a potential for even minor conflicts to fester and eventually escalate into violent strife (Kuran 1993). In Rwanda during 1988-93, the buildup of land issues led to a gradual increase in the potential for conflict and provided the conditions that finally led to the outbreak of civil war in 1994 (Andre and Platteau 1998). Investigators have identified the lack of adequate mechanisms for resolving conflict or clarifying the nature of land transactions as prime reasons for continued ethnic cleavages in Ghana (Fred-Mensah 1999) and Côte d'Ivoire (Chauveau 2000), where recent events illustrate the link to more generalized violence. Devoting sufficient attention and resources to establishing mechanisms to facilitate the systematic monitoring and resolution of land-related conflicts is particularly relevant, because land tenure issues are often strongly related to ethnicity and for conflict to escalate along this dimension is often easy.

Setting up a legal framework that minimizes the emergence of new conflicts and provides accessible mechanisms and procedures for settling old ones is a necessary, but insufficient, condition for a sustainable reduction of the conflict potential. The latter also requires the creation of an administrative or judicial infrastructure that can quickly and authoritatively settle conflicting claims. In doing so, documentary evidence, proven traditions, and oral testimony may need to be accepted as evidence of established rights where appropriate. The case of Mexico illustrates the magnitude of the claims that can be involved and the attention that may need to be given to establishing appropriate mechanisms for conflict resolution, including informal ones. Following far-reaching legal changes, the government launched an intensive program of providing legal assistance to make those affected aware of their rights and established a decentralized system of 42 agrarian courts covering the whole country. To make resolution of land conflicts more agile and accessible to beneficiaries, and at the same time preclude overburdening the judicial system, the court system was to accept only cases where prior efforts to arrive at a settlement using nonjudicial means of conflict resolution had failed. Despite the reduction in the number of cases this implied, the judiciary spent more than four years dealing with the accumulated backlog of cases (Zepeda 2000). This highlights the need to adopt procedures that, while being accessible to those in need of redress, make efficient use of public resources, possibly by complementing the formal apparatus with a system of alternative conflict resolution mechanisms.

Limited outreach or credibility of state institutions can create a vacuum that leads to a power struggle at the local level. Where this is the case, working with and building on existing institutions in an incremental fashion may be the only option. This is illustrated by the case of Burkina Faso, where, even though the state nominally owns all the land, it often lacks the institutional presence and ability to enforce legislation, implying that state institutions are unable or unwilling to settle land disputes (Kevane and Gray 1999). Experience illustrates that such an approach to recognizing growing individual control over land could involve, for example, formal documentation of land transactions. Reliance on written records, signed by participants, could help eliminate part of the bias of existing informal systems toward the wealthy and powerful, and at the same time reduce the arbitrariness that arises from the ability to re-interpret historical facts according to the circumstances.

Avoiding escalation of conflicts requires clear rules and legitimate and representative institutions

Building on existing institutions is often the only option

163

Similar approaches could be adopted with respect to legal recognition of solutions found to specific conflicts (Lavigne Delville 2002). Such mechanisms for conflict resolution, and accessible institutions to resolve conflicts in an authoritative manner, will be particularly important to avoid the tendency for institutional shopping whereby those affected by conflict choose whatever institution they think will be most favorable to their case and may even pursue parallel channels. Experience illustrates that such parallelism leads to wastefully high spending on legal battles and implies that resolution of conflict through one channel may not resolve the issue, and often contributes to a situation of generalized insecurity where the ability to bring (and through appropriate actions win) spurious claims can undermine the credibility of the entire property rights and associated judicial system.

Access to information is essential

In addition to using local institutions as much as possible and giving legal validity to informal resolution of conflicts, knowledge of the law and the institutional responsibilities by those who might be affected by conflicts is critical. Deficient knowledge about the applicable legal provisions and processes has been one reason why members of former cooperatives in Nicaragua failed to regularize their land ownership status. Their ignorance and the lack of clarity on institutional responsibilities was often exploited by powerful outsiders, with negative consequences for equity (Merlet and Pommier 2000). Similarly, in Russia and other CIS countries, limited awareness of legal provisions and ignorance about the proper institutional channels implies that new "landowners" are often unable to engage in collective action to resist pressures from individuals with better connections and to gain access to the inputs and markets they need to make productive use of the land. In many cases this has enabled former collective managers to gain temporary or permanent access to land for free or for extremely low payments. Case study evidence suggests that in such situations dissemination campaigns and the establishment of legal aid centers can have a significant impact (Prosterman and Hanstad 1999).

Access to information and proper channels for complaint and, if needed, appeal, are also relevant if land conflicts involve the state or its representatives. In China, for example, resolving conflicts between individuals and the collective is difficult, partly because farmers are unaware of their rights, and partly because the collective is often both judge and defendant. Yet the country has an effective approach for addressing conflicts between households. The new Land Contracting Law deals with these issues, but for it to become effective, wide dissemination and publicity involving specific examples will be required (Li 2002).

Land Taxation

THE LAST DECADE HAS WITNESSED A TREMENDOUS INCREASE in the decentralization of responsibilities to lower levels of government throughout the developing world (Bird 2000). At the same time central governments often assign responsibilities without making adequate resources available, and even in cases where they do so, the way in which resources are transferred often generates incentives that are inimical to effective service provision. For example, excessive reliance by local governments on central government transfers weakens fiscal responsibility and accountability to the users of such services. In the extreme, this can lead to a situation where unsustainable subnational debts can threaten macroeconomic stability, resources are spent in nontransparent ways, and the quality of service delivery is poor. A number of observers have identified the failure to devote sufficient attention to the availability of local revenue sources as a key deficiency of recent decentralization initiatives (Boadway 2001; Eaton 2001). Taxes on land and real property provide an ideal mechanism to increase fiscal responsibility in a way that has few distortionary effects. While such taxes have both advantages and disadvantages, they may have considerable potential to strengthen fiscal responsibility at the local level in a way that might encourage more effective use of land.

Because real property is immovable, implying that the only way in which households can react to differentials in property taxes is through relocation, taxing it will be much less distortionary than levying taxes on sales or income.[9] Moreover, property taxes will often be capitalized into property values in a particular community, thereby coming close to being a benefit tax. Land taxes have therefore traditionally been considered to be an ideal revenue source for local governments (Brueckner 2000). If a land tax is based on the potential monetary yield from a certain plot under normal conditions, it will have minimal disincentive and distortionary effects, and by taxing resource rents may contribute to more efficient use of a valuable natural resource. Indeed, local taxes are used extremely effectively in the United States, and some evidence indicates that levying taxes on land can actually induce development (Oates and Schwab 1997).[10] On this basis, observers often note that a land tax provides one of the few mechanisms to sustainably fund local governments without recourse to transfers, which may distort incentives and break the link between the level at which public services are provided and the payment for such services

Lack of adequate revenue affects the viability of local governments

Land taxes are ideal local taxes

Countries vary widely in the extent to which they use land taxes

Taxes on land and property are an important source of local revenue in many countries, and more so in developing than in industrial or transition countries.[11] In the 1990s land and property taxes accounted for 40 percent of all subnational taxes in developing countries, 35 percent (up from 30 percent in earlier decades) in industrial countries, but only 12 percent in transition countries (Bird and Slack 2002). They financed slightly more than 10 percent of subnational expenditure in industrial and developing countries in the 1990s, although only little more than half that much in transition countries. To assess the rationale underlying these large differences and what might be done to change this situation, the follows paragraphs review key issues that need to be taken into account with regard to property tax implementation.

To use land taxes effectively, an accurate cadastre and an assessment capacity are critical

Administering a tax on land effectively and equitably requires having an official record, or cadastre, of the size, value, and ownership status of each tract of land and its productive capacity along with information on the costs of outputs and inputs. Land tax administration also requires a property tax law that assigns property rights and tax obligations and an administrative organization that keeps the register up-to-date and assesses, collects, and enforces the tax (Bird 1974).

Taxes can be based on area occupied, on property value, or on a system of self-assessment and can be levied on the value of unimproved land or of land plus buildings. While levying a tax on unimproved land would be least distortionary from a theoretical perspective, land and buildings are normally subject to taxation. The assessment rates may be the same for land and buildings, or may be different, and possibly adjusted for location. Under an area-based assessment system, a charge is levied per square meter of land area or building space, something that can be extremely distortionary, because it does not adjust for differences in land quality. At the same time, determining a market value based on comparable sales, depreciated cost, or rental income may be difficult, especially where markets are thin, and mass appraisal techniques to deal with this problem have become increasingly widespread. A final possibility is self-assessment, that is, requiring property owners to place an assessed value on their own property, with different mechanisms applied to provide incentives for truthful declaration (Strasma 1965; Tanzi 2001). While appealing in theory, especially for poor countries with limited administrative capacity, such approaches have not been widely accepted, and any perceived lack of fairness may quickly undermine compliance. If land quality cannot be observed at low cost, a land tax may impose higher effective tax rates on landowners with low-quality land than on those with high-quality land. This effect may be large enough to make a land tax less desirable than an output tax (Skinner 1991).

Even though realization of the desirable features of a land tax requires that local governments are free to determine tax rates independently, in many developing countries local property taxes remain highly centralized. They are thus far from the ideal of responsible local autonomy, which combines the ability to set tax rates locally with a hard subnational budget constraint. In some countries, for example, Chile, Japan, Thailand, Tunisia, and Ukraine, the central government essentially sets the rate; in others, such as Colombia, Hungary, and the Philippines, some local discretion within a predetermined range is allowed; and in only a few, for example, Argentina, Canada, and Kenya, do local governments have complete discretion in setting tax rates.[12] Greater autonomy in setting tax rates can be highly desirable, especially in the case of CEE where, as discussed earlier, the privatization of enterprise land has largely stalled, because cities and local governments are unwilling to give up the secure and regular rent payments that they receive directly for vaguely defined property taxes over which, in many cases, they have little control.

In many countries poor tax administration rather than the more conceptual issues identified earlier imposes the greatest bottleneck on effective collection of property taxes. As a consequence, either the tax register does not include all taxable properties, and collection rates, as well as enforcement, remain low. Considerable devolution of power to subnational governments along with a strengthening of their administrative capacity may be needed to facilitate improvement.[13] The issues associated with administration are the typical technical ones and include identification, assessment, and collection. Identification is achieved through a fiscal cadastre that contains a description of each property, a definition of its boundaries, an indication of ownership, and the value of the land and improvements (for a more detailed review of cadastres see Dale and Mclaughlin 2000). In many countries, for example, Hungary, Latvia, and the Philippines, this information is dispersed among different agencies. Completeness of the revenue base is also a problem, for example, in Guinea and Kenya, where the fiscal cadastre covers only 33 percent and 20 to 70 percent of taxable property, respectively. As assessment requires specialized expertise, it may be contracted out rather than performed by local government employees. In addition to the problem of coordinating different government offices, key issues are the need to keep the system

Local governments need to have the authority to establish tax rates and the capacity to administer tax collection

up-to-date and to provide an appeals mechanism. Collection, by contrast, is mostly a local government function. Although tax arrears as a proportion of taxes collectible are low in most industrial countries, for instance, 3 to 4 percent in Japan and the United Kingdom, they can be large in developing and transition economies, and amount to 50 percent in Kenya and the Philippines and almost 70 percent in Russia.

Equity concerns need to be incorporated in the tax structure

The literature is clear that if risk is high and insurance markets are unavailable or imperfect, introducing a significant land tax (based on average incomes) can be disadvantageous to the poor, and in extreme cases can lead to greater land concentration, as Hamid (1983) shows for India. In addition, when insurance markets are imperfect, a mix of output taxes and land taxes is always superior to either tax in isolation for the same reason that a sharecropping contract is preferable to a fixed rental agreement (Hoff 1991). The simplest way of dealing with this concern is to have a land tax from which owners of extremely small holdings are exempt, as is the case in many countries. In addition to the positive effect on equity, this approach can also be justified by the high administrative cost that would be involved in taxing small holdings.

High visibility makes property taxes politically difficult

One of the reasons for the limited effectiveness of property taxes may be that because of their visibility they are difficult to introduce politically and fall largely on the rich who, at the local level, may hold political power, and thus effectively resist the collection of such taxes. Unlike income or sales taxes, property taxes are not withheld at source, but have to be paid directly. The implied visibility is desirable from a decisionmaking perspective, because it enhances the accountability of local governments and corresponds with the fact that property taxes normally finance local services, but that same visibility makes their introduction more difficult. This is further exacerbated by the fact that the values on which land taxes are based will rarely be available from impersonal markets, but have to be determined administratively. Moreover, the property tax base is relatively inelastic, implying that yields are unlikely to increase significantly over time.

A number of authors have argued that, conceptually, progressive land taxes would be more appropriate for reducing the tendency to hold land unproductively than land ownership ceilings and other instruments reviewed earlier. Taxes could reduce the scope for land speculation and induce large landowners to sell out or to use their land more intensively (Hayami, Quisumbing, and Adriano 1990). Because they encourage more intensive land use, land taxes could even be envisaged as a means to finance programs of redistributive land reform. Experience with this

Box 4.5   Land tax reform in Kenya and Indonesia

EXPERIENCE WITH LAND TAX REFORM IN KENYA and Indonesia illustrates the importance of simplicity and fairness in administering taxes. In Kenya, well-intentioned policies to strengthen local governments' capacity for tax collection have not had the desired success. Taxpayers did not feel they had received improved local services or that the taxes were administered fairly. Local governments had limited independence in setting tax rates, and incomplete tax rolls and varying valuation standards led to political resistance. By contrast, in Indonesia the enactment of a single tax, the land and building tax, with a single flat rate of 0.5 percent of land value helped to curtail exemptions for residential property and to considerably broaden the tax base. Revenues have already increased significantly, and the positive experience thus far will allow giving local governments some discretion over rate setting to increase local accountability and control over the amount of property taxes collected (Bird and Slack 2002).

in the past has not been encouraging. Many countries, including Argentina, Bangladesh, Brazil, Colombia, and Jamaica, tried to implement progressive land taxes. In all cases success was limited because of difficulties in valuation, in enforcing compliance, and in dealing with litigation surrounding the issue (Bird 1974; Strasma and others 1987). Part of the reason for the almost universal failure of taxes on rural land in these cases was undoubtedly the political clout of landlords in rural as compared with urban areas, their domination of local governments, and the formidable technical obstacles that created. Both were much higher when these reforms were attempted than they are today. Nonetheless, in view of both the political and administrative challenges associated with the implementation of land taxes, careful ex ante evaluation is needed and a simple, possibly flat, tax that may be waived for very small landowners may be more advisable than a complicated structure that invites evasion and political resistance (see box 4.5).

Devolution of Control of State Land

IN PRINCIPLE, STATE OWNERSHIP OF LAND DOES NOT PRECLUDE the award of secure, long-term leases to individuals that would allow entrepreneurs to make the investments needed to increase the productivity of the land and use it as a basis for enterprise development. In practice, however, unclear legal provisions, lengthy and nontransparent procedures, and a limited ability by either the central or local governments

State ownership of land can hamper private sector development

to credibly commit in the long term can all increase tenure insecurity, reduce investment incentives, and pose an obstacle to productive use of land. The areas involved can be substantial, for example, in Ghana estimates indicate that the state owns 40 percent of urban and peri-urban lands, most of which are left undeveloped (Kasanga and Kotey 2001). To the extent that such land is not used optimally, the transfer of land ownership or use rights, depending on the legal situation, to the private sector, could not only improve land use, but could also increase government revenue and eliminate a potential source of corruption.

In addition to legal issues, some of which have been discussed earlier, there are three areas of concern in relation to implementation, namely, (a) the recognition of adverse possession on state lands and speedy regularization procedures to occupants of such lands in peri-urban and rural areas; (b) the devolution of control of state land, either through long-term leases or through full ownership and the resolution of issues, for example, debts of predecessor enterprises, that might preclude such action; and (c) the clear circumscription of the state's right to expropriate land in the public interest that is linked to reduced scope for arbitrary and discretionary action by individual bureaucrats in this context.

The negative impact of land ownership arrangements on private investment is especially pronounced in Africa, where many newly independent states originally adopted the legal framework inherited from their colonial masters with few modifications, and subsequently often further increased rather than decreased bureaucrats' discretionary power over land. Purportedly to pursue equity and social justice, in the 1970s many African governments established state ownership or a monopoly of the state over land allocation, and in many cases nationalized land, something that has often given rise to high levels of mismanagement and corruption (Mabogunje 1992). In rural areas, this has often implied an attempt to replace traditional authorities that, while certainly not without shortcomings, were at least accessible and recognized at the local level, with a state bureaucracy with neither the necessary outreach nor the requisite social legitimacy or accountability. In situations where land is still relatively abundant, this can imply serious delays and obstacles to investment, and at the same time can reduce the scope for local communities to benefit from such investment. A study of 10 francophone Sub-Saharan African countries shows that with the exception of one country, the state has not yet renounced its monopoly on land, although the situation has improved in some countries (Durand-Lasserve and Royston 2002b).[14]

In many cases households have occupied state land for long periods of time, but the lack of formal recognition creates uncertainty and prevents occupants from making long-term investments, and in some cases even from using the land as collateral for credit, and may give them little recourse against evictions or extortion. In all these situations, the authorities provide a low-precision, and thus low-cost, certificate of usufruct that protects against eviction and can be gradually upgraded over time. Doing so can provide considerable benefits, as has been demonstrated in Brazil, where such certificates are known as *usucapios* (Fernandes 2002), or in India, where they are referred to as *pattas* (Banerjee 2002). By contrast, protection for possession of land in good faith in urban and rural areas is much weaker in Indonesia and nonexistent for state lands in Venezuela.

The ability to obtain legally recognized rights, even if unchallenged occupancy in good faith cannot be documented formally, but is instead based on oral evidence, is particularly important where administrative capacity is limited. In Mozambique, for example, legal provisions in favor of adverse possession provide immediate security to occupants independent of the government's limited capacity to survey and record such rights. Outside investors who want to obtain unoccupied land have to negotiate with neighboring communities, something that can effectively avoid land grabs and at the same time ensure that local communities derive net benefits from such investment (Negrao 2002). Respecting occupants' rights and making oral evidence admissible as proof of such rights has also proven to be critically important for a speedy transition toward stability at reasonable cost in postconflict situations, for example, in Cambodia, where any other system would have been infeasible. In instances where the same plot may be subject to complex and multiple layers of rights, slow maturing of possession into a fully recognized legal right can have equity and efficiency advantages and be much preferable to drawn-out and costly court proceedings.

The privatization of enterprise land and state farms in Eastern Europe and the CIS provides an example of the various pitfalls and consequences of government ownership of land. Most of these countries traditionally issue separate titles to land and buildings, and many are only now starting to privatize land, years after they began privatizing buildings on the land. The most pressing legal issue is to define the land to which building owners are entitled. Even though such land is currently subject to serious mismanagement (Kaganova and Nayyar-Stone 2000),[15] local governments perceive land ownership as a critical

Where state land has been occupied for a long time, giving rights to occupants can have large equity benefits

Devolution of state land can improve land utilization and spur investment

171

Box 4.6   The continuing challenge of state ownership

WHILE THE INCIDENCE OF INEFFICIENTLY MANAGED state land is particularly large in Eastern European transition economies, it is by no means confined to these. In Estonia, about 75 percent of land remains under state ownership and is being used on the basis of short-term leases, which is inimical to the necessary structural transformation. In the Czech Republic 800,000 hectares remain state owned and privatization is proceeding slowly. In the Slovak Republic most of the cooperatives continue to operate as before, and average almost 2,000 hectares. State ownership of the land of former state farms is still an issue in Poland, where less than 10 percent of land is private and about 70 percent of land

under the holding company APA is leased out, with 1.1 million hectares remaining fallow. In Romania about 1.7 million hectares of high-quality arable land continue to be administered under state farms. A 1999 law has removed the uncertainty about land ownership that had blocked progress, but remains to be fully implemented. In Croatia the privatization of the remaining collective structures is slow because of their size and the complexity of privatization procedures (Csaki and Nucifora 2002). While less prominent, state farms also remain a large part of the landscape in West Africa (Gueye, Ouedraogo, and Toulmin 2002) and northern Africa (Gharbi 2002).

---

revenue source that is more predictable than taxes, and in addition generally use their authority over such land to impose often arbitrary land use regulations. As a result, political opposition to eliminating public land ownership is strong, and given the insufficiency of the leases to provide a basis for investment, much of this land remains seriously underutilized, similar to much of the rural land in a number of countries (see box 4.6).

In countries with a history of collective land exploitation, the transfer of land to individuals is in many instances impeded by the fact that the land may have been used as collateral for loans, often to previously collective enterprises, that have not been repaid. To address this issue, it will often be necessary to combine the transfer of land rights from the state to individuals with a comprehensive debt workout. Although the details of such an arrangement will depend on the case at hand, experience shows that the social benefits from such an arrangement, in terms of increased investment and the ability to impose a hard budget constraint in the future, are often more than enough to quickly outweigh the costs of a write-off of part of the debt (Csaki and Lerman, 2000).

In many countries governments "own" considerable amounts of land in peri-urban areas, where high population density and rising land values imply high land values and considerable demand for such land. This land is often significantly underutilized. In this case, devising transparent mechanisms to transfer ownership to individuals or groups can have major benefits in terms of equity and, in the longer term, in terms of investment. Where equity concerns do not dictate otherwise, auctioning such land off to the highest bidder in a transparent fashion can benefit both local governments and private investors, as demonstrated by a number of successful privatizations (Rolfes 2002). If combined with a system of land taxation, this could yield significant economic benefits. For example, in China the auctioning off of use (now ownership) rights to peri-urban land has not only opened up a source of considerable revenue for local governments, but has also significantly improved urban land use (Dowall 1993).

National and local governments tend to have the authority to override private ownership rights using compulsory acquisition procedures for the broader public benefit. Governments should do so only for clear public purposes and with prompt payment of full market value as compensation, subject to a process that protects owners from abuse, for example, involvement by the courts. In many countries, the way in which governments have used their prerogative for zoning, eminent domain, and expropriation of land have often been a major source of political discontent and have lacked transparency. The extensive use of the powers of the state to expropriate property, the lack of a procedure for due process, or the failure to pay fair compensation seriously undermine the security of individual property rights, especially in peri-urban areas where land is rapidly appreciating. This undermines incentives for investment in areas where such investment would be most profitable or needed, and often leads to the accumulation of large tracts of land in the hands of the state or well-connected politicians and government representatives.

Attempts by the state to exercise its powers of eminent domain and pay only nominal compensation for land improvements made by private users are widespread virtually all over the world. In China, village officials frequently expropriate village land for nonagricultural uses, often factories, in the "public interest" or to rent out village land for use by nonvillagers. As the village owns the land, current users do not receive any compensation, even though the officials often derive handsome personal gains. A survey found that such practices affect about 20 percent of villages, that this practice is increasing rapidly, and that little consultation takes place with the villagers who have the primary right to the land. The pervasiveness of the practice led to a policy document that identifies it as one of the principal dangers to the integrity of landholdings at the village level and emphasizes that village authorities do not have the power to expropriate village land

Unregulated expropriation can affect governance and reduce efficiency and equity

Limiting discretionary bureaucratic behavior is particularly critical in peri-urban areas

173

(Li 2002). In Africa the taking of land by governments with minimal or no compensation is a key reason for landlessness in peri-urban areas (Kasanga and Kotey 2001; Kironde 2002). Anticipation of government expropriation often leads to informal land sales from the poor to richer and more influential entrepreneurs who can better protect their rights or obtain compensation in advance of expropriation. As prices charged are only between 10 and 20 percent of the market price when the risk of expropriation is high, this implies a significant transfer of resources from the poor to the rich (Kironde 2002). In Mexico users are unwilling to wait for expropriation with relocation or low compensation, but try to preempt it through by selling their land in the informal market, thereby contributing to further expansion of unplanned and informal settlement. This considerably increases the cost of providing infrastructure and services (World Bank 2002b).

Land Use Regulation and Zoning

Where externalities exist, limits on individuals' land use decisions are justified

EVEN THOUGH DIRECT MANAGEMENT OF LAND THROUGH government agencies has rarely been effective, there is a clear role for government to ensure that resources that embody broader social and cultural values and benefits, such as landscapes, biodiversity, historic sites, and cultural values, will not be irreversibly destroyed by myopic individual actions. Furthermore, public action is warranted to reduce undesirable externalities and nuisances, to provide incentives for the maintenance of positive external effects such as hydrological balances, and to facilitate cost-effective provision of government services. Ensuring that these goals can be met will first require attention to the nature of property rights and associated enforcement institutions, but can also involve the adoption of specific regulations. Environmental effects can often be internalized if property rights are designed in a way that encourages prudent management of natural resources, for example, by awarding property rights to groups that will be able to internalize the externalities arising from land use; by strengthening the capacity of these groups for collective action; or by making award of property rights, either to individuals or to groups, subject to certain restrictions or rewards for desirable behavior.

Governments employ zoning regulations to assign specific uses, or prohibit particular uses of certain lands, to overcome environmental and other externalities that would not be internalized if pure market forces were to determine land use. For example, local jurisdictions can use zoning regulations to prevent undesirable externalities, including cutting forests, converting agricultural land to specific uses (for example, industrial), or erecting specific types of buildings on a plot. In urban areas the objective of zoning is to prevent commercial or industrial activities from locating in residential areas and creating noise and pollution, to avoid congestion, to provide environmental benefits such as green space, and to preserve historical sites, views, and neighborhoods. Systems for zoning are also routinely used to lay out town plans and thereby facilitate orderly development and effective service provision. With the exception of establishing protected areas to serve environmental needs, zoning is more likely to be justified in urban and peri-urban than in rural areas (Brandão and Feder 1995), where the main focus is on regulatory intervention to avoid negative externalities from land use. In general terms, the purpose of government regulation is to enforce the rights of the broader public to environmentally acceptable land use against the rights of landowners to exploit the land for private benefit. Zoning standards will impose compliance costs, and should therefore be imposed only in cases where there is a clear external benefit or where negotiation and the imposition of restrictions at the community level would not yield the desired outcome.

In general, zoning is justified if negative externalities need to be reduced by more than the cost of zoning enforcement. This is likely to be the case if externalities are large, if policy instruments to deal with them are available, and if an apparatus to implement these instruments impartially exists (Malpezzi 1998). As earlier discussion illustrates, implementing regulation is never costless, and in developing countries in particular is likely to add to the demands placed on scarce administrative capacity. This implies that the requirements for implementing specific regulations must be matched to the available institutional and enforcement capacity. Where the state aims to regulate land use to avoid externalities and provide public goods, interventions should thus be based on broad and well-informed discussion of the costs and benefits and their incidence and a critical assessment of the state's capacity and comparative advantage to actually perform such a regulatory function. The latter is particularly important, because bureaucrats often tend to underestimate the scope for communities to establish and police standards locally based on voluntary cooperation. Indeed, in many instances, especially in rural areas, the government taking control has proved to be less effective and efficient, if not outright disastrous,

Key requirements for zoning regulations include implementation capacity, transparent and fair allocation of costs and benefits, and predictable rules designed to minimize compliance costs

175

than control by those directly affected (Curtis 1991). Investigators have documented that nationalizing forests previously governed by local user groups in India (Jodha 1996), Nepal (Jodha 1996), Niger (Thompson and Wilson 1994), and Thailand (Feeny 1989) has had often ambiguous effects on equity as well as efficiency. The imposition of state control over pastoral resources was relatively ineffective and may have contributed to open access situations (Ngaido and McCarthy 2002). Governments should therefore focus on issues that will not be adequately tackled either through markets or through community action at a more informal and voluntary level.

In any given situation, the costs of imposing certain zoning regulations, which will not be independent from the availability implementation capacity, should be clear to those who are involved and will eventually have to bear them as well as to those who make the decisions, and these costs should be allocated in a way that is perceived as fair. Evidence illustrates that failure to analyze the cost in advance can easily imply that well-intended regulation will end up hurting the poor. For example, restrictions on the conversion of agricultural land at the urban fringe are often inconsistent with the need to make land and services available for urban expansion at a reasonable cost. This has considerably increased land prices in peri-urban areas and driven land sales in these areas into informality, at a significant cost to the poor. For example, in Malaysia inappropriate zoning standards are a primary cause for housing prices being significantly above the costs of production. Recognition that this is likely to be a particular burden to the poor prompted the government to offer subsidies to this group as partial compensation. Evidence suggests that this has been costly and ineffective, and that the poor were more likely to choose informality (Malpezzi and Mayo 1997). The inverse relationship between informality and the imposition of regulations is also evident from India, where estimates put the size of the informal sector at 55 percent in Mumbai, where land markets are highly regulated; 40 percent in Ahmedabad; and only 22 percent in Bangalore, which has significantly fewer standards and restrictions on land markets (Durand-Lasserve and Royston 2002b).

Another frequent application of zoning is the declaration of certain places as parks, forests, or protected areas, which is associated with the prohibition of agricultural cultivation, and in addition precludes the acquisition of private property rights to such land. To avoid protecting areas with limited environmental value at a huge administrative expense, ways to quantify the costs and benefits of protection will be needed

(Deininger and Minten 2002). In cases where land is already owned by individuals or a group, the use of market substitutes, for example, through payments for the provision of environmental services, can provide an alternative to achieve the desired outcomes at low cost.

Where zoning is justified, regulations should be clear, predicable, and easy to implement. To be effective, government regulation needs to be matched by constraints on official discretion, transparent and effective rules, and formal and informal mechanisms for appeal and dispute resolution. Ensuring that regulations regarding land development are well justified is particularly important in developing countries, where both enforcement capacity and the ability to pay by those demanding housing is more limited. For example, in Africa overly rigorous permit systems impose large transaction costs and delay private investment, generate price distortions, breed corruption, and undermine governance (Mabogunje 1992). By contrast, a lack of regulation can greatly increase uncertainty over land rights if it gives rise to ambiguity and bureaucratic discretion. In a number of Eastern European countries, for example, lack of clarity about regulations pertaining to peri-urban land has considerably slowed the overall process of land privatization (Butler 2002). Economic preferences are often imposed in the guise of physical planning, thereby inducing corruption and interference in economic decisionmaking. This is particularly important because states have all too often used the need for appropriate land use regulation, especially in peri-urban areas, as a pretense to impose state ownership of land or other ambitious undertakings. When discretionary power was transferred to corrupt bureaucrats, this has often made landowners decidedly worse off, without clear benefits to society.

Zoning and other land use regulations should be established based on a clear assessment of the capacity needed to implement them, the costs of doing so, and the way in which both costs and benefits will be distributed. Failure to do so has often implied that centrally imposed regulations could either not be implemented with existing capacity, that doing so was associated with high costs that were predominantly borne by the poor, or that they degenerated into a source of corruption. Too little thought has often been given to providing mechanisms that would allow local communities to deal with such externalities in a more decentralized, and therefore a less costly, way. To facilitate this, it is essential that local governments have sufficient capacity and are aware of the advantages and disadvantages of different approaches. A gradual devolution of responsibility for land use regulation to local governments, if coupled with capacity building, could make a significant contribution to efforts toward more effective decentralization. Eventually, the decision on whether to impose land use restrictions is clearly a political one, and it will therefore be important to clarify the costs and trade-offs involved and to set priorities among competing objectives so as to maximize their contribution to overall welfare. The principle of having correspondence between the costs and benefits of zoning regulations implies that to the extent that the externalities are of a local rather than a global nature, land use planning and development control, like property valuation and taxation, should be at the discretion of local authorities.[16]

Putting Land Policy in Context

Land policy can help address structural issues that affect the poor

THE ANALYTICAL DISCUSSION IN THE PREVIOUS CHAPTERS, AS well as evidence from qualitative studies, demonstrates that insofar as the rules governing access to and the distribution of the benefits from one of the economy's main assets, land policy is important for poverty reduction, governance, economic growth, and environmental sustainability. This importance is often not reflected in countries' development strategies, where reference to land is either tangential or lacks specificity (Gueye, Ouedraogo, and Toulmin 2002). To be effective as an instrument for reducing chronic poverty and creating the preconditions for sustained long-term growth, the emphasis on delivery of basic services that characterizes much current thinking on development will need to be complemented with attention to more deeply rooted structural issues. This implies that factors related to tenure security, broader land access, and appropriate regulatory activity by the state discussed in this report will have to be translated into policies and programs within the context of specific countries. To do so, two principles are key. First, the long-term nature of the issues at stake will require a strategy that integrates actions in the legal, institutional, and policy arenas, taking into account the impact of other policies on land access and use wherever appropriate. In this context, key land policy indicators can have an important function, both for problem analysis and to measure progress toward achieving overarching policy goals and make comparisons across different countries. Second, even if addressed in a very technical fashion, land issues will always be highly political. It is therefore essential, especially in view of the wide range of stakeholders involved, to build local capacity to conduct policy dialogue and analysis.

Establishing a Land Policy Framework

In view of the wide variation of conditions across countries, it is impossible to implement "patent recipes" without an awareness of local conditions. Doing so can result in ad hoc interventions that can have serious negative impacts. For example, if the legal basis is inadequate, modernizing land administration institutions and land records may be of doubtful value. Issuing titles in the absence of a clear legal framework or in an environment where institutional responsibilities are not clearly delineated can easily increase rather than reduce conflict and may even become a source of higher tenure insecurity. Finally, where access to land is highly dualistic, property rights are insecure, information available to participants is scant, and access to institutions is wealth-biased, the activation of markets can easily bring about socially undesirable land concentration. The potential for such undesirable outcomes, together with the complexity and politically controversial nature of land issues, implies that the establishment of a land policy framework to guide the sequencing of specific interventions in the sector can have multiple benefits in generating consensus, helping to prioritize actions, and (by ensuring participation in the implementation and monitoring of these interventions) avoiding costly errors.

Given the long-term nature of interventions in the area of land policy (see box 4.7 for an example from Ghana), integration into the broader development strategy is particularly relevant to provide a basis for relating land policy to other interventions. Experience from Eastern European transition economies illustrates that having land markets function and contribute to greater productivity will be impossible if land rights are not well defined. Indeed, liberalizing markets in situations where either land rights are ambiguous or other markets do not function well has historically been one of the main facilitators of land grabbing. Clarifying land rights early on in the reform process, even if done in a very gradual manner as in China and Vietnam, is also important, because subsequent improvements such as infrastructure will be capitalized in land values, thereby tending to cement existing ownership relations. As sacrificing quality for quantity is not desirable either, low-cost methods of land registration are often sufficient initially and can be complemented by a more elaborate procedure at a later stage.

In line with the broad topics discussed earlier, an overarching framework for land policy should address (a) the property rights to land and tenure security and its impacts, (b) the scope for accessing land and the functioning and impact of market and nonmarket channels, and (c) the

Land policy needs to be integrated into a long-term strategy

179

Box 4.7 Ghana: an example of a comprehensive land policy

THE GOVERNMENT OF GHANA'S LAND POLICY, which it elaborated over a period of about two years of policy discussion, illustrates the type of issues to be tackled in such a strategy. These include

- *Reviewing the legal situation with a view to endorsing pluralism.* Customary owners control about 78 percent of the land, with the remaining area owned by the state either directly (20 percent) or indirectly with the state holding legal interests and the community holding beneficial interests (2 percent). This implies that no land policy can afford to neglect the issue of customary tenure, something that is reinforced by the fact that in many areas the state does not have enough institutional presence or resources to fully assume responsibility for the multitude of functions associated with land administration. This would imply that the best option would be to focus on a regulatory role and leave implementation to customary institutions and the private sector.

- *Privatizing government land that is not needed.* Eliminating state ownership over vast tracts of urban and peri-urban land that the government is unable to develop would not only remove a major impediment to increased investment, but would also send a powerful signal and stimulate the development of the private sector. In cases where charging for this land will not have a negative equity impact, the money gained would be used in part to compensate those whose lands had been expropriated in the past without proper compensation. At the same time, land revenue that is currently paid to central or local governments would be re-assigned to customary owners in return for them assuming essential functions in transparent and accountable land administration and management.

- *Ensuring security of tenure.* Preconditions for secure title are systematic registration of allodial (root) title, adequate education of communities,

and registration of all group members holding a beneficial interest in land (as opposed to just the leaders, who may then be able to dispose of the land without the knowledge of other group members). This will go a long way toward ensuring investors' confidence in the land sector.

- *Ensuring access to land.* The agricultural system is still largely effective in guaranteeing access to land, but in urban areas the powers of compulsory acquisition need to be curtailed. All disposal of public land has to be done in the open market, and compulsory acquisition has to be strictly circumscribed to the public interest. Adequate and prompt compensation, resettlement for those displaced, and a right of preemption if the land is not used as designated are not guaranteed. All surplus acquired land should be returned and past compensation claims should be settled (probably as annual rents or by using equity shares).

- *Restructuring land institutions.* The institutions dealing with land are overstaffed, underpaid, and have a reputation for lacking transparency. The land policy envisages bringing them together under one independent commission responsible for assuring title and managing public land that would be fully self-financing to ensure autonomy from political pressure. Also the management of community lands and revenues, which is currently one of the functions of the public sector at the central level, would be discontinued and given back to communities. At the same time, mechanisms to monitor the performance of traditional institutions and hold them accountable to specific standards would be established.

- *Increasing community involvement in managing forest reserves.* This would reduce state intervention in the management of these resources and instead increase communities' stake in promoting long-term, sustainable management.

Source: Adapted from Kasanga and Kotey (2001).

broader regulatory framework governing land and related sectors. Box 4.8 contains a series of questions and quantitative indicators. Most of the information needed should be available either from standard household surveys or can be included at little cost if it is not, or from administrative records. Even though not all of these will be relevant in a given situation and others might need to be added, they can provide a useful frame of reference, as well as a tool for initial analysis and a basis for discussion among stakeholders, in addition to permitting international comparison across countries. In doing so they can help to obtain consensus on the most urgent measures and generate backing for implementing specific policy measures. Building a strategy based on these indicators will also provide a foundation for monitoring to assess the extent to which specific policies have the desired effect and contribute to overarching policy goals. In this context, capacity building, piloting, and further research will all help to monitor and gradually refine indicators as implementation proceeds.

Even though linking land policy to the broader policy environment and sequencing interventions in light of an overall strategy are important, the formulation of a policy framework must not be an excuse for inaction. Indeed, the initiation of pilot activities often permits confronting vested interests and initiating a meaningful policy dialogue. To prevent such dialogue from degrading into a repetition of familiar prejudices, it should from the beginning be combined with the implementation of pilots and their careful and independent evaluation (or the conduct of field studies) to inform the debate. This is particularly important, because implementation of the general principles identified earlier in any given context will require that they be adapted to the specific legal and institutional context prevailing in a given country. To maximize the learning effect from pilot projects they will have to be designed appropriately and in a way that resists the temptation to use anecdotal evidence rather than rigorous evaluation to measure success. Careful design and rigorous evaluation of pilot activities generate benefits beyond the country conducting the pilot, and such pilots would therefore be an appropriate area for international funding.

Pilots can be important in situations where, even though agreement on the problem to be addressed has been reached, the benefits and costs of certain actions are not well established, or where debate about the specific approach to be taken is ongoing. Pilots can test different approaches in parallel, thereby providing input into the policy discussion as well as evidence about the extent to which a specific approach can be implemented in a given situation and can help evaluate the impact of specific measures before progressing to large-scale implementation.

Pilot projects can be used to develop solutions adapted to local conditions if they are replicable and carefully evaluated

Box 4.8   Elaborating and monitoring a land policy framework: key issues and indicators

INDICATORS THAT CAN BE USED TO MEASURE THE performance of institutions and the extent to which policy is contributing toward overall objectives are of great relevance to demonstrate that progress is being made toward meeting certain policy objectives over time and to facilitate comparison across countries. Although not all of them will be relevant in any given situation and the list is by no means exhaustive, a number of criteria and indicators that can serve as a reference and starting point to assess the need for more in-depth investigation in each of the main areas discussed in this report follows:

Tenure security. What is the overall amount of land held under different, formal and informal, tenure regimes and what is the tenure security associated with each of them? What is the share of land held de jure and de facto by women under different forms (individual, joint, and so on)? What share of parcels and of the total area are formally registered? What is the cost in terms of time and money for landowners to register a plot of land under different tenure systems? Are institutional responsibilities clear? What is the subsidy element involved and how does this compare with the value of the land? Are the rights of indigenous people or herders appropriately protected? How important is land as an asset and a source of livelihood for the poor? What is the inequality of the ownership or operational distribution of land? How much land in rural or urban areas (public and private) is informally occupied by squatters? What criteria and mechanisms allow squatters to obtain recognized property rights? What is the number of land conflicts, where are they concentrated, and how many new conflicts arise each year? How long does resolving a "typical" conflict take, what are the obstacles, and are solutions considered to be fair? Are mechanisms of appeal available? How much land does the state hold, what is the justification for such landholdings, and what mechanisms could be used to divest such land?

Markets and productivity. What share of land is transacted annually in sales and rental markets? How do prices for different types of land compare with each other and with the profits from agricultural cul-tivation? Are prices of past land transactions available to interested parties or the public? Is mortgage financing for land acquisition available? Is inheritance regulation unfavorable to women? Is there evidence of undue fragmentation, and if so, what are proximate reasons and suggested remedies? What are interest rates and other requirements? Are rents controlled, and if so, what is the share of land to which such controls are applicable? What is the level of informal land transactions? Is a land reform program in effect? Are there administrative restrictions on land sales or the prices to be paid in such transactions? If so, what are the mechanisms used and how much land has been transferred at what cost to how many beneficiaries over the last five years? What is the cost (in terms of fees, other monetary expenses, and time, absolute and relative to the value of the land) to register a land transaction and to subdivide land? What are the prices of average pieces of land under different tenures in rural and urban areas?

Regulatory framework. What is the land conversion multiplier and the price ratio of agricultural to non-agricultural land? Are big price differences apparent between different types of land that cannot be explained by differences in inherent quality characteristics? What are the tax rates on agricultural land, who has the authority to set them, who receives the money, and how much of the potential revenue is actually collected? How much of the land base is state owned and how does its productivity compare with that of comparable privately owned land? Are maps and cadastral and registry information readily available and at low cost to those who request them? What is the share of costs recovered from fees for service? What percentage of the land is held as collateral by financial institutions, and how much of it is in default? How long does it take a local or a foreign investor to get a permit in rural areas and in urban ones? How long does it take (and what does it cost to register a mortgage? Can creditors foreclose on property that is in default? How long does it take to complete the process, what is the cost, and what is the likely price that a creditor is going to obtain in a forced sale?

Well-designed and thoroughly evaluated pilots can be particularly useful to identify mechanisms and procedures (including the provision of legal assistance) appropriate for land regularization in a given context. They are likely to be essential to develop approaches to informally resolve conflict that are adapted to local realities, and are therefore effective. Similarly, even though strengthening women's land rights is an imperative that does not appear to lend itself to pilot approaches, the earlier discussion illustrates that large gaps are often apparent between the intention of laws and their actual impact. This implies not only considerable scope for monitoring in general, but also that evaluating specific instruments to improve women's rights, including awareness campaigns to inform women about their rights, may be appropriate. Another area where pilots to close gaps in knowledge concerning appropriate policy interventions would be suitable revolves around instruments for pro-poor land administration, in particular, means to protect and manage the rights of occupants at low cost at the local level. The same is true with respect to mechanisms that could help redistribute land through market and nonmarket channels.

Aspects of Process and Political Economy

Initiatives in the area of land policy entail institutional and other changes that will almost inevitably have to confront powerful vested interests, making it essential that they be based on solid analysis that is backed by local capacity and a broad policy dialogue. In cases where the focus of land policy has shifted or where little attention had been paid to land issues in the past, building the capacity to move ahead with implementation will be critical. This is particularly relevant where existing land institutions have been established under different circumstances and may be too fragmented or not have the skills needed to respond effectively to the requirements of an agreed land policy that enhances tenure security, provides broad access to land, and uses government regulation to prevent externalities and provide public goods. In many cases this will include a decentralization strategy and involvement by the private sector, local governments, and other stakeholders to ensure that the strategy addresses the appropriate concerns in an analytically justifiable way.

The presence of vested interests requires paying attention to political economy aspects

While the earlier discussion has already addressed many of the substantive principles that are important in developing a land policy

Process issues are important

183

framework, the process of going about this task is likely to be equally important. Examples show that the process of consensus building, which includes the private sector, NGOs, and academics, in addition to government representatives, is extremely important, both for the ability to implement and to identify priority activities in light of existing budget constraints and links to a poverty reduction strategy. The importance of a policy dialogue to gain political acceptance can be illustrated by comparing the cases of Colombia and Mozambique, both countries where conflict related at least partly to land played a major role. Postwar Mozambique had to repatriate about 5 million refugees and, more important, increase communities' rights to the land while at the same time helping to foster investment. To achieve this the government initiated a broad and participatory process that led to the formulation of an innovative law that has contributed significantly to the re-establishment of peace and broader economic development (Tanner 2002). By contrast, in 1994 Colombia passed a land reform law with little public discussion. As a consequence, finalizing the most basic regulations took almost three years, making the required institutional adjustments was impossible, and during 1995-97 a large amount of resources and political capital was spent on implementing a law that was poorly suited to realities on the ground (Gruszcynski and Jaramillo 2002).

Building local capacity is essential

The need to adapt land policies to the socioeconomic realities of a given situation implies that local capacity, both technical and socioeconomic, is an essential element in any process of policy reform that no amount of foreign technical assistance will be able to substitute for. Support to establish the necessary technical expertise poses considerable challenges, especially in a decentralized environment with rapidly changing technology, and constitutes an area where broad international support will be appropriate. The example of the United Nations Working Party on Land Administration in Eastern Europe illustrates that considerable advances can be made even within a short time frame. At the same time the need to complement technical skills with expertise on social, financial, legal, and economic issues, depending on the specific context, is likely to increase. This capacity building could include providing knowledge about land valuation and taxation; running legal literacy campaigns; and training local bodies in mediation and informal conflict resolution, land use planning, and basic economic concepts. Even though the specific approach to land issues will need to be country specific, sharing experience on common elements can add considerable value and enrich the policy dialogue.

Conclusion: Continuity and Change since 1975

THIS REPORT DOCUMENTS THE EVOLUTION OF THINKING ON land policy and some of the emerging areas of consensus. Highlighting how the experience gained during recent decades has expanded the scope of land policy compared with the World Bank's (1975) *Land Reform Policy Paper* permit demonstrating these changes and at the same time identifying challenges for the future, both in terms of the general relevance of land issues, and more specifically in the areas of land tenure, land markets, and land access and use. Such challenges arise both in terms of implementation and in identifying areas where evaluation of past and emerging experience could help improve knowledge and the ability to design more appropriate interventions in the area of land policies.

While development practitioners have long recognized the importance of property rights and land policy for long-term development and poverty reduction, recent research and operational experience, as illustrated in this report, have improved understanding of these issues in ways that are highly relevant for policy. Research has improved our understanding of the links between the distribution of assets, the channels for accessing land that are open to households and entrepreneurs, and longer-term economic and social development. These links include not only the scope for investment and access to other markets, but also the empowerment of the poor and their resulting ability to have their voice heard and to hold accountable local institutions that often derive much of their power from the ability to control access to land. Recent research also indicates the potentially far-reaching impact of insecure tenure, inequality in land access, and ill-functioning land and factor markets on a wide range of development outcomes and some of the channels through which such impacts may come about.

Other areas that were not covered in the 1975 paper include the relevance of land for broader social conflict, the need to pay particular attention to the vulnerable in designing and implementing land policy interventions, and the broader repercussions of the design of land-related institutions on governance and the accessibility of government services. This implies that despite the historical and institutional complexity of land issues and the long-term nature of any programs to deal with them, interventions in the area of land will have far-reaching implications and a narrow focus on only one or two policy instruments may not be appropriate. Evaluation of the wide variety of innovative approaches that have been implemented in different places and at different times can be utilized in a

The relevance of land issues is now appreciated

185

more systematic fashion to stimulate the policy dialogue, build capacity, and inform policymakers. More systematic learning from the successes and failures of the past could probably help to save considerable amounts of resources, while at the same time facilitating the policy dialogue, especially across countries. At the same time, support for strategies to implement new land legislation and careful monitoring of the impact these have on governance and social capital, provision of public goods, and private investment at the local level could provide interesting insights regarding the broader impact of land tenure arrangements.

Different ways to increase tenure security have been recognized

Tenure security, one of the key goals of public land policies, can be achieved under different modalities of land ownership. Instead of an often ideological stance in favor of full private ownership rights, long-term secure and transferable leases will convey many of the same benefits to owners and may be preferable where full ownership rights and titles would be politically controversial or too costly. Also, in the past land policy interventions often paid too little attention to protecting the rights of women and the vulnerable. Failure to do so can have negative economic and social consequences. Rather than striving to "modernize" the institutions that manage land rights at the local level, building on, and where needed adapting, existing ones is often more effective and efficient. This implies not only paying greater attention to existing institutions, but also emphasizing dissemination and assistance to create awareness and to help people exercise their rights, even where a good legal basis is available. A greater focus on local institutions is also warranted because, in some instances, central government institutions managing land rights have developed into a source of ambiguity, corruption, and red tape. As reforms will run counter to powerful vested interests, local technical and socioeconomic capacity to help support them is essential. Financial sustainability is required to make the institutions administering land rights contribute effectively to secure tenure and, through low-cost implementation, the long-term sustainability of the land administration system. While the earlier report did not deal with institutions, it is now recognized that failure to do so can jeopardize implementation and should therefore be avoided.

Land issues often become most acute in peri-urban and urban areas. Because the same regulatory and institutional framework will apply to rural and urban land even though modalities of implementation may vary, separation between the two is frequently difficult to justify, and approaches now often deal with both simultaneously. Better definition of property rights to reduce uncertainty can make a significant contribution to enhancing the functioning of markets, reducing the scope for discretionary bureaucratic intervention, and improving the climate for private sector investment. Better evaluation of innovative approaches that build on these conceptual advances would include in-depth assessment of the effect of formal recognition of women's land rights on their ability to assert their interests in intrahousehold bargaining; their vulnerability and risk-coping options; and their propensity to make land- and nonland-related investments, for example, starting businesses, and to accumulate and transfer human and physical capital across generations. Similarly, the broader impact of land-related policies and legislation on economic and social outcomes and the interaction between different types of interventions in bringing them about needs to be reviewed.

Considerable conceptual advances have also been made in relation to the operation of land markets and their impact. The experience of transition economies demonstrates that markets are complex institutions that do not emerge automatically, and that even where they can be made to work well, they are not an end in themselves, but should contribute to broader social goals. Through its macroeconomic policies, the legal framework, and the institutions to implement it, government plays a critical role in creating the conditions and incentives within which markets operate. At the same time, a long history of failed interventions in land sales and rental markets has illustrated that in most cases the best contribution government can make is to provide secure land rights, reduce the costs associated with land transactions, provide infrastructure to eliminate credit market imperfections, and offer safety nets to avoid distress sales. This has a number of implications.

Overemphasis on sales markets compared with rental markets is unwarranted. Given that wealth constraints and credit market imperfections pose considerable barriers to land access by the poor, relying on sales markets as the primary means for land access would be inappropriate. Rental markets are more important quantitatively and can make an important contribution to productivity, and often to poverty reduction as well. Steps to increase tenure security and reduce transaction costs through standardized contracts and better means of enforcement and dispute resolution and more systematic dissemination of information will be critical to fully realize the potential of rental markets and facilitate the emergence of long-term contracts.

Where administrative restrictions on the functioning of tenancy persist, there is a strong case for better documenting the economic losses, especially for the poor, that such restrictions are likely to cause, and for

Markets for rental and sales are better understood

187

identifying opportunities to eliminate such barriers that are beneficial to all parties—for example, by combining policy reforms that would improve the opportunities for rental markets with explicit recognition of the rights acquired by sitting tenants and an improvement of tenure security for both landlords and tenants. Direct government intervention in markets to bring about "desirable" outcomes is rarely effective, but tends to weaken property rights and decentralized land transactions. It also encourages bureaucratic discretion, which will reduce not only the confidence of private investors, but in most cases be particularly inimical to the poor who will be least able to afford the added costs thus created. In situations where land rental markets work well and demand for sales markets is unsatisfied, steps to ensure access to financial markets, including the use of assets other than land as collateral, could help reduce the need for distress sales and provide potential buyers with the necessary liquidity. Encouraging land sales markets can take various forms, ranging from taxing land and promoting the functioning of markets to providing direct grants for establishing small production units or expropriating nonproductive land (with compensation).

Even though our understanding of the way in which land rental and sales markets operate has improved, the equity benefits from land access through rental markets, the obstacles faced in the process, and the possible long-term impact of such access remain imperfectly understood. Assessing the impacts of land access and ownership on household welfare, the circumstances under which land rental can be an effective tool for poverty reduction, and the scope for renters to make the transition to owners is important. More systematic assessment and quantification of the potential for government policy to activate rental markets and to help to prevent socially and economically undesirable results, and of the potential advantages of eliminating such intervention in cases where it does not provide such benefits, is needed. Where real incomes are relatively high and increasing, but where land ownership remains highly fragmented, many think that projects aimed at land consolidation will be justified. Careful evaluation of the costs and benefits of experiments involving flexible and low-cost market and nonmarket approaches to consolidation is of great interest.

Governments have a role in ensuring effective land use

In situations where a combination of historical processes and policy distortions has led to a land distribution that implies substantial underutilization of productive economic resources, the operation of markets alone will not provide the poor with access to land at the level and speed required to deal with deep-rooted problems of structural backwardness and deprivation. Where land and other policies have discriminated against specific groups in the past, actions to empower the poor by providing them with equal access to economic opportunities will be justified.

Given the multiple channels through which a highly unequal distribution of land ownership can reduce economic and social development and the immediate welfare and productivity benefits that can often be derived from measures to transfer land from large, unproductive holdings to small producers, government involvement to hasten such restructuring can be justified as an investment in a country's long-term future. This has led the World Bank to provide loans, based on a case by case approval, for use in land redistribution efforts that are targeted toward the poor and can be shown to have a clear productivity benefit.

Note that such interventions constitute investments that can yield direct and indirect economic benefits in the form of more intensive land use, higher productivity, and greater incomes for beneficiaries. Where these benefits can be demonstrated and are shown to be superior to alternative options, and where transparency in beneficiary selection is ensured, there is no reason for outside donors not to support such interventions both technically and financially. In addition to their important role in helping to adjust operational approaches toward redistributive efforts that use land as a catalyst for improving beneficiaries' welfare, such evaluation is also likely to provide significant insights into the broader role of access to land and other assets as a means of overcoming poverty. In relation to the benefits and costs of helping landless or tenants make the jump to landowners, a number of programs of redistributive land reform can provide evidence that would facilitate a comparison of different approaches, while longitudinal evidence on past beneficiaries of land reform could provide insights on the longer-term impact.

Different options for interventions to bring land use closer in line with social needs constitute a second area where a considerable amount of innovation has taken place, and where the evaluation of experience could provide insights that are likely to be of value beyond the immediate context in which such policies were implemented.

Although the focus of this report is on the substantive issues, the fact that land issues are highly country specific, of a long-term nature, and often politically controversial, implies that identifying priority areas and integrating these into an agreed long-term framework becomes essential. In view of the wide variation in conditions across, and even within, countries and regions, more work will be needed to adapt the principles identified in this report to specific contexts. This will imply

Implementing these insights is a challenge for the future

189

spelling out which of the various policy options will be the most appropriate; how they can be translated and adapted to a specific institutional framework; whether any changes in the legal and regulatory context will be necessary; how changes should be prioritized and sequenced; and how to devise indicators for monitoring and impact assessment that would indicate not only whether implementation keeps up with expectations but, more important, what the expected impact has been and how it might compare with outcomes from alternative strategies and approaches.

Given the complex nature, the cost, and the long-term horizon of land-related interventions, any attempt to address them in a sustainable way will have to use the synergies derived from collaboration with others. As this report documents, thinking on land policy has evolved considerably over the last decade, leading to a modification of ideological positions and a considerable convergence of opinion on basic principles among major stakeholders. The challenge ahead is to translate the emerging agreement into specific programs at the national and regional level that can be integrated into countries' broader development strategies. The hope is that this report provides the basis for a policy discussion that would allow this, and that in so doing it will be possible to continue the spirit of open discussion and collaboration that has characterized the preparation of this report.

Notes

1. In Hungary, the use of financial rather than physical restitution has reduced the administrative requirements and delays associated with the latter. It also allowed giving priority to current occupants of land, thereby reducing the possible negative impacts on productivity.

2. In Romania, for example, the courts were inundated with real estate cases expected to take up to five years to resolve (Dumitru 2002).

3. Households plots, which emerged in the 1930s, entitle households to small plots for home consumption.

4. This would be consistent with the interpretation of land reform as a piecemeal strategy by the rich to avoid the imminent threat of revolt—with backtracking as soon as the threat weakens, as modeled by Horowitz (1993).

5. The case of Colombia, where in recent years about 75 percent of the land reform budget has been spent on the operational costs of the land reform institute and about 25 percent on acquiring land and settling beneficiaries, illustrates this dilemma (Rojas 2001).

6. Economic distortions—for instance, marketing restrictions or differential subsidies to products from large farms, as well as noneconomic interventions such as subdivision acts, that were established to maintain large farms—need to be eliminated if land reform is to have any chance of success.

7. Many land reform programs make the rights given to beneficiaries conditional on "efficient" use and impose restrictions on the ability to transact and inherit. Even if well intended, this has often given rise to politically motivated manipulation.

8. The rapid undoing of land reform by beneficiaries in many countries legally or illegally selling their properties to large landlords, often the former owners, illustrates the importance of an undistorted policy environment.

9. Fischel (2001), for example, has argued that the property tax in the United States is like a benefit tax, because taxes approximate the benefits received from local services. To the extent that this is the case, using local property taxes to finance local services will promote efficient public decisions, because taxpayers will support those measures for which the benefits exceed the taxes. Both the benefits derived from such local services as good schools and better access to roads and transportation and the taxes used to finance such services are capitalized into property values.

10. Purchase of development rights pays the landowner for the unearned increment of land values in exchange for strong deed restrictions that limit the use of the property, whereas land value taxation taxes land more heavily than improvements, thereby encouraging the development of land. While these two elements might appear to be opposing fiscal policies, they could be employed together as part of a regional planning strategy to encourage infill development within and near cities and to curb sprawl by retaining farm, forest, and ranch lands (Daniels 2001).

11. For the last year for which all data were available (1995), the highest property tax to gross domestic product ratio (4.1 percent) was in Canada, followed by the United States (2.9 percent) and Australia (2.5 percent). That all three are rich federations is unlikely to be a coincidence.

12. A minimum rate would be desirable to avoid tax competition whereby rich local governments with a strong tax base reduce rates to attract businesses, while a maximum rate would help to avoid tax exporting, that is, the levying of high tax rates on industries in the belief that the tax burden will ultimately be borne by nonresidents, thereby severing the connection between taxpayers and beneficiaries (Boadway 2001).

13. Bird (2000) develops this argument in more detail in the context of different systems for intergovernmental transfers.

14. Better definition of some land reserves, but also the emergence of civil society and of improved democracy at the local level, were conducive to such progress (Durand-Lasserve and Royston 2002b).

15. In Eastern Europe and the CIS, where state land still makes up a large share of the total, the management of such public property is often highly inefficient, often without any integrated strategy or policy, and is undertaken by multiple agencies and without performance indicators. This causes not only economic and financial losses to the public sector, but also distorts real estate markets and, by creating artificial scarcity of land in areas where demand is high, contributes to inefficient spatial development. Identifying good practices and ensuring that managers of public assets implement them is therefore extremely important.

16. We therefore do not deal with global externalities even though some interesting issues are involved. These include protecting fragile environments that, through various channels (biodiversity, hydrological flows, carbon sinks) provide local or global public goods. Indeed, a number of innovative mechanisms, such as tradable permits, now permit achieving environmentally sustainable outcomes in a decentralized way rather than through direct government intervention.

Regional Workshops

Regional Workshop on Land Issues in Central and Eastern Europe
Budapest, Hungary, April 3–6, 2002

Summary Program

Keynote: Land in the Broader Context of Economic Development

Presenter: *Peter Dale,* Honorary President, International Federation of Surveyors

Political Economy of Land Issues and Sequencing of Policy Reforms

Chair: *Laszlo Vajda,* Ministry of Agriculture and Regional Development, Hungary

Presenters: *Klaus Frohberg* and *Peter Tillack,* University of Halle, Germany

Konrad Hagedorn, Humboldt University of Berlin, Germany

Discussants: *Vladimir Nossick,* Land Initiative Project, Ukraine

Valeriu Bulgari, Private Farmer Assistance Project, Moldova

Making the Legal Basis for Private Land Rights Operational and Effective

Chair: *Mario Thurner,* Center of Legal Competence, Austria

Presenter: *Leonard Rolfes,* Rural Development Institute, United States

Discussants: *Aleksei Pulin,* Vladimir Oblast Center for Land Reform Support, Russia

Stephen Butler, United States

Farm Restructuring and Land Ownership

Chair: *Sergio Botezatu,* U.S. Agency for International Development Mission, Moldova

Moderator: *Csaba Csaki,* World Bank

Panelists: *Renata Yanbykh,* Federal Ministry of Agriculture, Russia
                Nadir Huseinbekov, Azerbaijan Land Cadastre, Azerbaijan
                Gejza Blaas, Agriculture and Food Economics Institute, Slovakia
                Thomas Doucha, Institute for Agricultural Economics, Prague, Czech Republic
                Alexander Muravschi, Private Farmer Assistance Program, Moldova

Comparative Analysis of Land Administration Systems
Chair: *John Manthorpe,* Her Majesty's Land Register, United Kingdom
Presenter: *Gavin Adlington,* United Kingdom
Discussants: *David Egiashvili,* Department of Land, Georgia
                Bozena Lipej, Department of Surveying and Mapping, Slovenia
                Mihaly Szabolcs, Institute of Geodesy, Hungary
                Joseph Salukvadze, German Technical Assistance, Georgia

Land Markets and Land Consolidation in Different Contexts
Chair: *Holger Magel,* International Federation of Surveyors
Moderator: *Zvi Lerman,* The Hebrew University, Israel
Panelists: *Alexei Overchuk,* Federal Land Cadastre Service, Russia
                Natalya Korchakovar, Center for Land Reform Policy, Ukraine
                Doina Nisto, Consulting and Credit in Agriculture, Moldova
                David Arsenashvili, Land Market Project, Georgia
                Christian Graefen, Gesellschaft für Technische Zusammenarbeit, Germany
                Fritz Rembold, Food and Agriculture Organization of the United Nations, Budapest Office

Improving the Functioning of Land and Financial Markets
Chair: *Geoffrey Hamilton,* United Nations Economic Commission for Eastern Europe
Presenter: *Alexander Sarris,* University of Athens, Greece
Discussants: *Juris Cebulis,* Mortgage and Land Bank, Latvia
                Victor Chiriac, BizPRO Microlending, Moldova
                Hayk Sahakyan, State Cadastral Committee, Armenia

Jozsef Toth, Budapest University of Economic Sciences, Hungary

Lela Shatirishvili, Land Market Project, Georgia

Land and Property Taxation in a Framework of Decentralized Governance

Chair: *Helge Onsrud,* United Nations Economic Commission for Eastern Europe, Working Party on Land Administration

Presenter: *Enid Slack,* University of Toronto, Canada

Discussants: *J. Eckert,* KPMG, United States

David Kirvalidze, Minister of Agriculture, Georgia

Istvan Feher, Hungary Agriculture University, Hungary

Country Case Studies

Albania: *Katherine Kelm,* legal adviser

Bulgaria: *Diana Kopeva,* Institute for Market Economics

Georgia: *Jaba Ebanoidze,* Association for the Protection of Landowners' Rights

Kyrgyz Republic: *Kachkynbai Kadyrkulov,* Rural Advisory Service

Moldova: *Alexander Muravschi,* Private Farmers Assistance Program

Romania: *Mihai Dumitru,* European Union delegation

Russia: *Vasiliy Yakimovich Uzun,* Agrarian Institute

Ukraine: *Pavlo Kulinich,* U.S. Agency for International Development Land Titling Project

Regional Workshop on Land Issues in Africa and the Middle East

Kampala, Uganda, April 29–May 2, 2002

Summary Program

Keynote: Land Access and Land Tenure in Africa: Historical Perspectives and Current Challenges

Presenter: *W. Kisamba Mugerwa,* Minister of Agriculture, Uganda

Social, Political, and Equity Aspects of Land and Property Rights

Chair: *Philippe Ospital,* Ministry of Foreign Affairs, France

Presenter: *Francis Ssekandi,* African Development Bank, Côte d'Ivoire

Panelists: *Jean Pierre Chauveau,* Institut de Recherche et Développement, France

Christian Graefen, Gesellschaft für Technische Zusammenarbeit, Germany

Martin Adams, Government of Botswana

Legal Basis for Land Administration in an African Context

Chair:	*H. E. Baguma-Isoke,* Minister of Water Lands and Environment, Uganda
Presenter:	*H. Okoth-Ogendo,* University of Nairobi, Kenya
Discussants:	*Hubert Ouedraogo,* LandNET West Africa, Burkina Faso
	Patrick McAuslan, Birkbeck College, University of London, United Kingdom
	Liz Alden Wily, international consultant, United Kingdom
	Chris Tanner, Food and Agriculture Organization of the United Nations Mozambique

Customary to Modern Transition: Challenges and Recent Advances

Chair:	*Paul Van Der Molen,* Dutch Kadaster
Presenter:	*Philippe Lavigne Delville,* Groupe de Recherche et d'Echanges Technologiques, France
Discussants:	*Scott Drimie,* Human Sciences Research Council, South Africa
	Andre Teyssier, Centre de Coopération Internationale en Recherche Agronomique pour le Développement, France
	Hamadou Ousman, Centre de Coopération Internationale en Recherche Agronomique pour le Développement, France
	Julian Quan, Department for International Development, United Kingdom

Pastoral Land Rights

Chair:	*Berhanu Gebremedhin,* International Livestock Research Institute, Ethiopia
Presenter:	*Tidiane Ngaido,* International Food Policy Research Institute, United States
Discussants:	*Michael Odhiambo,* Resources Conflict Institute, Kenya
	Véronique Ancey, Centre de Coopération Internationale en Recherche Agronomique pour le Développement, Madagascar
	Thomas Price, Centre de Coopération Internationale en Recherche Agronomique pour le Développement, Côte d'Ivoire

Land as a Source of Conflict and in Postconflict Settlement

Chair: *Joan Atherton,* U.S. Agency for International Development

Moderator: *Jean Daudelin,* senior researcher, North South Institute, Canada

Panelists: *Jose Negrão,* The Land Campaign, Mozambique
Mahamadou Zongo, University of Ouagadougou, Burkina Faso
Eugene Rurangwa, Ministry of Lands, Rwanda
Ruth Hall, Centre for Rural Legal Studies, South Africa

Land Markets in Africa: Preconditions, Potential, and Limitations

Chair: *Paul Matthieu,* Catholic University of Louvain, Belgium

Moderator: *Frank Place,* International Livestock Research Institute, Kenya

Panelists: *Honorat Edja,* LandNet West Africa, Benin
Camilla Toulmin, International Institute for Environment and Development, United Kingdom
Jean-Louis Arcand, University of Clermont-Ferrand, France

Land Reform

Chair: *Yves Gillet,* European Union, Uganda

Moderator: *Rogier van den Brink,* World Bank, South Africa

Panelists: *Glenn Thomas,* Department of Land Affairs, South Africa
Vincent Hungwe, Government of Zimbabwe, Zimbabwe
Ben Cousins, University of Western Cape, South Africa
Odenda Lumumba, Kenya Land Alliance, Kenya

Management of Peri-Urban Land and Land Taxation

Chair: *Klaus Deininger,* World Bank

Presenter: *Alain Rochegude,* Paris University, France

Discussants: *Rex Ahene,* Malawi
Alain Durand-Lasserve, Centre National de la Recherche Scientifique, France
J. M. Lussuga Kironde, University College for Lands and Architectural Studies, Tanzania

Ensuring Women's Land Access

Chair: *Salome Sijoana,* Permanant Secretary, Ministry of Lands Tanzania

Moderator: *Cherryl Walker,* Independent Consultant, South Africa

Panelists: *Harriet Busingye,* Uganda Land Alliance
Elizabeth Kharono, Initiative for the Advancement of Women, Uganda
Michael Kevane, Santa Clara University, United States
Esther Kasalu-Coffin, African Development Bank, Côte d'Ivoire

Designing Viable Land Administration Systems

Chair: *Kaori Izumi,* Food and Agriculture Organization of the United Nations, Harare
Moderator: *Tommy Oosterberg,* Swedesurvey, Sweden
Panelists: *Clarissa Fourie,* University of Cape Town, South Africa
Seth Asiama, Kumasi University of Science and Technology, Ghana
Fidelis Mutakyamilwa, Ministry of Lands, Tanzania
Michel Pescay, Centre de Coopération Internationale en Recherche Agronomique pour le Développement, France

Regional and Country Case Studies

Côte d'Ivoire: *Léon Desiré Zalo,* Ministry of Lands
Ethiopia: *Berhanu Nega,* Ethiopian Economic Policy Research Institute
Ghana: *Kasim Kasanga,* Minister of Lands
Kenya: *George Onyioro,* Ministry of Lands and Settlement
Lesotho: *Qhobela Selebalo,* Chief Surveyor
Mozambique: *Maria Conceicão da Quadros,* National Land Commission
Namibia: *H. K. Katali,* Deputy Minister of Land
Rwanda: *Eugene Rurungwa* and *Annie Kairaba,* Ministry of Lands and Rwanda Initiative for Sustainable Development
Southern
Africa: *Sue Mbaya,* LandNET Southern Africa
Tanzania: *Salome Sijoana,* Permanent Secretary, Ministry of Lands
Tunisia: *Mohamed Gharbi,* National Land Agency
Uganda: *Joanne Bosworth,* Ministry of Lands, Water, and Environment
West Africa: *Bara Gueye, H. Ouedraogo,* and *Camilla Toulmin,* LandNet West Africa and International Institute for Environment and Development

Regional Workshop on Land Issues in Latin America and the Caribbean
Pachuca (Hidalgo), Mexico, May 19–22, 2002

Summary Program

Keynote: Land Policy and Access to Assets in the Droader Development Context
Presenters: *Jose Abrão,* Minister of Agrarian Reform, Brazil
                  Edson Teofilo, Núcleo para Estudios Agrarios, Brazil

Political and Equity Aspects of Land Rights
Chair: *Isaías Rivera Rodríguez,* Procurador Agrario, Mexico
Presenter: *Gustavo Gordillo de Anda,* Food and Agriculture Organization of the United Nations Regional Office for Latin America, Chile
Discussants: *Alain de Janvry,* University of California at Berkeley, United States
                  Mario Pastore, Central Bank, Paraguay

The Legal and Institutional Basis for Effective Land Administration in Latin America and the Caribbean
Chair: *Jan van Hemert,* Cadastre International, Netherlands
Presenters: *Isabel Lavadenz,* World Bank
                  Jolyne Sanjak, U.S. Agency for International Development
Discussants: *Anthony Burns,* Land Equity, Australia
                  Thackwray Driver, Ministry of Agriculture, Lands, and Marine Resources, Trinidad and Tobago
                  Felix Garrid Safie, Centro Nacional de Registros, El Salvador
                  Gabriel Montes, Inter-American Development Bank, United States

Land and Other Factor Markets in Latin America
Chair: *Manoel dos Santos,* Confederação Nacional dos Trabalhadores na Agricultura, Brazil
Moderator: *Michael Carter,* University of Wisconsin, United States
Panelists: *Elisabeth Sadoulet,* University of California at Berkeley, United States
                  Wilson Navarro, Fondo Ecuatoriano Populorum Progressio, Ecuador

Pedro Tejo, United Nations Economic Commission for Latin America and the Caribbean, Chile

Javier Molina, Food and Agriculture Organization of the United Nations, Chile

Indigenous Land Rights and Natural Resource Management: Legal and Institutional Issues

Chair: *Shelton Davis,* World Bank

Presenter: *Roque Roldan,* Centro de Cooperación al Indígena, Colombia

Discussants: *Soren Hvalkof,* Nordic Agency for Development and Ecology, Denmark

                 Francisco Chapela, Estudios Rurales y Asesoría Campesina, Mexico

                 Jaime Urrutia, Grupo Permanente de Trabajo sobre Comunidades Campesinas, Peru

                 Xavier Albo, Programa de Educación Intercultural Bilingüe para los Países Andinos, Bolivia

Land in Conflict and Postconflict Situations

Chair: *Juerg Benz,* Swiss cooperation, Nicaragua

Presenter: *Jean Daudelin,* North South Institute, Canada

Discussants: *Carlos Camacho,* United Nations Verification Mission in Guatemala, Guatemala

                 Margarita Flores, United Nations Economic Commission for Latin America and the Caribbean, Mexico

                 Edin Barrientos, Minister of Agriculture, Guatemala

                 Juan Guillermo Ferro, Javeriana University, Colombia

Policies to Enhance Land Access

Chair: *Dittmar Jenrich,* Gesellschaft für Technische Zusammenarbeit, Guatemala

Moderator: *Klaus Deininger,* World Bank

Panelists: *Antonio Marcio Buainain,* University of Campinas, Brazil

                 Byron Garoz, Confederación Guatemalteca de Cooperativas, Guatemala

                 Miguel Urioste, Fundación Tierra, Bolivia

                 Jonathan Conning, Williams College, United States

Gender Dimensions of Land Access

Chair: *Maria Correia,* World Bank

Moderator: *Carmen Diana Deere,* University of Massachusetts at Amherst, United States

Panelists: *Lara Blanco,* Fundación Arias para la Paz y el Progreso Humano, Costa Rica

   Elizabeth Katz, St. Mary College, United States

   Jorge Edmundo Beyer Esparza, Procuraduría Agraria, Mexico

Land Taxation and Land Valuation

Chair: *Efrain Diaz,* Honduras

Presenter: *Enid Slack,* University of Toronto, Canada

Discussants: *John Strasma,* University of Wisconsin, United States

   Marino Henao, U.S. Agency for International Development, El Salvador

   Mark Gallagher, Dev Tech Systems, United S tates

Urban and Peri-Urban Lands

Chair: *Patricia de Jager,* Federation of Municipalities of the Central American Isthmus, Guatemala

Moderator: *Ernesto Alva Martinez,* Secretaría de Desarrollo Rural, Mexico

Panelists: *Wendy Quintero Gallardo,* Fideicomiso Fondo Nacional de Fomento Ejidal, Mexico

   Carolina Roullion, Comisión de Formalización de la Propiedad Informal, Peru

   Olivier Delahaye, Central University of Venezuela, Republica Bolivariana de Venezúela

Country Case Studies

General overview: *Ruben Echeverría,* Inter-American Development Bank

Bolivia: *Jose Justiniano,* Minister for Sustainable Development

Brazil: *Edson Teofilo,* Núcleo para Estudios Agrarios

Colombia: *Diana Grusczynski,* National Planning Department

Guatemala: *Edgar Gutiérrez* and *Carlos Cabrera,* Ministry of Agriculture

Honduras: *Anibal Delgado Fiallos,* Universidad Nacional Autónoma de Honduras

Jamaica: *Jacqueline da Costa,* Permanent Secretary, Ministry of Land and Environment

Mexico: *Sergio Sarmiento,* Instituto de Investigaciones Sociales

Regional Workshop on Land Issues in Asia
Phnom Penh, Cambodia, June 3–6, 2002

Summary Program

Keynote: Access to Assets and Land, Poverty Reduction, and Economic Development in Asia

Speaker: *Michael Lipton,* University of Sussex, United Kingdom

Land Registration for Security, Transparency, and Sustainable Resource Management

Chair: *Abdul Majid Mohamed,* Malaysian Land Registry
Presenter: *Anthony Burns,* Land Equity, Australia
Discussants: *Lutfi Nasution,* National Land Agency, Indonesia
                    Wanna Rakyao, Thailand Land Titling Project
                    Sek Setha, Ministry of Land, Cambodia

Improving Functioning of Land Markets in Asia

Chair: *Robin Palmer,* Oxfam, United Kingdom
Presenter: *Michael Carter,* University of Wisconsin, United States
Discussants: *Chan Sophal,* Cambodia Rural Development Institute, Cambodia
                    Eric Penot, Centre de Coopération Internationale en Recherche Agronomique pour le Développement, Indonesia
                    W.K.K. Kumarisiri, Secretary, Ministry of Lands, Sri Lanka

Improving Land Access through Land Reform

Chair: *R. B. Singh,* Food and Agriculture Organization of the United Nations, Thailand
Moderator: *Klaus Deininger,* World Bank
Panelists: *Myoung Chae Joung,* Korean Rural Economics Institute, Republic of Korea
                    Raj Lumsalee, Association of District Development Committees of Nepal, Nepal
                    Ronald Herring, Cornell University, United States

Enhancing Land Access and Land Rights for the Marginalized: Regional Overview in an International Context

Chair: *Cynthia Bantilan,* International Crops Research Institute for the Semi Arid Tropics, India

Presenter: *Keijiro Otsuka,* Foundation for Advanced Studies on International Development, Japan

Discussants: *Sediono M.P. Tjondronegoro,* Agricultural Institute Bogor, Indonesia

Jean-Philippe Fontenelle, Groupe de Recherche et d'Echanges Technologiques, Cambodia

Bharat Shrestha, Mobilization and Development, Nepal

Shaun Williams, Oxfam, Malawi

Ensuring Land Access in Postconflict Situations

Chair: *Bruno Vindel,* director, Ministry of Agriculture, France

Moderator: *Jean Daudelin,* North South Institute, Canada

Panelists: *Jon Lindsay,* Food and Agriculture Organization of the United Nations, Italy

Oun Visounnalad, Department of Lands, Lao People's Democratic Republic

Willi Zimmermann, Gesellschaft für Technische Zusammenarbeit, Cambodia

Thun Saray, Cambodian Human Rights Action Committee, Cambodia

Bencyrus Ellorin, Center for Alternative Rural Technology, Philippines

Land Management in Urban and Peri-Urban Areas

Chair: *Christian Graefen,* Gesellschaft für Technische Zusammenarbeit, Germany

Presenter: *Michael Kirk,* University of Marburg, Germany

Discussants: *Geoffrey Payne,* United Kingdom

Mylene Albano, Land Administration and Management Programme, Philippines

Muhammed Kamaluddin, Association for Realization of Basic Needs, Bangladesh

Country Case Studies

Cambodia: *Sar Sovann,* Ministry of Land Management, Urban Planning, and Construction

China: *Li Ping,* Rural Development Institute

India: *R. Deshpande,* Institute for Social and Economic Change

Indonesia: *Sujana Royat,* National Development Planning Agency

Lao People's Democratic Republic:	*Phoumy Vongleck,* Department of Land Use Planning and Development
Philippines:	*Marife Ballesteros,* National Economic and Development Agency
Sri Lanka:	*R. M. Ratnayake* and *W. K. K. Kumarasiri,* Ministry of Finance

Glossary

Collective farm: A farm jointly owned and operated under a single management for the benefit of and with work input from the owners of the collective.

Communal ownership system: A system of land ownership in which specific plots of land are assigned temporarily or permanently to members for family cultivation, while other areas are held in common for pasture, forestry, and collection of wild plants and game. Individual plots may or may not be inheritable or tradable in internal rental or sales markets, but sales to nonmembers are always forbidden or subject to community approval.

Contract farming: A form of production whereby farmer and purchaser enter into a contract in advance of the growing season for a specific quantity, quality, and date of delivery of an agricultural output at a price or price formula fixed in advance. The contract provides the farmer an assured sale of the crop and sometimes technical assistance, credit, services, or inputs from the purchaser.

Corvée: Unpaid labor and sometimes the service of draft animals provided by serfs, tenants, or usufruct right holders to owners of manorial estates or other landlords.

Family farm: A farm operated primarily with family labor, with some hiring in or out of labor. Family farming systems may be socially stratified, with wide variation in farm sizes and technology levels.

Hacienda: A manorial estate in which part of the land is cultivated as the home farm of the owner and part is cultivated as the home plots of serfs, usufructuary rights holders, or tenants.

Home farm: That part of the manorial estate or large ownership holding cultivated by the lord, landlord, or owner under his or her own management using *corvée* and sometimes partly remunerated labor.

Landlord estate: A manorial estate in which all the land is cultivated by tenants or usufructuary right holders.

Junker estate: A large ownership holding producing a diversified set of commodities operated under a single management with hired labor. As part of their remuneration, laborers may receive a house and garden plot for purposes of own cultivation.

Manorial estate: An area of land allocated temporarily or as a permanent ownership holding to a manorial lord who has the right to tribute, taxes, or rent in cash, in kind, or in *corvée* labor of the peasants residing on the estate. Manorial estates can be organized as haciendas or as landlord estates.

Sharecropping: A land rental arrangement whereby landlord and tenant share output according to a formula agreed on in advance rather than, as in a fixed rent contract, a cash payment that has to be made irrespective of the production obtained. In some cases the sharing arrangement involves the provision of certain inputs or credit through the landlord.

References

The word "processed" describes informally reproduced works that may not be commonly available through libraries.

Abt Associates. 1999. "The Land Tenure System in Sri Lanka." Bethesda, Md.

Acemoglu, D., and J. A. Robinson. 1999. "A Theory of Political Transitions." Working Paper: no. 99/26. Massachusetts Institute of Technology, Department of Economics, Cambridge, Mass.

_____. 2000. "Why Did the West Extend the Franchise? Democracy, Inequality, and Growth in Historical Perspective." *Quarterly Journal of Economics* 115(4): 1167–99.

Acemoglu, D., and T. Verdier. 1998. "Property Rights, Corruption, and the Allocation of Talent: A General Equilibrium Approach." *Economic Journal* 108(450): 1381–1403.

Adams, M. 2000. *Breaking Ground: Development Aid for Land Reform.* London: Overseas Development Institute.

Adelman, I., C. T. Morris, and S. Robinson. 1976. "Policies for Equitable Growth." *World Development* 4(7): 561–82.

Adesina, A. A., and J. Chianu. 2002. "Determinants of Farmers' Adoption and Adaptation of Alley Farming Agroforestry Technology in Nigeria." In C. B. Barrett, F. Place, and A. Aboud, eds., *Natural Resources Management in African Agriculture: Understanding and Improving Current Practices.* Wallingford, U.K.: CAB International.

Adesina, A. A., and K. K. Djato. 1996. "Farm Size, Relative Efficiency, and Agrarian Policy in Côte d'Ivoire: Profit Function Analysis of Rice Farms." *Agricultural Economics* 14(2): 93–102.

_____. 1997. "Relative Efficiency of Women as Farm Managers: Profit Function Analysis in Côte d'Ivoire." *Agricultural Economics* 16(1): 47–53.

Adlington, G. 2002. "Comparative Analysis of Land Administration Systems with Special Reference to Armenia, Moldova, Latvia, and Kyrgyzstan." Paper presented at the World Bank Regional Land Policy Workshop, April 3–6, Budapest, Hungary.

Agarwal, B. 1994. *A Field of One's Own: Gender and Land Rights in South Asia.* South Asian Studies. Cambridge, U.K.; New York; and Melbourne: Cambridge University Press.

Aghion, P., E. Caroli, and C. Garcia-Penalosa. 1999. "Inequality and Economic Growth: The Perspective of the New Growth Theories." *Journal of Economic Literature* 37(4): 1615–60.

Ahuja, V. 1998. "Land Degradation, Agricultural Productivity, and Common Property: Evidence from Côte d'Ivoire." *Environment and Development Economics* 3(1): 7–34.

Ai, C., J. L. Arcand, and F. Ethier. 1997. "De l'Efficacité Allocative des Contrats Agricoles: Cheung Avait-il Raison?" *Revue d'Economie du Développement* 0(2): 103–27.

Alden-Wily, L. 2002. "Comments on the Legal Basis for Land Administration in an African Context." Paper presented at the World Bank Regional Land Policy Workshop, April 29–May 2, Kampala, Uganda.

Ali, F., A. Parikh, and M. K. Shah. 1996. "Measurement of Economic Efficiency Using the Behavioral and Stochastic Cost Frontier Approach." *Journal of Policy Modeling* 18(3): 271–87.

Allen, D., and D. Lueck. 1992. "Contract Choice in Modern Agriculture: Cash Rent Versus Cropshare." *Journal of Law and Economics* 35(2): 397–426.

Allen, R. C. 1998. "Urban Development and Agrarian Change in Early Modern Europe." Discussion Paper no. 98/19. University of British Columbia, Department of Economics, Vancouver, Canada.

Alston, L. J., G. D. Libecap and B. Mueller. 1999a. "A Model of Rural Conflict: Violence and Land Reform Policy in Brazil." *Environment and Development Economics* 4(2): 135–60.

———. 1999b. *Titles, Conflict, and Land Use: The Development of Property Rights and Land Reform on the Brazilian Amazon Frontier.* Ann Arbor: University of Michigan Press.

———. 2000. "Land Reform Policies, the Sources of Violent Conflict, and Implications for Deforestation in the Brazilian Amazon." *Journal of Environmental Economics and Management* 39(2): 162–88.

Alston, L. J., G. D. Libecap, and R. Schneider. 1995. "Property Rights and the Preconditions for Markets: The Case of the Amazon Frontier." *Journal of Institutional and Theoretical Economics* 151(1): 89–107.

———. 1996. "The Determinants and Impact of Property Rights: Land Titles on the Brazilian Frontier." Working Paper no. 5405. National Bureau of Economic Research, Cambridge, Mass.

Amanor, K. S., and M. K. Diderutuah. 2001. *Share Contracts in the Oil Palm and Citrus Belt of Ghana.* London: International Institute for Environment and Development.

Amanor, K., D. Brown, and M. Richards. 2002. "Poverty Dimensions of Public Governance and Forest Management in Ghana." Final Technical Report: NRSP Project R7957. Overseas Development Institute, London, and the Institute of African Studies, University of Ghana, Legon.

Amelina, M. 2000. "Why Russian Peasants Remain in Collective Farms: A Household Perspective on Agricultural Restructuring." *Post-Soviet Geography and Economics* 41(7): 483–511.

Anderson, C. L., and E. Swimmer. 1997. "Some Empirical Evidence on Property Rights of

First Peoples." *Journal of Economic Behavior and Organization* 33(1): 1–22.

Anderson, T. L., and D. Lueck. 1992. "Land Tenure and Agricultural Productivity on Indian Reservations." *Journal of Law and Economics* 35(2): 427–54.

Andolfatto, D. 2002. "A Theory of Inalienable Property Rights." *Journal of Political Economy* 110(2): 382–93.

Andre, C., and J. P. Platteau. 1998. "Land Relations under Unbearable Stress: Rwanda Caught in the Malthusian Trap." *Journal of Economic Behavior and Organization* 34(1): 1–47.

Angel, S. 2000. *Housing Policy Matters: A Global Analysis.* Oxford, U.K.: Oxford University Press.

Angelsen, A. 1999. "Agricultural Expansion and Deforestation: Modelling the Impact of Population, Market Forces, and Property Rights." *Journal of Development Economics* 58(1): 185–218.

Appu, P. S. 1997. *Land Reforms in India: A Survey of Policy, Legislation, and Implementation.* New Delhi: Vikas Publishing House.

Arcand, J. L., and M. Rambonilaza. 1999. "Is Adverse Selection Relevant? Spence-Mirlees Meets the Tunisian Peasant." Document no. 99–23. University of Auvergne, Centre d'Etudes et Recherches sur le Développment. International Studies, Clermont-Ferrand, France.

Arnold, J. E. M. 2001. "Devolution of Control of Common Pool Resources to Local Communities: Experiences in Forestry." In A. de Janvry, G. Gordillo, J. P. Platteau, and E. Sadoulet, eds., *Access to Land, Rural Poverty, and Public Action.* Oxford, U.K.: Oxford University Press.

Arrunada, B., and N. Garoupa. 2002. "The Choice of Titling System in Land." Working Paper. University of Pompeu Fabra, Barcelona, Spain; and the New University of Lisbon, Lisbon, Portugal.

Atwood, D. A. 1990. "Land Registration in Africa: The Impact on Agricultural Production." *World Development* 18(5): 659–71.

Aw-Hassan. 2001. "Impact of Land Tenure Policy Modelling of the Trade-Off between Agricultural Development and Land Degradation— The Sudan Case." *Journal of Policy Modeling* 23(8): 847–74.

Ayalew, D., S. Dercon, and P. Krishnan. 2000. "Demobilisation, Land, and Household Livelihoods: Lessons from Ethiopia." Working Paper no. WPS/00/25. Centre for the Study of African Economies, Oxford, U.K.

Baker, M. 2001. "Property Rights by Squatting: Land Ownership Risk and Adverse Possession Statutes." *Land Economics* 77(3): 360–70.

_____. 2002. "Optimal Title Search." *Journal of Legal Studies* 31(1): 139–58.

Baland, J. M. 1996. *Halting Degradation of Natural Resources. Is There a Role for Rural Communities?* New York and Oxford, U.K.: Oxford University Press and Clarendon Press.

Baland, J. M., and J. P. Platteau. 1998. "Division of the Commons: A Partial Assessment of the New Institutional Economics of Land Rights." *American Journal of Agricultural Economics* 80(3): 644–50.

Balcazar, A. 1990. "Tamño de la Finca, Dinámica Tecnológica y Rendimientos Agrícolas." *Coyuntura Agropecuaria* 7(3): 107–25.

Bandiera, O. 2002. "Contract Duration and Investment Incentives: Evidence from Land Tenancy Agreements." Centre for Economic Policy Research Discussion Paper no. 3032. London School of Economics, London, U.K.

Banerjee, A. V. 1999. "Prospects and Strategies for Land Reform." In B. Pleskovic and J. Stiglitz, eds., *Annual World Bank Conference on Development Economics*. Washington, D.C.: World Bank.

Banerjee, A. V., P. J. Gertler, and M. Ghatak. 2002. "Empowerment and Efficiency: Tenancy Reform in West Bengal." *Journal of Political Economy* 110(2): 239–80.

Banerjee, B. 2002. "Security of Tenure in Indian Cities." In A. Durand-Lasserve and L. Royston, eds., *Holding Their Ground: Secure Land Tenure for the Urban Poor in Developing Countries*. London: Earthscan.

Banks, T. 2001. "Property Rights and the Environment in Pastoral China: Evidence from the Field." *Development and Change* 32(4): 717–40.

Bardhan, P., and M. Ghatak. 1999. "Inequality, Market Imperfections, and Collective Action Problems." Working Paper no. C99/108. University of California, Center for International and Development Economics Research, Berkeley.

Bardhan, P., S. Bowles, and H. Gintis. 2000. "Wealth Inequality, Wealth Constraints, and Economic Performance." In A. B. Atkinson and F. Bourguignon, eds., *Handbook of Income Distribution*. Amsterdam: North-Holland.

Barham, B., M. Carter, and K. Deininger. 2003. "Making Land Market Liberalization Work for the Welfare of the Rural Poor in Honduras." Report prepared for the European Union Food Security Program. Madison, Wisc. Processed.

Barham, B., M. R. Carter, and W. Sigelko. 1995. "Agro-Export Production and Peasant Land Access: Examining the Dynamic between Adoption and Accumulation." *Journal of Development Economics* 46(1): 85–107.

Barraclough, S. L. 1970. "Agricultural Policy and Land Reform." *Journal of Political Economy* 78(4): 906–47.

_____. 1999. "Land Reform in Developing Countries: The Role of the State and Other Actors." United Nations Research Institute for Social Development, Geneva.

Barrows, R., and M. Roth. 1990. "Land Tenure and Investment in African Agriculture: Theory and Evidence." *Journal of Modern African Studies* 28(2): 265–97.

Barry, P. J. 2000. "Lease Pricing for Farm Real Estate." *Review of Agricultural Economics* 22(1): 2–16.

Barzel, Y. 2000. "Dispute and Its Resolution: Delineating the Economic Role of the Common Law." *American Law and Economics Review* 2(2): 238–58.

Bastiaan, P. R., and L. A. Plata. 2002. "Intervençáo Estatal no Mercado de Terras: A Experiência Recente no Brasil." Public University of Campinas and National Institute for Colonization and Agrarian Reform, São Paulo, Brazil.

Basu, K. 1992. "Limited Liability and the Existence of Share Tenancy." *Journal of Development Economics* 38(1): 203–20.

Basu, K., and P. M. Emerson. 2000. "The Economics of Tenancy Rent Control." *Economic Journal* 110(466): 939–62.

Benjamin, D. 1995. "Can Unobserved Land Quality Explain the Inverse Productivity Relationship?" *Journal of Development Economics* 46(1): 51–84.

Benjamin, D., L. Brandt, and S. Rozelle. 2000. "Aging, Well-Being, and Social Security in Rural Northern China." *Population and Development Review* 26(0): 89–116.

Bentley, J. 1987. "Economic and Ecological Approaches to Land Fragmentation: In Defense of a Much Maligned Phenomenon." *Annual Review of Anthropology* 16: 31–67.

Berry, A. 2001. "When Do Agricultural Exports Help the Rural Poor? A Political-Economy Approach." *Oxford Development Studies* 29(2): 125–44.

Berry, R. A., and W. R. Cline. 1979. *Agrarian Structure and Productivity in Developing Countries.* Baltimore, Md.: The Johns Hopkins University Press.

Berry, S. 1993. *No Condition Is Permanent.* Madison: University of Wisconsin Press.

Besley, T. 1995. "Property Rights and Investment Incentives: Theory and Evidence from Ghana." *Journal of Political Economy* 103(5): 903–37.

Besley, T., and R. Burgess. 2000. "Land Reform, Poverty Reduction, and Growth: Evidence from India." *Quarterly Journal of Economics* 115(2): 389–430.

Bhalla, S. S., and P. Roy. 1988. "Misspecification in Farm Productivity Analysis: The Role of Land Quality." *Oxford Economic Papers* 40(1): 55–73.

Bidinger, P. D., T. S. Walker, B. Sarkar, A. R. Murty, and P. Babu. 1991. "Consequences of Mid-1980s Drought: Longitudinal Evidence from Mahbubnagar." *Economic and Political Weekly* 26: 105–14.

Bierlen, R. 2000. "Land Leasing and Debt on Farms: Substitutes or Complements?" *Quarterly Journal of Business and Economics* 39(2): 18–38.

Binswanger, H. P., and K. Deininger. 1995. *World Bank Land Policy: Evolution and Current Challenges.* Washington, D.C.: World Bank.

Binswanger, H. P., and M. Elgin. 1988. "What Are the Prospects for Land Reform?" In A. Maunder and A. Valdes, eds., *Agriculture and Governments in an Interdependent World. Proceedings of the 20th International Conference of Agricultural Economists.* Aldershot, U.K.: Ashgate.

Binswanger, H. P., K. Deininger, and G. Feder. 1995. "Power, Distortions, Revolt, and Reform in Agricultural Land Relations." In J. Behrman and T. N. Srinivasan, eds., *Handbook of Development Economics.* Amsterdam, New York, and Oxford: Elsevier Science, North-Holland.

Bird, R. M. 1974. *Taxing Agricultural Land in Developing Countries.* Cambridge, Mass.: Harvard University Press.

Bird, R. M. 2000. "Subnational Revenues: Realities and Prospects." Paper presented at the World Bank Intergovernmental Fiscal Relations and Local Financial Management Conference, April 17–21, Almaty, Kazakhstan.

Bird, R. M., and E. Slack. 2002. "Land and Property Taxation around the World: A Review." Paper presented at the World Bank Land Workshop, April 3–6, Budapest, Hungary.

Birdsall, N., and J. L. Londono. 1997. "Asset Inequality Matters: An Assessment of the World Bank's Approach to Poverty Reduction." *American Economic Review* 87(2): 32–37.

Blarel, B., P. Hazell, F. Place, and J. Quiggin. 1992. "The Economics of Farm Fragmentation: Evidence from Ghana and Rwanda." *World Bank Economic Review* 6(2): 233–54.

Blewett, R. A. 1995. "Property Rights as a Cause of the Tragedy of the Commons: Institutional Change and the Pastoral Masai of Kenya." *Eastern Economic Journal* 21(4): 477–90.

Boadway, R. 2001. "Intergovernmental Fiscal Relations: The Facilitator of Fiscal Decentralization." *Constitutional Political Economy* 12(2): 93–121.

Borras, S. M., Jr. 2001. "State-Society Relations in Land Reform Implementation in the Philippines." *Development and Change* 32(3): 545–75.

Boserup, E. 1965. *Conditions of Agricultural Growth: The Economics of Agrarian Change under Population Pressure.* New York: Aldine Publishing.

Bosworth, J. 2002. "Country Case Study: Uganda." Paper presented at the World Bank Regional Workshop on Land Issues, April 29–May 2, Kampala, Uganda.

Boucher, S., B. Barham, and P. Useche. 2001. "The Long and Grinding Road of Inegalitarian Agrarian Structure in Honduras: Impacts of Market Reforms and Hurricane Mitch." Paper presented at the Latin American Studies Association Meeting, September 6–8, Washington, D.C.

Bourguignon, F., and T. Verdier. 2000. "Oligarchy, Democracy, Inequality, and Growth." *Journal of Development Economics* 62(2): 285–313.

Brandão, A. S. P., and G. Feder. 1995. "Regulatory Policies and Reform: The Case of Land Markets." In C. Frischtak, ed., *Regulatory Policies and Reform: A Comparative Perspective.* Washington, D.C.: World Bank.

Brandão, A. S. P., and G. C. de Rezende. 1992. "Credit Subsidies, Inflation, and the Land Market in Brazil: A Theoretical and Empirical Analysis." World Bank, Washington, D.C.

Brasselle, A. S., F. Gaspart, and J. P. Platteau. 2002. "Land Tenure Security and Investment Incentives: Puzzling Evidence from Burkina Faso." *Journal of Development Economics* 67(2): 373–418.

Braverman, A., and J. E. Stiglitz. 1982. "Sharecropping and the Interlinking of Agrarian Markets." *American Economic Review* 72(4): 695–715.

Brenner, R. 1997. "Property Relations and the Growth of Agricultural Productivity in Late Medieval and Early Modern Europe." In A. Bhaduri and R. Skarstein, eds., *Economic Development and Agricultural Productivity.* London: Elgar.

Breusers, M. 2001. "Searching for Livelihood Security: Land and Mobility in Burkina Faso." *Journal of Development Studies* 37(4): 49–80.

Briggs, J., and D. Mwamfupe. 2000. "Peri-Urban Development in an Era of Structural Adjustment in Africa: The City of Dar es Salaam, Tanzania." *Urban Studies* 37(4): 797–809.

Brits, A. M., C. Grant, and T. Burns. 2002. "Comparative Study of Land Administration Systems with Special Reference to Thailand, Indonesia, and Karnataka (India)." Paper presented at the World Bank Regional Land Workshop, June 4–6, Phnom Penh, Cambodia.

Brockett, C. D. 1984. "Malnutrition, Public Policy, and Agrarian Change in Guatemala." *Journal of Interamerican Studies and World Affairs* 26(4): 477–97.

Brooks, K., and U. Koester. 1997. "Agriculture and German Reunification." Discussion Paper no. 355. World Bank, Washington, D.C.

Brueckner, J. K. 2000. "Fiscal Decentralization in Developing Countries: The Effects of Local Corruption and Tax Evasion." *Annals of Economics and Finance* 1(1): 1–18.

Brummer, B., and J. P. Loy. 2000. "The Technical Efficiency Impact of Farm Credit Programmes: A Case Study of Northern Germany." *Journal of Agricultural Economics* 51(3): 405–18.

Buainain A. M., J. M. da Silveira, H. M. Souza, and M. M. Magalhães. 2002. "Perfil dos Beneficiários PCT e INCRA 2001." Brazil Land Reform Program Technical Advisory Committee, Agricultural Economics Unit and Agricultural Economics and Development Unit, Brasilia, Brazil.

Burger, A. 2001. "Agricultural Development and Land Concentration in a Central European Country: A Case Study of Hungary." *Land Use Policy* 18(3): 259–68.

Burgess, R. 1997. "Land, Welfare, and Efficiency in Rural China." London School of Economics, London.

_____. 2001. "Land and Welfare: Theory and Evidence from China." Working Paper. London School of Economics, London.

Bush, R. 2000. "An Agricultural Strategy without Farmers: Egypt's Countryside in the New Millennium." *Review of African Political Economy* 27(84): 235–49.

Butler, S. 2002. "Comments: Making the Legal Basis for Private Land Rights Operational and Effective." Paper presented at the World Bank Land Workshop, April 3–6, Budapest, Hungary.

Cain, M. 1981. "Risk and Insurance: Perspectives on Fertility and Agrarian Change in India and Bangladesh." *Population and Development Review* 7(3): 435–74.

Callison, C. S. 1983. *Land-to-the-Tiller in the Mekong Delta : Economic, Social, and Political Effects of Land Reform in Four Villages of South Vietnam.* Lanham, Md: University Press of America.

Calvo, G. A., and S. Wellisz. 1978. "Supervision, Loss of Control, and the Optimum Size of the Firm." *Journal of Political Economy* 86(5): 943–52.

Cardenas, J. C. Forthcoming "Real Wealth and Experimental Cooperation: Experiments in the Field Lab." *Journal of Development Economics.*

Carter, M. R. 1984. "Identification of the Inverse Relationship between Farm Size and Productivity: An Empirical Analysis of Peasant Agricultural Production." *Oxford Economic Papers* 36 (1): 131–45.

_____. 1993. *Can Production Cooperatives Resolve the Conundrum of 'Exclusionary Growth?' An Econometric Evaluation of Land Reform Cooperatives in Honduras and Nicaragua.* Boulder, Colo.: Westview Press.

_____. 2002. "Land and other Factor Markets in Latin America." Paper presented at the World Bank Regional Land Workshop, May 19–22 Pachuca, Mexico.

Carter, M. R., and J. S. Chamorro. 2002. "The Economics of Liberalizing Segmented Land Markets: Theory and Evidence from Nicaragua." Paper presented at the American Agricultural Economics Association Meeting, July 26–31, Chicago.

Carter, M. R., and L. Galeano. 1995. "Campesino, Tierra y Mercado." Asunción, Paraguay: Confederación Empresarial Española de Economía Social.

Carter, M. R., and J. May. 1999. "Poverty, Livelihood, and Class in Rural South Africa." *World Development* 27(1): 1–20.

Carter, M. R., and D. Mesbah. 1993. "Can Land Market Reform Mitigate the Exclusionary Aspects of Rapid Agro-Export Growth?" *World Development* 21(7): 1085–1100.

Carter, M. R., and P. Olinto. 2003. "Getting Institutions Right for Whom? Credit Constraints and the Impact of Property Rights on the Quantity and Composition of Investment." *American Journal of Agricultural Economics* 85(1): 173–86.

Carter, M. R., and R. Salgado. 2001. "Land Market Liberalization and the Agrarian Question in Latin America." In A. de Janvry, J. P. Platteau, and E. Sadoulet, eds., *Land Access, Rural Poverty, and Public Action.* Oxford, U.K.: Oxford University Press.

Carter, M. R., and K. Wiebe. 1990. "Access to Capital and Its Impact on Agrarian Structure and Productivity in Kenya." *American Journal of Agricultural Economics* 721146–50.

Carter, M. R., and Y. Yao. 2002. "Local Versus Global Separability in Agricultural Household Models: The Factor Price Equalization Effect of Land Transfer Rights." *American Journal of Agricultural Economics* 84(3): 702–15.

Carter, M. R., and E. Zegarra. 2000. "Land Markets and the Persistence of Rural Poverty in Latin America: Post-Liberalization Policy Options." In A. Valdes and R. Lopez, eds., *Rural Poverty in Latin America: Analytics, New Empirical Evidence and Policy Options.* New York: Palgrave MacMillan Press.

Carter, M. R., and F. J. Zimmerman. 2000. "The Dynamic Cost and Persistence of Asset Inequality in an Agrarian Economy." *Journal of Development Economics* 63(2): 265–302.

Carter, M. R., B. Barham, and D. Mesbah. 1996. "Agro-Export Booms and the Rural Poor in Chile, Paraguay, and Guatemala." *Latin American Research Review* 31(1): 33–65.

Carter, M. R., Y. Yao, and K. Deininger. 2002. "Land Rental Markets under Risk: A Conceptual Model for China." University of Wisconsin, Madison. Processed.

Cattaneo, A. 2001. "Deforestation in the Brazilian Amazon: Comparing the Impacts of Macroeconomic Shocks, Land Tenure, and Technological Change." *Land Economics* 77(2): 219–40.

Cavendish, W. 2000. "Empirical Regularities in the Poverty-Environment Relationship of Rural Households: Evidence from Zimbabwe." *World Development* 28(11): 1979–2003.

Chaudhuri, A., and P. Maitra. 2001. "Tenant Characteristics and the Choice of Tenurial Contracts in Rural India." *Journal of International Development* 13(2): 169–81.

Chauveau, J.-P., 2000. "Question Foncière et Construction Nationale en Côte d'Ivoire." *Politique Africaine* 78: 94–125.

Chen, F., and J. Davis. 1998. "Land Reform in Rural China since the Mid 1980s." *Land Reform* 2(1):23–37.

Chen, K., and C. Brown. 2001. "Addressing Shortcomings in the Household Responsibility System: Empirical Analysis of the Two-Farmland System in Shandong Province." *China Economic Review* 12(4): 280–92.

Cheung, S. N. S. 1969. "Irving Fisher and the Red Guards." *Journal of Political Economy* 77(3): 430–33.

Chiriac, V. 2002. "Improving Functioning of Financial Markets in the Republic of Moldova." Paper presented at the Regional Workshop on Land Issues in Eastern Europe and the Commonwealth of Independent States, April 3–6, Budapest, Hungary.

Chuma, H., K. Otsuka, and Y. Hayami. 1990. "On the Dominance of Land Tenancy over Permanent Labor Contracts in Agrarian Economies." *Journal of the Japanese and International Economy* 4(2): 101–20.

Cliffe, L. 2000. "Land Reform in South Africa." *Review of African Political Economy* 27(84): 273–86.

Collier, P. 1989. "Contractual Constraints on Labour Exchange in Rural Kenya." *International Labour Review* 128(6): 745–68.

Conning, J. 2002. "Latifundia Economics." Working Paper no. 02/1. Hunter College, Department of Economics, New York.

Conning, J., and J. A. Robinson. 2002. "Land Reform and the Political Organization of Agriculture." Working Paper no. 3204. Centre for Economic Policy Research, London.

Crisologo-Mendoza, L., and D. Van de Gaer. 2001. "Population Growth and Customary Land Law: The Case of Cordillera Villages in the Philippines." *Economic Development and Cultural Change* 49(3): 631–58.

Csaki, C., and H. Kray. 2001. "The Agrarian Economies of Central-Eastern Europe and the CIS: An Update on Status and Progress in 2000." Working Paper no.32. World Bank, Environmentally and Socially Sustainable Development Sector of Europe and Central Asia, Washington, D.C.

Csaki, C., and Z. Lerman. 2000. "Structural Change in the Farming Sectors in Central and Eastern Europe: Lessons for EU Accession." Technical Paper no. 465. World Bank, Washington, D.C.

Csaki, C., and A. Nucifora. 2002. "The Agrarian Economies of Central-Eastern Europe and the CIS." Working Paper no. 36. World Bank, Environmentally and Socially Sustainable Development Sector of Europe and Central Asia, Washington, D.C.

Csaki, C., G. Feder, and Z. Lerman. 2002. "Land Policies and Evolving Farm Structures in Transition Countries." Policy Research Working Paper no. 2794. World Bank, Washington, D.C.

Csaki, C., A. Valdes, and A. Fock. 1998. "The Estonian Rural Sector: The Challenge in

Preparing for EU Accession." Working Paper no. 5. World Bank, Environmentally and Socially Sustainable Development Sector of Europe and Central Asia, Washington, D.C.

Cungu, A., and J. F. M. Swinnen. 1999. "Albania's Radical Agrarian Reform." *Economic Development and Cultural Change* 47(3): 605–19.

Curtis, D. 1991. *Beyond Government: Organizations for Common Benefit.* London: Macmillan.

Dale, P. F., and J. Mclaughlin. 2000. *Land Administration (Spatial Information Systems).* Oxford, U.K; and New York: Oxford University Press.

Daniels, T. L. 2001. "Coordinating Opposite Approaches to Managing Urban Growth and Curbing Sprawl: A Synthesis." *American Journal of Economics and Sociology* 60(1): 229–43.

Dasgupta, S., T. O. Knight, and H. A. Love. 1999. "Evolution of Agricultural Land Leasing Models: A Survey of the Literature." *Review of Agricultural Economics* 21(1): 148–76.

David, C., and V. Cordova. 1994. "Technological Change, Land Reform, and Income Distribution in the Philippines." In C. David and K. Otsuka, eds., *Modern Rice Technology and Income Distribution in Asia.* Boulder, Colo.: Lynne Rienner.

Davidova, S., M. Gorton, T. Ratinger, K. Zawalinska, B. Iraizoz, B. Kovács, and T. Mizo. 2001. "The Productivity and Profitability of Individual Farms in the Czech Republic." Paper presented at the Food and Agriculture Organization of the United Nations Workshop on Individual Farms in Central and Eastern Europe: Issues and Policy, September 18, Budapest, Hungary.

Dayton-Johnson, J. 2000. "Choosing Rules to Govern the Commons: A Model with Evidence from Mexico." *Journal of Economic Behavior and Organization* 42(1): 19–41.

Deere, C. D., and M. Leon. 2001. *Empowering Women: Land and Property Rights in Latin America.* Pitt Latin America Series. Pittsburgh: University of Pittsburgh Press.

De Franco, M., and H. Rose. 2002. "Políticas de Tenencia de Tierra en Nicaragua." Paper presented at the World Bank Regional Land Workshop, May 19–22, Pachuca, Mexico.

Deininger, K. 1995. "Collective Agricultural Production: A Solution for Transition Economies?" *World Development* 23(8): 1317–34.

_____. 1999. "Making Negotiated Land Reform Work: Initial Experience from Colombia, Brazil, and South Africa." *World Development* 27(4): 651–72.

_____. 2002. "Agrarian Reforms in Eastern European Countries: Lessons from International Experience." *Journal of International Development* 14(7): 987–1003.

Deininger, K., and H. P. Binswanger. 1995. "Rent Seeking and the Development of Large-Scale Agriculture in Kenya, South Africa, and Zimbabwe." *Economic Development and Cultural Change* 43(3): 493–522.

Deininger, K., and R. Castagnini. 2002. "Incidence and Impact of Land Conflict in Uganda." Discussion Paper. World Bank, Washington, D.C.

Deininger, K., and J. S. Chamorro. Forthcoming. "Investment and Income Effects of Land Regularization: The Case of Nicaragua." *Agricultural Economics.*

Deininger, K., and M. A. Gonzalez. 2002. "Land Markets and Land Reform in Colombia." Discussion Paper. World Bank, Washington, D.C.

Deininger, K., and S. Jin. 2002. "Land Rental Markets as an Alternative to Government Reallocation? Equity and Efficiency Considerations in the Chinese Land Tenure System." Policy Research Working Paper no. 2930. World Bank, Washington, D.C.

_____. 2003. "Land Sales and Rental Markets in Transition: Evidence from Rural Vietnam." Discussion Paper. World Bank, Washington, D.C.

Deininger, K., and J. May. 2000. "Can There Be Growth with Equity? An Initial Assessment of Land Reform in South Africa." Working Paper no. 2451. World Bank, Washington, D.C.

Deininger, K., and B. Minten. 2002. "Determinants of Deforestation and the Economics of Protection: An Application to Mexico." *American Journal of Agricultural Economics* 84(4): 943–60.

Deininger, K., and P. Mpuga. 2002. "Land Markets in Uganda: Incidence, Impact, and Evolution over Time." Discussion Paper. World Bank, Washington, D.C.

Deininger, K., and P. Olinto. 1998. "Why Liberalization Alone Has Not Improved Agricultural Productivity in Zambia: The Role of Asset Ownership and Working Capital Constraints." Working Paper no. 2302. World Bank, Washington, D.C.

_____. 2000. "Asset Distribution, Inequality, and Growth." Policy Research Working Paper no. 2375. World Bank, Washington, D.C.

Deininger, K., and A. Sarris. 2002. "Improving the Functioning of Land and Financial Markets." Paper presented at the World Bank Regional Land Policy Workshop, April 3–6, Budapest, Hungary.

Deininger, K., and S. Savastano. 2002. "Do Rental Markets Transfer Land to more Productive Producers? Evidence from Six Central European Countries." Discussion Paper. World Bank, Washington, D.C.

Deininger, K., and L. Squire. 1997. "Economic Growth and Income Inequality: Reexamining the Links." *Finance and Development* 34(1): 38–41.

_____. 1998. "New Ways of Looking at Old Issues: Inequality and Growth." *Journal of Development Economics* 57(2): 259–87.

Deininger, K., E. Zegarra, and I. Lavadenz. Forthcoming. "Determinants and Impacts of Rural Land Market Activity: Evidence from Nicaragua." *World Development.*

Deininger, K., F. Bresciani, I. Lavadenz, and M. Diaz. 2002. "Mexico's Second Agrarian Reform: Impact on Factor Markets and Household Welfare." Discussion Paper. World Bank, Washington, D.C.

Deininger, K., M. Maertens, P. Olinto, and F. Lara. 2002. "Redistribution, Investments and Human Capital Accumulation: The Case of Agrarian Reform in the Philippines." World Bank Discussion Paper. Washington D.C.

Deininger, K., S. Jin, B. Adenew, S. Gebre-Selassie, and M. Demeke. 2003. "Market and Nonmarket Transfers of Land in Ethiopia: Implications for Efficiency, Equity, and Nonfarm

Development." Policy Research Paper no. 2992. World Bank, Washington, D.C.

Deininger, K., S. Jin, B. Adenew, S. Gebre-Selassie, and B. Nega. 2003. "Tenure Security and Land-Related Investment: Evidence from Ethiopia." Policy Research Paper no. 2991. World Bank, Washington, D.C.

de Janvry, A., and E. Sadoulet. 1989. "A Study in Resistance to Institutional Change: The Lost Game of Latin American Land Reform." *World Development* 17(9): 1397–1407.

_____. 2002. "Comments on Political and Equity Aspects of Land Rights." Paper presented at the World Bank Land Workshop, May 19–22, Pachuca, Mexico.

de Janvry, A., E. Sadoulet, and W. Wolford. 2002. "The Changing Role of the State in Latin American Land Reforms." In A. de Janvry, E. Sadoulet and G. Gordillo, eds., *Land Reform and Public Policy*. Oxford, U.K.: Oxford University Press.

de Janvry, A., G. Gordillo, J. P. Platteau, and E. Sadoulet. 2001. *Access to Land, Rural Poverty, and Public Action*. Oxford, U.K.: Oxford University Press.

Delahaye, O. 2001. *Politicas de Tierras en Venezuela en el Siglo XX*. Caracas, Republica Boliviari-ana de Venezúela: Fondo Editorial Tropykos.

Delville, P. L. 2002. "Customary to Modern Transition." Paper presented at the World Bank Regional Land Workshop, April 29–May 2, Kampala, Uganda.

De Meza, D., and J. Gould. 1992. "The Social Efficiency of Private Decisions to Enforce Property Rights." *Journal of Political Economy* 100(3): 561–580.

Deshpande, R. S. 2002. "Country Case Study India." Paper presented at the World Bank Regional Land Workshop, June 4–6, Phnom Penh, Cambodia.

DeSilva, S. 2000. "Skills, Partnerships, and Tenancy in Sri Lankan Rice Farms." Discussion Paper no. 819. Yale University, Economic Growth Center, New Haven, Conn.

de Soto, H. 1993. "The Missing Ingredient: What Poor Countries Need to Make Their Markets Work." *The Economist* 328(7): 8–28.

_____. 2000. *The Mystery of Capital: Why Capitalism Triumphs in the West and Fails Everywhere Else*. New York: Basic Books.

Diaz, A. 2000. "On the Political Economy of Latin American Land Reforms." *Review of Economic Dynamics* 3(3): 551–71.

Do, Q. T., and L. Iyer. 2002. "Land Rights and Economic Development: Evidence from Vietnam." Massachusetts Institute of Technology, Department of Economics, Cambridge, Mass.

Dolan, C. S. 2001. "The 'Good Wife': Struggles over Resources in the Kenyan Horticultural Sector." *Journal of Development Studies* 37(3): 39–70.

Dong, X. Y. 1996. "Two-Tier Land Tenure System and Sustained Economic Growth in Post-1978 Rural China." *World Development* 24(5): 915–28.

Dong, X. Y., and L. Putterman. 2000. "Prereform Industry and State Monopsony in China." *Journal of Comparative Economics* 28(1): 32–60.

Dorner, P., and W. C. Thiesenhusen. 1990. "Selected Land Reforms in East and Southeast Asia: Their Origins and Impacts." *Asian-Pacific Economic Literature* 4(1): 65–95.

Dorward, A. 1999. "Farm Size and Productivity in Malawian Smallholder Agriculture." *Journal of Development Studies* 35(5): 141–61.

Doss, C. R. 1996. "Testing among Models of Intrahousehold Resource Allocation." *World Development* 24(10): 1597–1609.

Dowall, D. E. 1993. "Establishing Urban Land Markets in the People's Republic of China." *Journal of the American Planning Association* 59(2): 182–92.

Dowell, D. E., and M. Leaf. 1992. "The Price of Land for Housing in Jakarta." In K. A. Kim, ed., *Spatial Development in Indonesia, Review and Prospects.* Aldershot, U.K.: Avebury.

Downs, R. W., and S. P. Reyna. 1978. *Land and Society in Contemporary Africa.* Hanover, N.H., and London: University Press of New England.

Drimie, S. 2002. "Comments: Customary to Modern Transition: Challenges and Recent Advances." Paper presented at the Regional Workshop on Land Issues in Africa and the Middle East and North Africa Region, April 29–May 2, Kampala, Uganda.

Dubois, P. 2002. "Moral Hazard, Land Fertility, and Sharecropping in a Rural Area of the Philippines." *Journal of Development Economics* 68(1): 35–64.

Dumitru, M. 2002. "Country Case Studies: Romania." Paper presented at the World Bank Land Workshop, April 3–6, Budapest, Hungary.

Duncan, J. 2000. "Agricultural Land Reform and Farm Reorganization in Tajikistan." Reports

on Foreign Aid and Development no. 106. Rural Development Institute, Seattle, Wash.

Durand-Lasserve, A., and L. Royston. 2002a. *Holding Their ground: Secure Land Tenure for the Urban Poor in Developing Countries.* London: Earthscan Publications.

_____. 2002b. "International Trends and Country Contexts: From Tenure Regularisation to Tenure Security." In A. Durand-Lasserve and L. Royston, eds., *Holding Their Ground: Secure Land Tenure for the Urban Poor in Developing Countries.* London: Earthscan Publications.

Easterly, W., and R. Levine. 2001. "Tropics, Germs, and Crops: How Endowments Influence Economic Development." Working Paper no. W 9106. National Bureau of Economic Research, Cambridge, Mass.

Eaton, K. 2001. "Political Obstacles to Decentralization: Evidence from Argentina and the Philippines." *Development and Change* 32(1): 101–27.

Echenique, J., and N. Rolando. 1991. *Tierras de Parceleros: ¿Donde Están?* Santiago, Chile: Agraria.

Eckstein, S. D., and G. D. Horton. 1978. "Land Reform in Latin America: Bolivia, Chile, Mexico, Peru, and Venezuela." Working Paper no. 275. World Bank, Washington, D.C.

Eckstein, Z., and I. Zilcha. 1994. "The Effects of Compulsory Schooling on Growth, Income Distribution, and Welfare." *Journal of Public Economics* 54(3): 339–59.

Edja, H. 2001. "Land Rights under Pressure: Access to Resources in Southern Benin." International Institute for Environment and Development, London.

Eggertsson, T. 1996. "No Experiments, Monumental Disasters: Why It Took a Thousand Years to Develop a Specialized Fishing Industry in Iceland." *Journal of Economic Behavior and Organization* 30 (1): 1–23.

El Ghonemy, M. R. 1990. *The Political Economy of Rural Poverty: The Case for Land Reform.* London and New York: Routledge.

El Ghonemy, M. R. 1999. "The Political Economy of Market-Based Land Reform." Discussion Paper no. DP104. United Nations Research Institute for Social Development, Geneva.

Ellickson, R. C. 1993. "Property in Land." *Yale Law Journal* 102(6): 1315–1400.

Enriquez, L. J. 1992. *Harvesting Change: Labor and Agrarian Reform in Nicaragua, 197–1990.* Chapel Hill, N.C.: University of North Carolina Press.

Estudillo, J. P., A. R. Quisumbing, and K. Otsuka. 2001. "Gender Differences in Land Inheritance and Schooling Investments in the Rural Philippines." *Land Economics* 77(1): 130–43.

Eswaran, M. and A. Kotwal. 1985a. "A Theory of Contractual Structure in Agriculture." *American Economic Review* 75(3): 352–67.

_____. 1985b. "A Theory of Two-Tier Labor Markets in Agrarian Economies." *American Economic Review* 75(1): 162–77.

Everingham, M. 2001. "Agricultural Property Rights and Political Change in Nicaragua." *Latin American Politics and Society* 43(3): 61–93.

Fafchamps, M., and A. R. Quisumbing. 1999. "Human Capital, Productivity, and Labor Allocation in Rural Pakistan." *Journal of Human Resources* 34(2): 369–406.

_____. 2002. "Control and Ownership of Assets within Rural Ethiopian Households." *Journal of Development Studies* 38(6): 47–82.

Falk, B., B. S. Lee, and R. Susmel. 2001. "Fads Versus Fundamentals in Farmland Prices: Reply." *American Journal of Agricultural Economics* 83(4): 1078–81.

Fearnside, P. M. 2001. "Land-Tenure Issues as Factors in Environmental Destruction in Brazilian Amazonia: The Case of Southern Para." *World Development* 29(8): 1361–72.

Feder, G. 1985. "The Relation between Farm Size and Farm Productivity: The Role of Family Labor, Supervision, and Credit Constraints." *Journal of Development Economics* 18(2–3): 297–313.

_____. 1988. *Land Policies and Farm Productivity in Thailand.* Baltimore, Md.; and London: The Johns Hopkins University Press.

_____. 2002. "The Intricacies of Land Markets: Why the World Bank Succeeds in Economic Reform through Land Registration and Tenure Security." Paper presented at the Conference of the International Federation of Surveyors, April 19–26, Washington, D.C.

Feder, G., and D. Feeny. 1991. "Land Tenure and Property Rights: Theory and Implications for Development Policy." *World Bank Economic Review* 5(1): 135–53.

Feder, G., and A. Nishio. 1999. "The Benefits of Land Registration and Titling: Economic and Social Perspectives." *Land Use Policy* 15(1): 143–69.

Feder, G., and R. Noronha. 1987. "Land Rights Systems and Agricultural Development in Sub-Saharan Africa." *World Bank Research Observer* 2(2): 143–70.

Feder, G., L. J. Lau, J. Y. Lin, and X. Luo. 1992. "The Determinants of Farm Investment and Residential Construction in Postreform China." *Economic Development and Cultural Change* 41(1): 1–26.

Feeny, D. 1989. "The Decline of Property Rights in Man in Thailand, 1800–1913." *Journal of Economic History* 49(2): 285–96.

Feher, I. 2001. "Functioning of the Land Factor Market in France and Hungary: Opportunities and Constraints for Farming Sector Restructuring." Paper presented at the World Bank Workshop on Pension Reform, April 3–6, Budapest, Hungary.

Feldstein, M. 1980. "Inflation, Portfolio Choice, and the Prices of Land and Corporate Stock." *American Journal of Agricultural Economics* 62(5): 910–16

Fenoaltea, S. 1976. "Risk, Transaction Costs, and the Organization of Medieval Agriculture." *Explorations in Economic History* 13(2): 129–75.

Fernandes, E. 2002. "Providing Security of Land Tenure for the Urban Poor: The Brazilian Experience." In A. Durand-Lasserve and L. Royston, eds., *Holding Their Ground: Secure Land Tenure for the Urban Poor in Developing Countries.* London: Earthscan Publications.

Field, E. 2002. "Entitled to Work: Urban Property Rights and Labor Supply in Peru." Princeton University, Industrial Relations Section Firestone Library, Princeton, N.J..

Finan, F., E. Sadoulet, and A. de Janvry. 2002. "Measuring the Income-Generating Potential of Land in Rural Mexico." Working paper. University of California, Berkeley.

Firmin-Sellers, K., and P. Sellers. 1999. "Expected Failures and Unexpected Successes of Land Titling in Africa." *World Development* 27(7): 1115–28.

Fischel W. 2001. "The Homevoter Hypothesis: How Home Values Influence Local Government Taxation, School Finance, and Land-Use Policies." Dartmouth College, Hanover, N.H. Processed.

Foldvary, F. E. 1998. "Market-Hampering Land Speculation: Fiscal and Monetary Origins and Remedies." *American Journal of Economics and Sociology* 57(4): 615–37.

Foster, A. D., and M. R. Rosenzweigh. 2001. "Democratization, Decentralization, and the Distribution of Local Public Goods in a Poor Rural Economy." Working Paper. University of Pennsylvania, Philadelphia.

Fourie, C. 2002. "Comments: Designing Viable Land Administration." Paper presented at the Regional Workshop on Land Issues in Africa and the Middle East and North Africa Region, April 29–May 2, Kampala, Uganda.

Fred-Mensah, B. K. 1999. "Capturing Ambiguities: Communal Conflict Management Alternative in Ghana." *World Development* 27(6): 951–65.

Frisvold, G. B. 1994. "Does Supervision Matter? Some Hypothesis Tests Using Indian Farm-Level Data." *Journal of Development Economics* 43(2): 217–38.

Galassi, F. L., and J. S. Cohen. 1994. "The Economics of Tenancy in Early 20th Century Southern Italy." *Economic History Review* 47(3): 585–600.

Galor, O., and J. Zeira. 1993. "Income Distribution and Macroeconomics." *Review of Economic Studies* 60(1): 35–52.

Gardner, B., and E. Serova. 2002. "Constraints to Growth in Russian Agriculture." Brief no. 7. BASIS Collaborative Research Support Program. University of Wisconsin-Madison, Madison, Wis.

Gavian, S., and M. Fafchamps. 1996. "Land Tenure and Allocative Efficiency in Niger." *American Journal of Agricultural Economics* 78(2): 460–71.

Gerard, D. 2001. "Transaction Costs and the Value of Mining Claims." *Land Economics* 77(3): 371–84.

Gharbi, M. 2002. "Country Case Study Tunisia." Paper presented at the World Bank Regional Workshop on Land Issues, April 29–May 2, Kampala, Uganda.

Ghatak, M., and P. Pandey. 2000. "Contract Choice in Agriculture with Joint Moral Hazard in Effort and Risk." *Journal of Development Economics* 63(2): 303–26.

Giovarelli, R. 2002. "How to Start Your Land Consolidation Project: The Legal Issues." Rural Development Institute, Seattle, Wash. Processed.

Giovarelli, R., C. Aidarbekova, J. Duncan, K. Rasmussen, and A. Tabyshalieva. 2002. "Women's Rights to Land in the Kyrgyz Republic." World Bank, Washington, D.C. Draft.

Glover, D. 1990. "Contract Farming and Outgrower Schemes in East and Southern Africa." *Journal of Agricultural Economics* 41(3): 303–15.

Godoy, R. E. A. 1998. "The Role of Tenure Security and Private Time Preference in Neotropical Deforestation." *Land Economics* 74(2): 162–70.

Goldstone, J. A. 1991. *Revolution and Rebellion in the Early Modern World.* Berkeley: University of California Press.

Gonzalez, J. G., and A. Velez. 1995. "Intra-Industry Trade between the United States and the Major Latin American Countries: Measurement and Implications for Free Trade in the Americas." *International Trade Journal* 9(4): 519–36.

Gopal, G., and M. Salim. 1998. *Gender and Law—Eastern Africa Speaks: Proceedings of the Conference Organized by the World Bank and the Economic Commission for Africa.* Washington, D.C.: World Bank.

Gordillo, G., A. de Janvry, and E. Sadoulet. 1998. "Between Political Control and Efficiency Gains: The Evolution of Agrarian Property Rights in Mexico." *CEPAL Review* 0(66): 151–69.

Graham, A. W., and M. A. G. Darroch. 2001. "Relationship between the Mode of Land Redistribution, Tenure Security, and Agricultural Credit Use in KwaZulu-Natal." *Development Southern Africa* 18(3): 295–308.

Gray, L. C., and M. Kevane. 2001. "Evolving Tenure Rights and Agricultural Intensification in Southwestern Burkina Faso." *World Development* 29(4): 573–87.

Graziano da Silva, J. 2001. "Quem Precisa de uma Estratégia de Desenvolvimiento?" Discussion paper no. 2, 5–53. Núcleo de Estudos Agrários e de Desenvolvimiento (Center for Agrarian and Development Studies), Brasilia, Brazil.

Grindle, M. S. 1990. "Agrarian Reform in Mexico: A Cautionary Tale." In R. L Prosterman, M. N. Temple, and T. M. Hanstad, eds., *Agrarian Reform and Grassroots Development, Ten Case Studies.* Boulder, Colo.: L. Rienner.

Grossman, H. I. 2001. "The Creation of Effective Property Rights." *American Economic Review* 91(2): 347–52.

_____. 2002. "'Make Us a King': Anarchy, Predation, and the State." *European Journal of Political Economy* 18(1): 31–46.

Grossman, H. I., and M. Kim. 1995. "Swords or Plowshares? A Theory of the Security of Claims to Property." *Journal of Political Economy* 103(6): 1275–88.

Grossman, H. I., and J. Mendoza. 2001. "Butter and Guns: Complementarity between Economic and Military Competition." *Economics of Governance* 2(1): 25–33.

Gruszczynski, D., and C. F. Jaramillo. 2002. "Country Case Study Colombia." Paper presented at the World Bank Regional Land Workshop, May 19–22, Pachuca, Mexico.

Gueye, B., H. Ouedraogo, and C. Toulmin. 2002. "Country Case Study West Africa." Paper presented at the World Bank Regional Workshop on Land Issues in Africa and the Middle East and North Africa Region, April 29–May 2, Kampala, Uganda.

Guinnane, T. W., and R. I. Miller. 1997. "The Limits to Land Reform: The Land Acts in Ireland, 1870–1909." *Economic Development and Cultural Change* 45(3): 591–612.

Gunjal, K., S. Williams, and R. Romain. 1996. "Agricultural Credit Subsidies and Farmland Values in Canada." *Canadian Journal of Agricultural Economics* 44(1): 39–52.

Gunning, J. W., J. Hoddinott, B. Kinsey, and T. Owens. 2000. "Revisiting Forever Gained: Income Dynamics in the Resettlement Areas of Zimbabwe, 1983–96." *Journal of Development Studies* 36(6): 131–54.

Haddad, L. 1997. *The Scope of Intrahousehold Resource Allocation Issues.* Baltimore, Md.; and London: The Johns Hopkins University Press.

Hall A. L. 1990. "Land Tenure and Land Reform in Brazil." In R. L Prosterman, M. N. Temple, and T. M. Hanstad, eds., *Agrarian Reform and Grassroots Development, Ten Case Studies.* Boulder, Colo.: L. Rienner.

Hall, R. 1998. "Design for Equity: Linking Policy with Objectives in South Africa's Land Reform." *Review of African Political Economy* 25(77): 451–62.

Hamid, N. 1983. "Growth of Small-Scale Industry in Pakistan." *Pakistan Economic and Social Review* 21(1–2): 37–76.

Hamman, J., and J. Ewert. 1999. "A Historical Irony in the Making? State, Private Sector, and Land Reform in the South African Wine Industry." *Development Southern Africa* 16(3): 447–54.

Hayami, M. 2000. "The U.S. and Japanese Economies: Reflections of a Central Banker." *Economic and Financial Review* 7(4): 189–96.

Hayami, Y. 2001. "Ecology, History, and Development: A Perspective from Rural Southeast Asia." *World Bank Research Observer* 16(2): 169–98.

Hayami, Y., and M. Kikuchi. 2000. *A Rice Village Saga: Three Decades of Green Revolution in the Philippines.* London: Macmillan.

Hayami, Y., and K. Otsuka. 1993. *The Economics of Contract Choice: An Agrarian Perspective.* Oxford, U.K.; New York; Toronto; and Melbourne: Oxford University Press and Clarendon Press.

Hayami, Y., and V. W. Ruttan. 1985. *Agricultural Development: An International Perspective.* Baltimore, Md.: The Johns Hopkins University Press.

Hayami, Y., A. R. Quisumbing, and L. Adriano. 1990. *Toward an Alternative Land Reform Paradigm: A Philippine Perspective.* Manila: Ateneo de Manila University Press.

Heath, J. 1994. "Land Management in Côte d'Ivoire." Working Paper. World Bank, Washington, D.C.

Heltberg, R. 2001. "Determinants and Impact of Local Institutions for Common Resource Management." *Environment and Development Economics* 6(2): 183–208.

Hernandez, M. A. 2001. "Ejemplos de Políticas de Tierra en Varios Paises de Europa Occidental, Espana, Francia, Portugal, Italia, Dinamarca." IRAM. Processed.

Herring, R. J. 1999. "Persistent Poverty and Path Dependency—Agrarian Reform: Lessons from the United States and India." *IDS Bulletin* (University of Sussex, Institute of Development Studies, Brighton, U.K.) 30(2): 13–22.

Heston, A., and D. Kumar. 1983. "The Persistence of Land Fragmentation in Peasant Agriculture: An Analysis of South Asian Cases." *Explorations in Economic History* 20(2): 199–220.

Hilton, R. 1978. *The Transition from Feudalism to Capitalism.* London: New Left Books.

Hirtz, F. 1998. "The Discourse That Silences: Beneficiaries' Ambivalence towards Redistributive Land Reform in the Philippines." *Development and Change* 29(2): 247–75.

Ho, P. 2000. "China's Rangelands under Stress: A Comparative Study of Pasture Commons in the Ningxia Hui Autonomous Region." *Development and Change* 31(2): 385–412.

Hodgson, S., C. Cullinan, and K. Campbell. 1999. "Land Ownership and Foreigners: A Comparative Analysis of Regulatory Approaches to the Acquisition and Use of Land by Foreigners." Food and Agriculture Organization of the United Nations Legal Papers Online no. 6. Available on: http://www.fao.org/Legal/Prs-OL/hodgson.pdf.

Hoff, K. 1991. "Land Taxes, Output Taxes, and Sharecropping: Was Henry George Right?" *World Bank Economic Review* 5(1): 93–111.

Horowitz, A. W. 1993. "Time Paths of Land Reform: A Theoretical Model of Reform Dynamics." *American Economic Review* 83(4): 1003–10.

Hossain, M. 1978. "Factors Affecting Tenancy: The Case of Bangladesh Agriculture." *Bangladesh Development Studies* 6(2): 139–62.

Hotte, L. 2001. "Conflicts over Property Rights and Natural-Resource Exploitation at the Frontier." *Journal of Development Economics* 66(1): 1–21.

Huizer, G. 1972. *The Revolutionary Potential of Peasants in Latin America.* Lexington, Mass.: Lexington Books.

Hvalkof, S. 2002. "Indigenous Land Rights and Natural Resource Management: Legal and Institutional Issues." Paper presented at the World Bank Land Workshop, May 19–22, Pachuca, Mexico.

Ibbotson, R. G., L. B. Siegel, and K. S. Love. 1985. "World Wealth: Market Values and Returns." *Journal of Portfolio Management* 12(1): 4–23.

Jacoby, H. G., and G. Mansuri. 2002. "Incomplete Contracts and Investment: A Study of Land and Tenancy in Pakistan." Discussion Paper. World Bank, Washington, D.C.

Jacoby, H. G., G. Li, and S. Rozelle. 2002. "Hazards of Expropriation: Tenure Insecurity and Investment in Rural China." *American Economics Review* 92(5): 1420–47.

Jaramillo, C. F. 1998. "El Mercado Rural de Tierras en América Latina: Hacia una Nueva Estrategia B." Technical Report no. ENV-124. Inter-American Development Bank, Washington, D.C.

_____. 2001. "Liberalization, Crisis, and Change: Colombian Agriculture in the 1990s." *Economic Development and Cultural Change* 49(4): 821–46.

Jarvis, L. S. 1985. "Chilean Agriculture under Military Rule: From Reform to Reaction, 1973–1980." University of California, Institute of International Studies, Berkeley.

_____. 1989. "The Unraveling of Chile's Agrarian Reform, 1973–1986." In W. Thiesenhusen, ed., *Searching for Agrarian Reform in Latin America.* Boston: Unwin Hyman.

_____. 1991. "Overgrazing and Range Degradation in Africa: Is There Need and Scope for Government Control of Livestock Numbers?" *Eastern Africa Economic Review* 7(1): 95–116.

Jensen, M. C,. and W. H. Meckling. 1976. "Theory of the Firm: Managerial Behavior, Agency Costs, and Ownership Structure." *Journal of Financial Economics* 3(4): 305–60.

Jeon, Y. D., and Y. Y. Kim. 2000. "Land Reform, Income Redistribution, and Agricultural Production in Korea." *Economic Development and Cultural Change* 48(2): 253–68.

Jimenez, E. 1984. "Tenure Security and Urban Squatting." *Review of Economics and Statistics* 66(4): 556–67.

Jodha, N. S. 1984. "Agricultural Tenancy in Semi-arid Tropical India." In H. P. Binswanger and R. Rosenzweig, eds., *Contractual Arrangements, Employment, and Wages in Rural Labor Markets in Asia.* New Haven, Conn.; and London: Yale University Press.

_____. 1990. "Depletion of Common Property Resources in India: Micro-Level Evidence." In G. McNicholl and M. Cain, eds., *Rural Development and Population: Institutions and Policy.* New York: Population Council and Oxford University Press.

_____. 1996. *Property Rights and Development.* Washington, D.C.: Island Press.

Joireman, S. F. 2001. "Property Rights and the Role of the State: Evidence from the Horn of Africa." *Journal of Development Studies* 38(1): 1–28.

Jonakin, J. 1996. "The Impact of Structural Adjustment and Property Rights Conflicts on Nicaraguan Agrarian Reform Beneficiaries." *World Development* 24(7): 1179–91.

Juma, S., and S. Christensen. 2001. "Bringing the Informal Settlers under the Register: The Namibian Challenge." Paper presented at the International Conference on Spatial Information for Sustainable Development, October 2–5, Nairobi, Kenya.

Just, R. E., and J. A. Miranowski. 1989. "U.S. Land Prices: Trends and Determinants." In A. Maunder and A. Valdes, eds., *Agriculture and Governments in an Interdependent World. Proceedings of the 20th International Conference of Agricultural Economists.* Aldershot, U.K.: Ashgate.

Kaganova, O., and R. Nayyar-Stone. 2000. "Municipal Real Property Asset Management: An Overview of World Experience, Trends, and Financial Implications." *Journal of Real Estate Portfolio Management* 6(4): 307–26.

Kalabamu, F. T. 2000. "Land Tenure Management Reforms in East and Southern Africa: The Case of Botswana." *Land Use Policy* 17(4): 305–19.

Kanazawa, M. T. 1996. "Possession Is Nine Points of the Law: The Political Economy of Early Public Land Disposal." *Explorations in Economic History* 33(2): 227–49.

Kantor, S. E. 1998. *Politics and Property Rights: The Closing of the Open Range in the Postbellum South.* Chicago and London: University of Chicago Press.

Kasanga, K., and N. Kotey. 2001. *Land Management in Ghana: Building on Tradition and Modernity.* London: International Institute for Environment and Development.

Katz, E., and J. S. Chamorro. 2002. "Gender, Land Rights, and the Household Economy in Rural Nicaragua and Honduras." Paper presented at the Regional Workshop on Land Issues in Latin America and the Caribbean, May 19–22, Pachuca, Mexico.

Kawagoe, T. 1999. "Agricultural Land Reform in Postwar Japan: Experiences and Issues." Working Paper no. 2111. World Bank, Washington, D.C.

Keefer, P., and S. Knack. 2002. "Polarization, Politics, and Property Rights: Links between Inequality and Growth." *Public Choice* 111(1–2): 127–54.

Kevane, M. 1996. "Agrarian Structure and Agricultural Practice: Typology and Application to Western Sudan." *American Journal of Agricultural Economics* 78(1): 236–45.

Kevane, M., and L. C. Gray. 1999. "A Woman's Field Is Made at Night: Gendered Land Rights and Norms in Burkina Faso." *Feminist Economics* 5(3): 1–26.

Key, N., J. Muñoz-Piñand, A. de Janvry, and E. Sadoulet. 1998. "Social and Environmental Consequences of the Mexican Reforms: Common Pool Resources in the *Ejido* Sector." University of California-Berkeley, Department of Agricultural and Resource Economics, Berkeley.

Khadiagala, L. S. 2001. "The Failure of Popular Justice in Uganda: Local Councils and Women's Property Rights." *Development and Change* 32(1): 55–76.

Kijima, Y., T. Sakurai, and K. Otsuka. 2000. "*Iriaichi:* Collective Versus Individualized Management of Community Forests in Postwar Japan." *Economic Development and Cultural Change* 48(4): 866–86.

King, R. 1977. *Land Reform: A World Survey.* London: G. Bell and Sons.

Kinsey, B. H., and H. P. Binswanger. 1993. "Characteristics and Performance of Resettlement Programs: A Review." *World Development* 21(9): 1477–94.

Kironde, L. 2002. "Comments on Management of Peri-Urban Land and Land Taxation." Paper presented at the World Bank Regional Land Workshop, April 29–May 2, Kampala, Uganda.

Kochar, A. 1997. "Does Lack of Access to Formal Credit Constrain Agricultural Production? Evidence from the Land Tenancy Market in Rural India." *American Journal of Agricultural Economics* 79(3): 754–63.

Koo, A. Y. C. 1973. "Towards a More General Model of Land Tenancy and Reform." *Quarterly Journal of Economics.* 87(4): 567–80.

Kopeva, D. 2002. "Bulgaria Country Case Study." Paper presented at the World Bank Land Workshop, April 3–6, Budapest, Hungary.

Kranton, R. E., and A. V. Swamy. 1999. "The Hazards of Piecemeal Reform: British Civil Courts and the Credit Market in Colonial India." *Journal of Development Economics* 58(1): 1–24.

Kriger, N. J. 1992. *Zimbabwe's Guerrilla War, Peasant Voices.* Cambridge, U.K.: Cambridge University Press.

Kung, J. K.-S. 2000. "Common Property Rights and Land Reallocations in Rural China: Evidence from a Village Survey." *World Development* 28(4): 701–19.

Kuran, T. 1993. "Sparks and Prairie Fires: A Theory of Unanticipated Political Revolution." In U. Witt, ed., *Evolutionary Economics.* Aldershot, U.K.: Edward Elgar Press.

Kutcher, G. P., and P. L. Scandizzo. 1981. "The Agricultural Economy of Northeast Brazil." World Bank, Washington, D.C.

Laffont, J.-J., and M.-S. Matoussi. 1995. " Moral Hazard, Financial Constraints, and Sharecropping in El Oulja." *Review of Economic Studies* 62(3): 381–99.

Lanjouw, J. O. 1999. "Information and the Operation of Markets: Tests Based on a General Equilibrium Model of Land Leasing in India." *Journal of Development Economics* 60(2): 497–527.

Lanjouw, J. O., and P. Levy 1998. "Untitled: A Study of Formal and Informal Property Rights in Urban Ecuador." Discussion Paper no. 788. Yale Economic Growth Center, New Haven, Conn.

Lansink, A. O., K. Pietola, and S. Backman. 2002. "Efficiency and Productivity of Conventional and Organic Farms in Finland 1994–1997." *European Review of Agricultural Economics* 29(1): 51–65.

Lastarria-Cornhiel, S. 1997. "Impact of Privatization on Gender and Property Rights in Africa." *World Development* 25(8): 1317–33.

Lavadenz, I., and K. Deininger. 2002. "Land Policies." In M. M. Giugale, O. Lafourcade, C. Luff, eds., *Colombia: The Economic Foundation of Peace.* Washington, D.C.: World Bank.

Lavigne Delville, P. 2000. "Harmonising Formal Law and Customary Land Rights in French-Speaking West Africa." In C. Toulmin and J. Quan, eds., *Evolving Land Rights, Policy, and Tenure in Africa.* London: International Institute for Environment and Development.

Lavigne Delville, P., C. Toulmin, J.-P. Colin, and J.-P. Chauveau. 2002. *Negotiating Access to Land in West Africa: A Synthesis of Findings from Research on Derived Rights to Land.* London: International Institute for Environment and Development and Groupe de Recherche et d'Echange Technologiques.

227

Lence, S. H. 2001. "Farmland Prices in the Presence of Transaction Costs: A Cautionary Note." *American Journal of Agricultural Economics* 83(4): 985–92.

Lerman, Z. 2001. "Agriculture in Transition Economies: From Common Heritage to Divergence." *Agricultural Economics* 26(2): 95–114.

Lerman, Z., and K. Brooks. 2001. "Turkmenistan: An Assessment of Leasehold-Based Farm Restructuring." Technical Paper no. 500, Europe and Central Asia Environmentally and Socially Sustainable Development Series. World Bank, Washington, D.C..

Lerman, Z., C. Csaki, and V. Moroz. 1998. "Land Reform and Farm Restructuring in Moldova: Progress and Prospects." Discussion Paper no. 398. World Bank, Washington, D.C.

Leroy de la Brière, B. 1996. "Household Behavior toward Soil Conservation and Remittances in the Dominican Republic." Working Paper. World Bank, Washington, D.C.

Leybourne M., F. Ghassali, A. S. Osman, T. Nordblom, and G. Gintzburger. 1993. "The Utilization of Fodder Shrubs (Atriplex spp., Salsola Vermicula) by Agropastoralists in the Northern Syrian Steppe." Pasture Forage and Livestock Program Annual Report. International Center for Agricultural Research in the Dry Areas, Aleppo, Syria.

Li, G., S. Rozelle, and L. Brandt. 1998. "Tenure, Land Rights, and Farmer Investment Incentives in China." *Agricultural Economics* 19(1): 63–71.

Li, P. 2002. "Rural Land System in China: Status and Recommendations." Case study presented at the Regional Workshop on Land Issues in Asia, June 4–6, Phnom Penh, Cambodia.

Libecap, G. D. 1986. "Property Rights in Economic History: Implications for Research." *Explorations in Economic History* 23(3): 227–52.

Lin, J. Y. 1992. "Rural Reforms and Agricultural Growth in China." *American Economic Review* 82(1): 34–51.

Lin, J. Y., F. Cai, and Z. Li. 1997. "The China Miracle: Development Strategy and Economic Reform." *Asia-Pacific Development Journal* 4(1): 165–69.

Lopez, R. 1997. "Land Titles and Farm Productivity in Honduras." World Bank, Washington, D.C. Processed.

Lopez, R., and A. Valdez. 2000. *Rural Poverty in Latin America.* New York and London: St. Martin's Press and Macmillan Press.

Lyne, M. C,. and M. A. G. Darroch. 1997. "Broadening Access to Land Markets: Financing Emerging Farmers in South Africa." *Development Southern Africa* 14(4): 561–68.

Mabogunje, A. L. 1992. "Perspective on Urban Land and Urban Management Policies in Sub-Saharan Africa." Technical Paper no. 196, Africa Technical Department Series. World Bank, Washington, D.C.

Macours, K., 2002. "Land Rental markets in Guatemala: Functioning and Potential." University of California at Berkeley. Processed.

Macours, K., and J. F. M. Swinnen. 2000a. "Causes of Output Decline in Economic Transition: The Case of Central and Eastern European Agriculture." *Journal of Comparative Economics* 28(1): 172–206.

_____. 2000b. "Impact of Initial Conditions and Reform Policies on Agricultural Performance in Central and Eastern Europe, the Former Soviet Union, and East Asia." *American Journal of Agricultural Economics* 82(5): 1149–55.

_____. 2002. "Patterns of Agrarian Transition." *Economic Development and Cultural Change* 50(2): 365–94.

Mahmood, M. 1990. "The Change in Land Distribution in the Punjab: Empirical Application of an Exogenous-Endogenous Model for Agrarian Sector Analysis." *Pakistan Development Review* 29(3–4): 149–289.

Malik, A., and R. M. Schwab. 1991. "Optimal Investments to Establish Property Rights in Land." *Journal of Urban Economics* 29(3): 295–309.

Malpezzi, S. 1998. "Welfare Analysis of Rent Control with Side Payments: A Natural Experiment in Cairo, Egypt." *Regional Science and Urban Economics* 28(6): 773–95.

Malpezzi, S., and S. K. Mayo. 1997. "Getting Housing Incentives Right: A Case Study of the Effects of Regulation, Taxes, and Subsidies on Housing Supply in Malaysia." *Land Economics* 73(3): 372–91.

Malpezzi, S., G. H. Chun, and R. K. Green. 1998. "New Place-to-Place Housing Price Indexes for U.S. Metropolitan Areas and Their Determinants." *Real Estate Economics* 26(2): 235–74.

Manyong, V., and V. Houndekon. 2000. "Land Tenurial Systems and the Adoption of Mucuna Planted Fallow in the Derived Savannas of West Africa." Working Paper no.4. International Food Policy Research Institute, Washington, D.C.

Mason, T. D. 1986. "Land Reform and the Breakdown of Clientelist Politics in El Salvador." *Comparative Political Studies* 18(4): 487–516.

Masri, A. 1991. "The Tradition of Hema as a Land Tenure Institution in Arid Land Management: The Syrian Arab Republic." Food and Agriculture Organization of the United Nations, Rome.

Mathijs, E., and J. F. M. Swinnen. 2001. "Production Organization and Efficiency during Transition: An Empirical Analysis of East German Agriculture." *Review of Economics and Statistics* 83(1): 100–07.

McAuslan, P. 1998. "Making Law Work: Restructuring Land Relations in Africa." *Development and Change* 29(3): 525–52.

McCarthy, N., A. de Janvry, and E. Sadoulet. 1997. "Land Allocation under Dual Individual-Collective Use in Mexico." International Livestock Research Institute, Nairobi, Kenya.

McCarthy, N., E. Sadoulet, and A. de Janvry. 2001. "Common Pool Resource Appropriation under Costly Cooperation." *Journal of Environmental Economics and Management* 42(3): 297–309.

McClintock, C. 1981. *Peasant Cooperatives and Political Change in Peru*. Princeton, N.J.: Princeton University Press.

McCloskey, D. N. 1975. *The Persistence of English Common Fields*. Princeton, N.J.: Princeton University Press.

McKean, M. A. 1996. *Common-Property Regimes as a Solution to Problems of Scale and Linkage*. Washington, D.C.: Island Press

McMillan, J. 1989. "A Game-Theoretic View of International Trade Negotiations: Implications for the Developing Countries." In J. Whalley, ed., *Developing Countries and the Global Trading System*, vol. 1, *Thematic Studies from a Ford Foundation Project*. London and Ann Arbor, Mich.: MacMillan and University of Michigan Press.

McMillan, J., J. Whalley, and L. Zhu. 1989. "The Impact of China's Economic Reforms on Agricultural Productivity Growth." *Journal of Political Economy* 97(4): 781–807.

Mearns, R. 1996. "Community, Collective Action, and Common Grazing: The Case of Post-Socialist Mongolia." *Journal of Development Studies* 32(3): 297–339.

Melmed-Sanjak, J. S., and M. R. Carter. 1991. "The Economic Viability and Stability of 'Capitalised Family Farming': An Analysis of Agricultural Decollectivisation in Peru." *Journal of Development Studies* 27(2): 190–210.

Melmed-Sanjak, J. S., and S. Lastarria-Cornhiel. 1998. "Development of Good Practice Guidelines for Land Leasing: Some Preliminary Considerations." Draft report for the Food and Agriculture Organization of the United Nations. University of Wisconsin, Land Tenure Center, Madison.

Merlet, M., and D. Pommier. 2000. "Estudios sobre Tenencía de la Tierra." Managua Institute for Research and Application of Development Methods, Managua, Nicaragua.

Messick, R. 1996. "Report on Informal Lending Organizations in Lima." Informal Note. Institute for Liberty and Democracy, Lima, Peru.

Migdal, J. S. 1974. *Peasants, Politics, and Revolution: Pressure toward Political and Social Change in the Third World.* Princeton, N.J.: Princeton University Press.

Migot-Adholla, S. 1993. *Indigenous Land Rights Systems in Sub-Saharan Africa: A Constraint on Productivity?* Oxford, U.K.; New York;

Toronto; and Melbourne: Oxford University Press.

Molina, J. 2002. "Credit for Land Purchases by the Rural Poor: Review of Experience." Food and Agriculture Organization of the United Nations, Office for Latin America and the Caribbean, Santiago, Chile.

Moll, P. G. 1988. "Transition to Freehold in the South African Reserves." *World Development* 16(3): 349–60.

_____. 1996. "Position Paper on Rural and Urban Land in Zambia." World Bank, Southern Africa Department, Washington, D.C.

Mookherjee, D. 1997. "Informational Rents and Property Rights in Land." In J. Roemer, ed., *Property Relations, Incentives, and Welfare.* New York: MacMillan Press.

Moore, B. 1966. *Social Origins of Dictatorship and Democracy: Lord and Peasant in the Making of the Modern World.* Boston: Beacon Press.

Moyo, S., B. Rutherford, and D. Amanor-Wilks. 2000. "Land Reform and Changing Social Relations for Farm Workers in Zimbabwe." *Review of African Political Economy* 27(84): 181–202.

Munoz, J. A. 1999. "Los Mercados de Tierras Rurales en Bolivia." Productive Development Series no. 61. Network for Agricultural Development, Santiago, Chile.

Munoz, J., and I. Lavadenz. 1997. "Reforming the Agrarian Reform in Bolivia." Discussion Paper. Harvard University, Harvard Institute for International Development, Cambridge, Mass.

Murphy, R. 2000. "Migration and Interhousehold Inequality: Observations from Wanzai County, Jiangxi." *China Quarterly* 0(164): 965–82.

Mushinski, D. W. 1999. "An Analysis of Offer Functions of Banks and Credit Unions in Guatemala." *Journal of Development Studies* 36(2): 88–112.

Nega, B., B. Adenew, and S. Gebre-Selassie. 2002. "Ethiopia Country Case Study." Paper presented at the World Bank Regional Workshop on Land Issues in Africa and the Middle East and North Africa Region, April 29–May 2, Kampala, Uganda.

Negrao, J. 2002. "Comments: Land as a Source of Conflict and in Post-Conflict Settlement." Paper presented at the Regional Workshop on Land Issues in Africa and the Middle East and North Africa Region, April 29–May 2, Kampala, Uganda.

Nelson, G. C., V. Harris, and S. W. Stone. 2001. "Deforestation, Land Use, and Property Rights: Empirical Evidence from Darien, Panama." *Land Economics* 77(2): 187–205.

Nesheiwat, K., T. Ngaido, and Q. Mamdoh. 1998. "Farmers and Communities in Low Rainfall Areas in Jordan: Implications of State Ownership over Rangelands." Paper presented at the Policy and Property Rights Research Workshop, November 24–29, Hammamet, Tunisia.

Newell, A., K. Pandya, and J. Symons. 1997. "Farm Size and the Intensity of Land Use in Gujarat." *Oxford Economic Papers* 49(2): 307–15.

Ngaido, T. 1993. "Implementing the Rural Code: Perceptions and Expectations of Rural Niger." Discussion Paper no. 7. University of Wisconsin, Land Tenure Center, Madison.

Ngaido, T., and N. McCarthy. 2002. "Pastoral Land Rights." Paper presented at the World Bank Regional Land Workshop, April 29–May 2, Kampala, Uganda.

Niamir-Fuller, M. 1999. *Managing Mobility in African Rangelands: The Legitimization of Transhumance.* London and Rome: Intermediate Technology Publications.

Nordblom, T. L., and F. Shomo. 1995. "Food and Feed Prospects to 2020 in the West Asia/ North Africa Region." Social Science Papers no. 2. International Center for Agricultural Research in the Dry Areas, Aleppo, Syria.

Noronha, R. 1985. "A Review of the Literature on Land Tenure Systems in Sub-Saharan Africa." Discussion Paper. World Bank, Washington, D.C.

Ntozi, J. P. M., and F. E. Ahimbisibwe. 1999. "Some Factors in the Decline of AIDS in Uganda." In J. C. Caldwell, I. O. Orubuloye, and J. P. M. Ntozi, eds., *The Continuing African HIV/AIDS Epidemic.* Canberra: Australian National University, National Centre for Epidemiology and Population Health, Health Transition Centre,.

Nugent, J., and J. Robinson. 2002. "Are Endowments Fate?" Discussion Paper no. 3206. Centre for Economic Policy Research, London.

Nugent, J. B., and N. Sanchez. 1998. "Common Property Rights as an Endogenous Response to Risk." *American Journal of Agricultural Economics* 80(3): 651–57.

Oates, W. E., and R. M. Schwab. 1997. "The Impact of Urban Land Taxation: The Pittsburgh Experience." *National Tax Journal* 50(1): 1–21.

Olinto, P. V. 1995. "Land Quality and the Inverse Relationship between Farm Size and

Productivity: A Panel Data Analysis of Paraguayan Farm Households." University of Wisconsin, Department of Agricultural Economics, Madison.

Österberg, T. 2002. "Designing Viable Land Administration Systems." Paper presented at the World Bank Regional Land Workshop, April 29–May 2, Kampala, Uganda.

Ortega, E. 1988. "Transformaciones Agrarias y Campesinado: De la Participación a la Exclusión." Corporation of Investigation for Latin America, Santiago, Chile.

Osman, A. F., N. H. Bahhady, and N. Murad. 1994. "Use of Fodder Shrubs in the Rehabilitation of Degraded Rangelands in Syria." Pasture Forage and Livestock Program Annual Report. International Center for Agricultural Research in the Dry Areas, Aleppo, Syria.

Ostrom, E. 1990. *Governing the Commons: The Evolution of Institutions for Collective Action.* Political Economy of Institutions and Decisions Series. Cambridge, U.K.; New York; and Melbourne: Cambridge University Press.

Otsuka, K. 1991. "Determinants and Consequences of Land Reform Implementation in the Philippines." *Journal of Development Economics* 35(2): 339–55.

_____. 2001. *Land Tenure and Natural Resource Management: A Comparative Study of Agrarian Communities in Asia and Africa.* Baltimore and London: The Johns Hopkins University Press.

_____. 2002. "Enhancing Land Access and Land Rights for the Marginalized: Regional Overview in an International Context." Paper presented at the World Bank Regional Land Workshop, June 4–6, Phnom Penh, Cambodia.

Otsuka, K., and Y. Hayami. 1988. "Theories of Share Tenancy: A Critical Survey." *Economic Development and Cultural Change* 37(1): 31–68.

Otsuka, K., H. Chuma, and Y. Hayami. 1992. "Land and Labor Contracts in Agrarian Economies: Theories and Facts." *Journal of Economic Literature* 30(4): 1965–2018.

_____. 1993. "Permanent Labour and Land Tenancy Contracts in Agrarian Economies: An Integrated Analysis." *Economica* 60(237): 57–77.

Overchuk, A. 2002. "Integrated Approach to Land Policy and Development of Land Administration Institutions in Russia." Paper presented at the World Bank Regional Land Policy Workshop, April 3–6, Budapest, Hungary.

Palmer, R. 1977. *Land and Racial Domination in Rhodesia.* Berkeley: University of California Press.

Pant, C. 1983. "Tenancy and Family Resources: A Model and Some Empirical Analysis." *Journal of Development Economics* 12(1–2): 27–39.

Pender, J. L., and J. M. Kerr. 1998. "Determinants of Farmers' Indigenous Soil and Water Conservation Investments in Semi-Arid India." *Agricultural Economics* 19(1–2): 113–25.

_____. 1999. "The Effects of Land Sales Restrictions: Evidence from South India." *Agricultural Economics* 21(3): 279–94.

Pescay, M. 2002. "Analyze Comparée des Expériences, de Côte d'Ivoire, du Bénin et de Guinée-Bissau." Paper presented at the Regional Workshop on Land Issues in Africa and the Middle East and North Africa Region, April 29–May 2, Kampala, Uganda.

Pinckney, T. C., and P. K. Kimuyu. 1994. "Land Tenure Reform in East Africa: Good, Bad, or Unimportant?" *Journal of African Economies* 3(1): 1–28.

Pingali, P. 1987. *Agricultural Mechanization and the Evolution of Farming Systems in Sub-Saharan Africa*. Baltimore and London: The Johns Hopkins University Press.

Place, F. 1995. "The Role of Land and Tree Tenure in the Adoption of Agroforestry Technologies in Zambia, Burundi, Uganda, and Malawi: A Summary and Synthesis." University of Wisconsin, Land Tenure Center, Madison.

_____. 2002. "Land Markets in Africa: Preconditions, Potentials, and Limitations." Paper presented at the Regional Workshop on Land Issues in Africa and the Middle East and North Africa Region, Kampala, Uganda.

Place, F., and K. Otsuka. 2001. "Population, Tenure, and Natural Resource Management: The Case of Customary Land Area in Malawi." *Journal of Environmental Economics and Management* 41(1): 13–32.

Platteau, J. P. 1996. "The Evolutionary Theory of Land Rights as Applied to Sub-Saharan Africa: A Critical Assessment." *Development and Change* 27(1): 29–86.

Platteau, J. P., and J.-M. Baland. 2001. "Impartial Inheritance Versus Equal Division: A Comparative Perspective Centered on Europe and Sub-Saharan Africa." In A. de Janvry, G. Gordillo, J. P. Platteau, and E. Sadoulet, eds., *Access to Land, Rural Poverty, and Public Action*. Washington, D.C.: World Bank.

Poffenberger, M. 2002. *Keepers of the Forest: Land Management Alternatives in Southeast Asia*. West Hartford, Conn.: Kumarian Press.

Pomfret, R. 2000. "Agrarian Reform in Uzbekistan: Why Has the Chinese Model Failed to Deliver?" *Economic Development and Cultural Change* 48(2): 269–84.

Powelson, J. P. 1988. "The Story of Land: A World History of Land Tenure and Agrarian Reform." Lincoln Institute of Land, Cambridge, Mass.

Powelson, J. P., and R. Stock. 1987. "The Peasant Betrayed: Agriculture and Land Reform in the Third World." Boston, Mass.: Oelgeschlager, Gunn, and Hain.

Prosterman, R. 2001. "Land Tenure, Food Security, and Rural Development in China." *Development* 44(4): 79–84.

Prosterman, R., and T. Handstad. 1999. *Legal Impediments to Effective Rural Land Relations in Eastern Europe and Central Asia: A Comparative Perspective*. Technical Paper no. 436. Europe and Central Asia Environmentally and Socially Sustainable Rural Development Series. Washington, D.C.: World Bank.

Prosterman, R. L., M. N. Temple, and T. M. Hanstad, eds. 1990. *Agrarian Reform and Grassroots Development, Ten Case Studies*. Boulder, Colo.: L. Rienner.

Quibria, M. G., and S. Rashid. 1986. "Sharecropping in Dual Agrarian Economies: A Synthesis." *Oxford Economic Papers* 38(1): 94–111.

Quisumbing, A. R. 2001. "Women's Land Rights in the Transition to Individualized Ownership: Implications for Tree-Resource Management in Western Ghana." *Economic Development and Cultural Change* 50(1): 157–81.

Quisumbing, A. R., and K. Otsuka. 2001. "Land, Trees, and Women: Evolution of Land

Tenure Institutions in Western Ghana and Sumatra." Research Report no. 121. International Food Policy Research Institute, Washington, D.C.

Radhakrishnan, P. 1990. "Land Reforms: Rhetoric and Reality." *Economic and Political Weekly* 25(47): 2617–21.

Rahmato, D. 1993. "Land, Peasants, and the Drive for Collectivization in Ethiopia." In T. J. Bassett and D. E. Crummey, eds., *Land in African Agrarian Systems.* University of Wisconsin Press, Madison.

_____. 1997. "Manufacturing Poverty: Rural Policy and Micro-Agriculture." Paper presented at the Land Tenure Project Workshop, September 20–21, Institute of Development Research, Addis Ababa, Ethiopia.

Ravallion, M., and D. van de Walle. 2001. "Breaking up the Collective Farm: Welfare Outcomes of Vietnam's Massive Land Privatization." Working Paper no. 2710. World Bank, Washington, D.C.

Ravenscroft, N., R. Gibbard, and S. Markwell. 1998. "Private Sector Tenancy Arrangements," vol. I, "Literature Review." Draft report to the Food and Agriculture Organization of the United Nations, Rome.

Rawal, V. 2001. "Agrarian Reform and Land Markets: A Study of Land Transactions in Two Villages of West Bengal, 1977–1995." *Economic Development and Cultural Change* 49(3): 611–29.

Ray, S. K. 1996. "Land System and Its Reforms in India." *Indian Journal of Agricultural Economics* 51(1): 220–37.

Ray, T. 1999. "Share Tenancy as Strategic Delegation." *Journal of Development Economics* 58(1): 45–60.

Ray, T., and N. Singh. 2001. "Limited Liability, Contractual Choice, and the Tenancy Ladder." *Journal of Development Economics* 66(1): 289–303.

Reid, J. D., Jr. 1977. "The Theory of Share Tenancy Revisited—Again." *Journal of Political Economy* 85(2): 403–07.

Renaud, B. 1999. "The Financing of Social Housing in Integrating Financial Markets: A View from Developing Countries." *Urban Studies* 36(4): 755–73.

Robison, L. J., D. A. Lins, and R. Venkataraman. 1985. "Cash Rents and Land Values in U.S. Agriculture." *American Journal of Agricultural Economics* 67(4): 795–805.

Rodrik, D. 1998. "Where Did All the Growth Go? External Shocks, Social Conflict, and Growth Collapses." Working Paper: no. 6350-27. National Bureau of Economic Research, Cambridge, Mass.

Rojas, M. E., 2001. "Evaluación de las Leyes 30/88 y 160/94 y Diseño de Indicadores para la Medición de la Reforma Agraria en Colombia." National Department for Planning, Bogotá, Colombia.

Rolfes, L., Jr. 2002. "Making the Legal Basis for Private Land Rights Operational and Effective." Paper presented at the World Bank Regional Land Policy Workshop, April 3–6, Budapest, Hungary.

Rosenzweig, M. R., and K. I. Wolpin. 1985. "Specific Experience, Household Structure, and

Intergenerational Transfers: Farm Family Land and Labor Arrangements in Developing Countries." *Quarterly Journal of Economics* 100(5): 961–87.

Roth, M., J. Bruce, and S. G. Smith. 1994. "Land Tenure, Land Markets, and Institutional Transformation in Zambia." University of Wisconsin, Land Tenure Center, Madison. Draft.

Roy, J., and K. Serfes. 2000. "Strategic Choice of Contract Lengths in Agriculture." Discussion Paper no. 00/17. University of Copenhagen, Institute of Economics, Copenhagen, Denmark.

Rueschemeyer, D., E. Huber, and J. D. Stephens. 1992. *Capitalist Development and Democracy.* Chicago: University of Chicago Press.

Sadoulet, E., S. Fukui, and A. de Janvry. 1994. "Efficient Share Tenancy Contracts under Risk: The Case of Two Rice-Growing Villages in Thailand." *Journal of Development Economics* 45(2): 225–43.

Salas C. 1986. "Jamaica Land Titling Project: Feasibility Report." Inter-American Development Bank, Washington, D.C.

Sanjak, J., and I. Lavadenz. 2002. "The Legal and Institutional Basis for Effective Land Administration in Latin America and the Caribbean." Paper presented at the World Bank Regional Land Policy Workshop, May 19–22, Pachuca, Mexico.

Sarap, K. 1998. "On the Operation of the Land Market in Backward Agriculture: Evidence from a Village in Orissa, Eastern India." *Journal of Peasant Studies* 25(2): 102–30.

Saxena, N. C. 1999. "Rehabilitation of Degraded Lands in India through Watershed Develop-

ment." Government of India, Planning Commission, New Delhi, India.

_____. 2002. "Tenancy Reforms Versus Open Market Leasing: What Would Serve the Poor Better?" Government of India, Planning Commission, New Delhi, India.

Schultz, T. P. 1999. "Women's Role in the Agricultural Household: Bargaining and Human Capital." Discussion Paper no. 803. Yale University, Economic Growth Center, New Haven, Connecticut.

Schwarzwalder, B. 2002. "China's New Land Law: Challenges and Opportunities." Rural Development Institute, Seattle, Wash.

Scott, J. C. 1976. *The Moral Economy of the Peasant: Rebellion and Subsistence in Southeast Asia.* New Haven, Conn.: Yale University Press.

Seligson, M. A. 1995. "Thirty Years of Transformation in the Agrarian Structure of El Salvador, 1961–1991." *Latin American Research Review* 30(3): 43–74.

Shaban, R. A. 1991. "Does the Land Tenancy Market Equalize Holdings?" Working Paper. University of Pennsylvania, Philadelphia.

Shackleton, C. M., S. E. Shackleton, and B. Cousins. 2001. "The Role of Land-Based Strategies in Rural Livelihoods: The Contribution of Arable Production, Animal Husbandry, and Natural Resource Harvesting in Communal Areas in South Africa." *Development Southern Africa* 18(5): 581–604.

Sharma, N., and J. Dreze. 1996. "Sharecropping in a North Indian Village." *Journal of Development Studies* 33(1): 1–39.

Shepherd, G. 1991. "The Communal Management of Forests in the Semi-Arid and Sub-Humid Regions of Africa: Past Practice and Prospects for the Future." *Development Policy Review* 19(1): 151–76.

Shetty, S. 1988. "Limited Liability, Wealth Differences, and Tenancy Contracts in Agrarian Economies." *Journal of Development Economics* 29(1): 1–22.

Shih, H. 1992. *Chinese Rural Society in Transition: A Case Study of the Lake Tai Area.* Berkeley: University of California Press.

Siamwalla, A. 1990. "The Thai Rural Credit System: Public Subsidies, Private Information, and Segmented Markets." *World Bank Economic Review* 4(3): 271–95.

Simons, S. 1987. "Land Fragmentation and Consolidation: A Theoretical Model of Land Configuration with an Empirical Analysis of Fragmentation in Thailand." Ph.D.thesis. University of Maryland, College Park.

Sjaastad, E., and D. W. Bromley. 1997. "Indigenous Land Rights in Sub-Saharan Africa: Appropriation, Security, and Investment Demand." *World Development* 25(4): 549–62.

_____. 2000. "The Prejudices of Property Rights: On Individualism, Specificity, and Security in Property Regimes." *Development Policy Review* 18(4): 365–89.

Skinner, J. 1991. "Prospects for Agricultural Land Taxation in Developing Countries." Symposium Series. World Bank, Washington, D.C.

Skocpol, T. 1979. *States and Social Revolutions: A Comparative Analysis of France, Russia, and China.* Cambridge, U.K.: Cambridge University Press.

Skoufias, E. 1991. "Land Tenancy and Rural Factor Market Imperfections Revisited." *Journal of Economic Development* 16(1): 37–55.

_____. 1995. "Household Resources, Transaction Costs, and Adjustment through Land Tenancy." *Land Economics* 71(1): 42–56.

Stanfield, D. 1990. "Rural Land Titling and Registration in Latin America and the Caribbean: Implications for Rural Development Programs." University of Wisconsin, Land Tenure Center, Madison.

Steele, S. R. 2001. "Property Regimes as Information Regimes: Efficiency and Economies of Joint Production." *Environmental and Resource Economics* 18(3): 317–37.

Stiglitz, J. E., and A. Weiss. 1981. "Credit Rationing in Markets with Imperfect Information." *American Economic Review* 71(3): 393–410.

Strasma, J. 1965. "Market-Enforced Self-Assessment for Real Estate Taxes." *Bulletin for International Fiscal Documentation* 1(9): 9–10.

_____. 2000. "Land Tenure in Nicaragua: Analysis and Future Perspectives." Working Paper. Food and Agriculture Organization of the United Nations, Land Tenure Service, Rome.

Strasma, J., J. Alsm, E. Shearer, and A. Waldstein. 1987. *Impact of Agricultural Land Revenue Systems on Agricultural Land Usage.* Madison: University of Wisconsin, Land Tenure Center.

Suyanto, S., T. P. Tomich, and K. Otsuka. 2001. "Land Tenure and Farm Management Efficiency: The Case of Paddy and Cinnamon Production in Customary Land Areas of Sumatra." *Australian Journal of Agricultural and Resource Economics* 45(3): 411–36.

Swallow, B. M., and A. D. Kamara. 1999. "The Dynamics of Land Use and Property Rights in Semi-Arid East Africa." In N. McCarthy, M. Kirk, and H. H. P. Grell, eds., *Property Rights, Risk, and Livestock Development in Africa.* Washington, D.C.: International Food Policy Research Institute.

Swamy, D. S. 1988. "Agricultural Tenancy in the 1970s." *Indian Journal of Agricultural Economics* 43(4): 555–68.

Swinnen, J. F. M. 2002. *Political Reforms, Rural Crises, and Land Tenure: A Historic Analysis of Land Leasing and Tenure Reforms in Western Europe.* Leuven, Belgium: Policy Research Group.

Takekoshi, Y. 1967. *The Economic Aspects of the History of the Civilization of Japan.* London: Macmillan.

Tanner, C. 2002. "Law Making in an African Context: The 1997 Mozambican Land Law." *Food and Agriculture Organization of the United Nations Legal Papers Online no. 26.* Available on: http://www.fao.org/Legal/Prs-OL/lpo26.pdf.

Tanzi, V. 2001. "Pitfalls on the Road to Fiscal Decentralization." Working Paper no. 19. Carnegie Endowment for International Peace, Washington, D.C.

Teofilo, E. 2002. "Country Case Study Brazil." World Bank Regional Workshop on Land Policy Issues, May 19–22, Pachuca, Mexico.

Thimmaiah, G. 2001. "New Perspectives on Land Reform in India." *Journal of Social and Economic Development* 3(2): 179–97.

Thompson, G. D., and P. N. Wilson. 1994. "Common Property as an Institutional Response to Environmental Variability." *Contemporary Economic Policy* 12(3): 10–21.

Thorat, S. 1997. "Trends in Land Ownership, Tenancy, and Land Reform." In M. D. Bhupat, ed., *Agricultural Development Paradigm for the Ninth Plan under the New Economic Environment.* New Delhi: Oxford and IBH Publishing.

Toulmin, C., and J. Quan. 2000. *Evolving Land Rights, Policy and Tenure in Africa.* London: International Institute for Environment and Development and Natural Resources Institute.

Townsend, R. F., J. Kirsten, and N. Vink. 1998. "Farm Size, Productivity, and Returns to Scale in Agriculture Revisited: A Case Study of Wine Producers in South Africa." *Agricultural Economics* 19(1–2): 175–80.

Tran, T. Q. 1998. "Economic Reforms and Their Impact on Agricultural Development in Vietnam." *ASEAN Economic Bulletin* 15(1): 30–46.

Turner, M. A. 1999. "Tradition and Common Property Management." *Canadian Journal of Economics* 32(3): 673–87.

Turner, M. A., L. Brandt, and S. Rozelle. 1998. "Property Rights Formation and the Organization of Exchange and Production in Rural China." Working Paper. University of Toronto, Department of Economics, Toronto, Canada.

Udry, C. 1996. "Gender, Agricultural Production, and the Theory of the Household." *Journal of Political Economy* 104(5): 1010–46.

_____. 1997. "Recent Advances in Empirical Microeconomic Research in Poor Countries: An Annotated Bibliography." *Journal of Economic Education* 28(1): 58–75.

Umbeck, J. 1977. "The California Gold Rush: A Study of Emerging Property." *Explorations in Economic History* 14(3): 197–226.

UNCHS (United Nations Centre for Human Settlements). 1999. "The Global Campaign for Secure Tenure." United Nations Human Settlements Commission, Geneva.

UNECE (United Nations Economic Commission for Europe). 1996. "Land Administration Guidelines, with Special References to Countries in Transition." ECE/HBP/96. New York and Geneva.

Uzun, V. Y. 2002. "Russia Country Case Study." Paper presented at the World Bank Land Workshop, April 3–6, Budapest, Hungary.

Valetta, W. 2000. "Completing the Transition: Lithuania Nears the End of Its Land Restitution and Reform Programme." Food and Agriculture Organization of the United Nations Legal Papers Online no. 11. Available on: http://www.fao.org/Legal/prs-ol/lpo11.pdf.

van den Brink, R., D. W. Bromley, and J. P. Chavas. 1995. "The Economics of Cain and Abel: Agro-Pastoral Property Rights in the Sahel." *Journal of Development Studies* 31(3): 373–99.

van den Brink, R., D. W. Bromley, and J. Cochrane. 1994. "Property Rights and Productivity in Africa: Is There a Connection?" *Development Southern Africa* 11(2): 177–82.

Verma, B. N., and D. W. Bromley. 1987. "The Political Economy of Farm Size in India: The Elusive Quest." *Economic Development and Cultural Change* 35(4): 791–808.

Wadhwa, D. C. 2002. "Guaranteeing Title to Land: The Only Sensible Solution." *Economics and Political Weekly* 23(50): 30–65.

Walker, C. 2002. "Ensuring Women's Land Access." Paper presented at the World Bank Regional Land Workshop, April 29–May 2, Kampala, Uganda.

Wallace, J., and S. Poerba. 2000. "Commercial Transactions in Land Security Interest in a Market System—Indonesian Context (Topic Cycle 6)." Government of the Republic of Indonesia, National Development Planning Agency and National Land Agency, Jakarta, Indonesia.

Wan, G. H., and E. Cheng. 2001. "Effects of Land Fragmentation and Returns to Scale in the Chinese Farming Sector." *Applied Economics* 33(2): 183–94.

Wang, Y. P., and A. Murie. 2000. "Social and Spatial Implications of Housing Reform in China." *International Journal of Urban and Regional Research* 24(2): 397–417.

Warriner, D. 1969. *Land Reform in Principle and Practice*. Oxford, U.K.: Clarendon Press.

Wenfang, Z., and J. Makeham. 1992. "Recent Developments in the Market for Rural Land Use in China." *Land Economics* 68(2): 139–62.

Werlin, H. 1999. "The Slum Upgrading Myth." *Urban Studies* 36(9): 1523–34.

Wickham-Crowley, T. 1991. *Exploring Revolution: Essays on Latin American Insurgency and Revolutionary Theory*. Armonk, N.Y.: M. E. Sharpe.

Woodhouse, P. 1997. "Governance and Local Environmental Management in Africa." *Review of African Political Economy* 24(74): 537–47.

World Bank. 1975. *Land Reform: Sector Policy Paper.* Washington, D.C.

_____. 1998. "Philippines: Land Management and Administration, Policy Note." East Asia and Pacific Region, Rural Development and Natural Resources Sector Unit, Washington, D.C.

_____. 2000. "Vietnam Rural Strategy." East Asia and Pacific Region, Rural Development and Natural Resources Sector Unit, World Bank, Washington, D.C.

_____. 2002a. "Mexico—Land Policy a Decade after the Ejido Reforms." World Bank, Rural Development and Natural Resources Sector Unit, Washington, D.C.

_____. 2002b. "Mexico—Urban Development: A Contribution to a National Urban Strategy." Latin America and Caribbean Department, Washington, D.C.

Yanbykh, R. 2002. "Country Case Study: Russia." Paper presented at the Regional Workshop on Land Issues in Eastern Europe and the CIS, April 3–6, Budapest, Hungary.

Yang, D. T. 1997. "China's Land Arrangements and Rural Labor Mobility." *China Economic Review* 8(2): 101–15.

Yao, Y. 1996. "Three Essays on the Implications of Imperfect Markets in Rural China." Ph.D. thesis, University of Wisconsin, Madison.

Yngstrom, I. 2002. "Women, Wives, and Land Rights in Africa: Situating Gender beyond the Household in the Debate over Land Policy and Changing Tenure Systems." *Oxford Development Studies* 30(1): 21–40.

Zamosc, L. 1989. "Peasant Struggles and Agrarian Reform." Latin American Issues no. 8. Allegheny College, Meadville, Pa.

Zegarra Méndez, E. 1999. "El Mercado de Tierras Rurales en el Perú." Productive Development Series no. 63. Economic Commission for Latin America and Caribbean, Santiago de Chile, Chile.

Zeller, M. A., A. Diagne, and V. Kisyombe. 1997. "Adoption of Hybrid Maize and Tobacco in Malawi's Smallholder Farms: Effects on Household Food Security." In F. Heidues and A. Fadani, eds., *Food Security and Innovations: Successes and Lessons Learned.* Frankfurt, Germany: Peter Lang Press.

Zepeda, G. 2000. "Transformación Agraria. Los Derechos de Propriedad en el Campo Mexicano bajo el Nuevo Marco Institucional." Central Independiente de Obreros Agrícolas y Campesionos, Mexico City, Mexico.

Zimmerman, F. J. 2000. "Barriers to Participation of the Poor in South Africa's Land Redistribution." *World Development* 28 (8): 1439–60.

Zimmermann, W. 2002. "Comments on Land in Conflict and Post-Conflict Situations." Paper presented at the World Bank Land Workshop, June 4–6, Phnom Penh, Cambodia.